Mekong Memoirs

Mekong Memoirs
A GI in Tan Tru, Long An Province, 1969–1970

L. Glen Inabinet

McFarland & Company, Inc., Publishers
Jefferson, North Carolina

Photographs by author unless otherwise credited

LIBRARY OF CONGRESS CATALOGING-IN-PUBLICATION DATA

Names: Inabinet, L. Glen, 1943– author.
Title: Mekong memoirs : a GI in Tan Tru, Long An Province, 1969-1970 /
    L. Glen Inabinet.
Description: Jefferson, North Carolina : McFarland & Company, Inc., Publishers, 2025. |
    Includes bibliographical references and index.
Identifiers: LCCN 2024049536 | ISBN 9781476696799 (paperback : acid free paper) ∞
    ISBN 9781476655079 (ebook)
Subjects: LCSH: Inabinet, L. Glen, 1943- | Vietnam War, 1961-1975—Personal
    narratives, American. | United States. Army. Field Artillery Regiment,
    4th. Battalion, 2nd. Battery C | Artillerymen—United States—Biography. |
    Soldiers—United States—Biography. | Vietnam War, 1961-1975—Vietnam—
    Long An (Province) | Vietnam War, 1961-1975—Campaigns—Mekong River
    Delta (Vietnam and Cambodia) | Vietnam War, 1961-1975—Artillery operations,
    American. | Orangeburg (S.C.)—Biography.
Classification: LCC DS559.5 .I533 2024 | DDC 959.704/342092 [B]—dc23/eng/20241115
LC record available at https://lccn.loc.gov/2024049536

ISBN (print) 978-1-4766-9679-9
ISBN (ebook) 978-1-4766-5507-9

© 2025 L. Glen Inabinet. All rights reserved

No part of this book may be reproduced or transmitted in any form
or by any means, electronic or mechanical, including photocopying
or recording, or by any information storage and retrieval system,
without permission in writing from the publisher.

Front cover image: Atop his bunker after being posted on perimeter guard,
a soldier reads a letter from home as day gives way to twilight
(author photograph).

Printed in the United States of America

McFarland & Company, Inc., Publishers
  Box 611, Jefferson, North Carolina 28640
    www.mcfarlandpub.com

Table of Contents

Acknowledgments — vii
Preface: Why I Am Writing — 1
Introduction: America's War in Vietnam to 1969 — 5

1. Personal Beginnings: *"We will draft you!"* — 9
2. Reception: *"Responsibilities which Americans inherit"* — 13
3. Basic Combat Training: *"In 8 weeks … teach you how to kill"* — 21
4. Bivouac: *"Really a mess … completely exhausted"* — 35
5. Training Post-Bivouac: *"Keeping us occupied and allowing us no sleep"* — 39
6. Advanced Individual Training: *"Different post, same Army"* — 44
7. 1969, a New Year: *"What I will be, I'm not sure; they haven't told us yet"* — 56
8. Officially Holdovers: *"The thought that some of them might not return"* — 65
9. RVN Training: *"Charlie has some really nasty booby traps"* — 73
10. Oakland Departure: *"So much to be thankful for and so much to return to"* — 76
11. Vietnam In-Country: *"A stench then unrecognized"* — 80
12. RTO: *"I didn't volunteer for this job but … I must … do my best"* — 96
13. Back in Charlie Battery: *"Mixed feelings leaving the grunts"* — 128
14. Monsoon, Mosquitos, Mortars: *"It don't mean nothing. It's only temporary."* — 137
15. Independence, Illness, Inspections: *"Wet, muddy, cold, and quite peeved"* — 151
16. Penta Prime, Photography, Pestering: *"I was on a treadmill"* — 163

v

17. Shorthanded on the Guns: *"Don't know ... if I'm a clerk or a cannoneer"* — 177

18. Tet 1970, a Two-digit Midget: *"We were keeping vigilant"* — 186

19. Extension: *"36 days remaining"* — 205

20. Coming Home: *"Stopped... That was not going to happen to me"* — 211

Afterword: "Young men taken way too soon" — 214

Bibliography — 219

Index — 221

Acknowledgments

During the fifty-five years since I separated from military service, I have shared experiences with numerous veterans. Some have been impromptu meetings when I encountered someone wearing a cap or other evidence of veteran status. I express my gratitude to pre–Vietnam and post–Vietnam veterans or offer a hearty "welcome home" to comrades of my generation. Invariably, in those latter happenstances, a dialogue ensues during which we compare when (chronologically) and where (geographically) and in which branch of the military we served. These conversations are sometimes brief but often evolve into more detailed accounts of military service and sharing of experiences.

I am an active member of the 40 & 8, Veterans of Foreign Wars, and American Legion Post 17, of which I am past commander. My valued associations with fellow members of these service organizations have also afforded my participation in conversations deeper than those more casual encounters on the sidewalks, in stores, or in parking lots. Every veteran has a story (or stories) to tell. Some are eager to speak while others are more reluctant. Experiences and sacrifices often make conversations difficult and even painful.

Occasionally a fellow Vietnam-era veteran might apologetically state that he served *during* the war but had not been deployed *to* Vietnam. My sincere response has always been that members of the military serve their country where they are sent and that they too sacrificed and their service was meaningful. The statement, "All gave some, some gave all," is not a trite expression, but rather is a profound and timeless manifestation of the service of every American veteran. Having served as a member of an artillery gun crew, an RTO embedded with the grunts in the field, and a TAERS clerk in a remote firebase, I witnessed and experienced the sacrifices of my comrades at all levels.

In addition to my general acknowledgment of all those comrades whose paths I have crossed, I specifically want to thank three friends with whom I served and with whom I continue to correspond: Lee Dudley,

Patrick McReynolds, and John Nesavich. From the time I began pulling memories and words together several years ago, they have offered encouragement and have helped me reconstruct events or recall names. They have also attempted to assist me in locating other comrades we remember but whose whereabouts are unknown. My only regret in writing this memoir has been my inability to locate other brothers-in-arms so that I might have honored them by including their actual names.

I am hopeful that my three children (and their spouses)—Julie (Shawn), Bill (Renata), and Greg (Jana)—and my grandchildren—Daniel, Matthew, Philip, Sarah, and James—will find merit in reading this book. It will help explain why over the last couple of years they so often found their daddy/granddaddy working on his laptop. More importantly, it may help them better understand why I believe a higher power watches over us; why I stand for the National Anthem or salute at the passing of the American flag; why I vote in every election, even when sometimes I am less than enthusiastic about some candidates; why I write letters to encourage—or chastise—my elected representatives; and why I believe development of citizenship and an understanding and support of our nation's Constitution with its system of checks and balances is crucial if our federal republic is to endure.

I would like to thank several professionals with expertise in scholarship and the publishing industry who agreed to read my manuscript. All were forthright and encouraging. My respected friend, Vietnam veteran Allen Stokes, director emeritus of the South Caroliniana Library at the University of South Carolina, was the first to offer meaningful insight and suggestions for my rough draft. I was cautioned from the beginning that a number of presses are moving out of the niche of military memoirs for perceived low reader interest. Regardless of that, a new acquaintance Michael McGandy, currently director of the University of South Carolina Press, offered to read my manuscript and discuss it with me. He suggested several other university presses for me to contact. One of these encouraging readers, Natalie O'Neal at the University Press of Kentucky, offered me recommendations that led to my eventual publisher, McFarland. I appreciate their confidence and assistance in my work.

Most importantly, I must acknowledge the contributions of my wife Joan, who has been my constant companion since we wed in 1966. Much of which I have written she actually or vicariously experienced as we corresponded during the time we were apart. When I began this writing project, she urged me on. She has been my fiercest encourager and my greatest critic. I am grateful for her willingness to proofread and assist me in final edits prior to submission. Her candor in pointing out areas where my words made little if any sense to someone who had never been in the military are much appreciated. If my corrections are inadequate, the blame is mine alone.

Preface:
Why I Am Writing

I AM A RETIRED EDUCATOR WHO CONTINUES to enjoy studying history, researching, writing, and photography. Usually I am writing about or illustrating other people and their lives. With this publication, I am writing as an ordinary person with everyday information that I personally kept during a troubling period of national history.

My wife Joan, also a retired educator, and I share a number of interests, ones that we held from the beginning of our long relationship or developed together over time. She has written several local history books, and we have co-edited two related publications, *Kershaw County Legacy: A Commemorative History* in 1976 and *Legacy II: Kershaw County History and Heritage* in 1983. I photographed collections for a friend's *The South Carolina Dispensary* and have provided images for other publications, especially ours, as well. Since our retirement, Joan and I have co-authored *A History of Kershaw County, South Carolina* (2011) and *The World of Jak Smyrl: South Carolina Artist, Journalist, Cartoonist* (2020), both published by the University of South Carolina Press. We are presently researching Revolutionary War topics in our home area of Camden for a book detailing the impact upon this South Carolina community when British forces occupied it as their backcountry headquarters for nearly a year in 1780–1781.

While writing history, we frequently compile evidence—wills, letters, family Bibles, census records, oral interviews, memoirs, and genealogy—to research our own respective families. All too often we find unidentified persons in a photograph, or a reference to an unknown name or place or event in a letter or document. At these times we find ourselves saying, "If only mother (father, grandmother, grandfather, aunt or uncle so-and-so) were around, they could identify those people and tell the story surrounding that incident or period."

We realize that, oftentimes, perhaps our elders did tell us some of those stories, but we were too young or too preoccupied with our own lives to appreciate the details, and we did not make record of the stories by writing them down or by using voice or video recording. By the time we were ready or able to listen and comprehend them fully, the old folk had passed away, or in some cases, no longer possessed the mental capacity to relate information.

A unique feature of my life was my military service, which coincided with a tumultuous time in United States history: 1968–1970 during the Vietnam War. I decided to chronicle my story while I was able to do so with the belief that my three children, five grandchildren, and potential progeny might find it of interest. There may be others whom I have known or whom I have never met who would find this story to be of interest as well.

This is a personal account, told through my recollections, most of them substantiated in details by the letters I wrote to Joan and the numerous color slides and black-and-white photographs I took with whatever camera I was able to have with me at the time. In "Ulysses," the English poet Alfred, Lord Tennyson, remarked, "I am a part of all that I have met." Desiring my story to be as authentic as possible, I wanted to use *actual names* of the people with whom I trained stateside and served in Vietnam. So that I may do so, my publisher required that I have permission from the individual named, or if a person is no longer alive, from a family member. Thus, I have endeavored to locate old acquaintances. Some of them I have found and we have had pleasant reunions, catching up through phone calls, emails, or text messages. In other cases, obituaries have revealed names of surviving family members and I have had opportunity to tell a sister, nephew, or other relative that my relationship with their kinsman had meaning in my life and that the individual has not been forgotten.

Unfortunately, by publication time some of my searches had yet to prove successful, in which case I have used a pseudonym rather than a real name. If anyone reads this book and recognizes himself but with a different name, know that it was with great regret that I was unable to locate him for permission to use his real name. Furthermore, I appreciate the permissions from friends who snapped photos of me with my camera. In those cases, I acknowledge such by including their names in parentheses after the captions. Except for any photos parenthetically acknowledged from the Army's public domain BCT cycle book I purchased at the time, all other photographs in this book were taken by me. In addition, for any dialogue that I have attempted to reproduce, I have done so to the best of my recollection.

I do not presume to represent everyone who served in Vietnam, nor do I claim to be a "typical" soldier in that conflict, if such an individual ever existed. The average age of a serviceman in Vietnam was 19. I turned 26 while I was there. Veterans who served in Vietnam in 1965 or during Tet of 1968 or during later Vietnamization in 1970 have different stories to tell. Those soldiers who fought near the Demilitarized Zone (DMZ) or in the Central Highlands fought a war different from that of the Mekong Delta where I was stationed. Each veteran's experience was different; yet, in various respects, there are similarities. I believe many Vietnam veterans will share a common bond with some of my experiences and feelings.

My personal story is not heroic. Today the term *hero* is so frequently overused to refer to anyone who puts on a uniform that it taints the deeds of those who truly deserve that exceptional epithet. I was simply a young man who was called to serve my country and did so to the best of my ability in the circumstances where I was placed. To be totally accurate, this is not just *my* story, but rather *our* story, because my wife Joan and I lived parts of it in common. As a young couple married less than two years when I was away in service, we shared the loneliness of separation, especially while I was in Vietnam, and we were unable to converse even by phone for nearly thirteen and a half months. Throughout all, we shared the anxiety of conditions over which we had no control.

However, we also shared a deep faith that we and our situations were in God's hands, and we both prayed for His protection. Unable to see or to speak to one another, we communicated through letters, often one each, every day. Those written words we treasured and kept. And it is those letters which now allow me to reconstruct the manner in which we led our lives—separated, yet united by our love and faith, even with the inescapable possibility that I might come home mentally or physically impaired, or not return at all. We have always humbly felt blessed that such did not befall us.

My hope is that our story of confronting the anguish of physical separation, the discomfort of monetary challenges, and the uncertainty of our future will encourage our posterity to face the ordeals of their lives with love, devotion, and faith.

Introduction: America's War in Vietnam to 1969

AMERICAN FOREIGN POLICY CONNECTIONS with Vietnam date to World War II when a nationalist group—the Viet Minh, led by Ho Chi Minh—carried on effective resistance efforts in Southeast Asia against invading Japanese forces in an area then known as French Indochina (later Laos, Cambodia, and Vietnam).

When World War II finally ended with the surrender of Japan in 1945, France, one of the Allied victors, desired to reassert its control over its former colony of Indochina. The Viet Minh felt their efforts against the Japanese entitled them to self-determination for their land and its people. In 1945 Ho Chi Minh established Hanoi as the capital of an independent nation, the Democratic Republic of Vietnam. The conflict of interests led to the first Indochina War (1946–1954), both a French struggle for reconquest and a civil war with Vietnamese divided fighting for and against the French.

In Europe the fragile coalition of war-time allies began to unravel. Democratic-leaning nations had concerns about the Soviet Union's intensifying efforts to undermine the governments of Greece and Turkey. The U.S. State Department perceived this conduct preliminary to a spread of communism into Western Europe and the Middle East. President Harry Truman requested that Congress appropriate funds to assist "free peoples who are resisting subjugation by armed minorities or by outside pressures." This concept became known as the Truman Doctrine.

As the "cold war" conflict between democratic and communist adversaries intensified, the Truman administration formulated a policy of containment. While having no intention to attempt to destroy communism where it existed, the United States would resist its spread. The Truman Doctrine and the containment policy became major elements guiding post-war United States diplomacy in Europe. The belief was that if a non-communist country fell to a communist faction, the result would be a chain reaction of neighboring nations falling like dominos. Developed as policy in Europe, the domino theory became the American government's justification for intervention *wherever in the world* communism was threatening to spread. By the end of the post-war decade, containment of communism became a concern in Southeast Asia as well.

In 1949 communist factions emerged dominant and established the People's Republic of China. The following year, the Republic began providing the Viet Minh with military advisors and weapons. Concerned that leader Ho Chi Minh in Vietnam was more of a communist than a nationalist, the United States feared the spread of communism into Indochina. In 1950 President Truman pledged $15 million in military aid to France as a countermeasure. South Vietnam was increasingly being viewed as the key domino in Southeast Asia. Accordingly, American aid to France incrementally increased. By 1954 America was bearing over three-fourths of France's war costs in Vietnam.

Despite this support, on May 7 of that year, France was decisively defeated at Dien Bien Phu, an action that sealed its departure, relinquishing its former colony. In July 1954 five nations holding interests in the area—the Democratic Republic of Vietnam, the People's Republic of China, the Soviet Union, the United Kingdom, and France—signed the Geneva Accords. This pact, which allowed France to withdraw its troops peacefully from Southeast Asia, also divided Indochina into three regions—Laos, Cambodia, and Vietnam.

Vietnam was temporarily divided midway at the 17th Parallel into two entities. The Viet Minh were to withdraw to the area north of the parallel (North Vietnam), whereas forces that had supported the French were to occupy land south of the parallel (South Vietnam). The Accords mandated that in 1956 elections would be held to allow the Vietnamese people to reunify into one nation. However, in October 1955, factions in South Vietnam created the "Republic of Vietnam," established its capital at Saigon, and in rigged elections chose Ngo Dinh Diem president.

By 1956 the U.S. military began training South Vietnamese forces to resist communism. As Ho Chi Minh, now supported by China *and* the Soviet Union, increased activity in Vietnam, the United States increasingly supported Diem's government in South Vietnam. Diem cancelled the 1956 elections, asserting that his nation, the Republic of Vietnam, had not signed the Geneva Accords and was not bound by terms of the agreement. Instead of being unified by ballots, Vietnam experienced unruliness by bullets as communist guerrillas began an insurgency south of the 17th Parallel.

In 1960 Ho Chi Minh's government in the north formed the National Liberation Front (NLF) within South Vietnam. This network of guerrilla operatives spread across the south with the goal of liberating it from Diem's government. Although led by communists, the NLF also included non-communist factions also opposed to Diem, who called the NLF the "Vietcong" (Vietnamese communists). This label rallied greater American support for Diem's perceived anti-communist government, despite his questionable, undemocratic rise to power.

In 1963 when Diem, a Catholic, ordered repressive actions against the Buddhist majority in South Vietnam, Buddhist monks protested by dousing themselves with gasoline and igniting it. Photographs and video in newscasts depicting the Buddhist self-immolations horrified the world. As a result of the chaos of Diem's actions, a coup of his own army arrested and assassinated him. A succession of leaders had no success in stabilizing South Vietnam, despite the presence of American advisors.

In early August of 1964, when a U.S. Navy destroyer surveilling in international waters off North Vietnam's Gulf of Tonkin reported attacks against the ship by North Vietnamese gunboats, President Lyndon Johnson apprised Congress of "aggression." On August 7 Congress passed the Gulf of Tonkin Resolution, authorizing the president to "take all necessary measures to repel any armed attack against forces of the United States and to prevent further aggression."

This was the closest Congress ever came to a declaration of war against North Vietnam, but the resolution was used to empower presidents Johnson and later Richard Nixon to order bombing missions and deploy ground troops and naval vessels in an escalating war in Vietnam, with America supporting South Vietnam against North Vietnam. After a decade that accumulated more than 400 deaths among American advisors in Vietnam, the first U.S. ground troops—numbering 3,500—were sent to protect the U.S. air base in Da Nang, arriving in March 1965.

When I landed in-country in March 1969, I was one of nearly 550,000 American servicemen, the largest military force ever to be assembled there.

In between the beginning of the First Indochina War and that highest-engagement statistic in 1969, American public opinion had shifted from lukewarm support to heated debates and protests, some of them violent, over involvement in Vietnam. My experience in the Army and in Vietnam covers a very small part of that period—from September 1968 to April 1970.

With Nixon having promised to end America's involvement in the war, his presidential election in November 1968 led to a policy of "Vietnamization"—gradually withdrawing U.S. ground troops while simultaneously increasing both the training and supplying of South Vietnam's military forces. That strategical process began shortly after my arrival in-country.

It was March 1973 when the last U.S. combat troops were withdrawn. Two years later, the last American personnel left South Vietnam on the day in April 1975 that Saigon fell to communist forces. Since that date, North and South Vietnam have melded into one country. A half-century later at the time of the publication of this book, the country is governed by the Communist Party of Vietnam. Today Hanoi is Vietnam's capital, and Ho Chi Minh City, formerly Saigon, is the nation's most populous city.

1

Personal Beginnings

"We will draft you!"

IN SPRING OF 1962, WHEN I GRADUATED from Orangeburg High School in Orangeburg, South Carolina, where I was born, I was like many others in America who had been paying only casual personal attention to United States foreign policy in the Republic of Vietnam. About six months before completing high school, I had routinely registered in my hometown with the Selective Service as legally required at age 18. The expectations that I thought lay ahead of me while alternately working and paying my way through college began to change in early 1967 when I was very close to reaching my goal.

I had recently gotten married and was living in Camden, where Joan was teaching high school English and freelancing in journalism, and I was commuting full-time 70 miles round-trip to Columbia to continue my classes at the University of South Carolina. I was taking my academic work seriously and was living up to the potential that high school teachers had reminded me about whenever they chastised me if I got lazy. I was doing well with my major in Spanish and was on track in a couple more semesters to graduate from college, the first person to do so in my immediate family. Joan and I were looking forward to my graduation with ambitious plans for interesting jobs with travel abroad before settling down to build a home and raise a family.

It was a great shock when I received a letter with the "Greetings" that I had been drafted. When our good friends and next-door apartment neighbors, Andrea and Bill Norris, read the news I handed them, Billy T. (as I call him) put his hand on my shoulder and intoned in deep seriousness, "Louie" (using my given name the draft board used instead of my familiar "Glen" friends and family used), "Somebody ain't treating you right."

I contacted my draft board in Orangeburg and scheduled an appeal at their next meeting. I had completed two years of college ROTC (Reserve Officer Training Corps) and was paying attention to the increasing potential of wartime service eligibility *after* I finished my education. However, I was not expecting to be called *before* graduation according to the general circumstances at the time. Within the next few days, I scurried around USC's campus collecting the affidavits that proved I was a student in good standing. Armed with those documents, I made the 65-mile drive down Highway 601 on a dark Monday night to plead my case to the Orangeburg draft board. It was necessary to travel there to meet them at the time of their choosing because my hometown was where I had registered, and no matter where I lived, this individual board of citizens retained legal authority over my draft status.

I do not remember the number of board members nor the name of the chairman. He read over the documents, paused, then confirmed that since I was on track to graduate at the end of the fall 1967 semester, my deferment would continue until that time. I vividly recall his emphatically proclaiming, "We will draft you then. Do not plan to go to graduate school. Do not get your wife pregnant. We *will* draft you."

Outwardly I was polite, yet internally I was seething at his suggestion. Somewhere on that long, dark, and lonesome drive back to Camden, I determined that I would not allow that board to *draft* me. I was not joining protesting hippies with peace signs or leaving my country to evade being called. I would serve my country, but I would serve on my own terms. I began to investigate National Guard and reserve components within a 40-mile radius of Camden. None had vacancies; all had lengthy waiting lists. I found myself among a growing number of others affected by the divisive controversies and effects of a huge buildup currently underway to supply additional personnel for America's expanding presence in Vietnam. As graduation approached, I went to the U.S. Army recruiter. After comparing various options, I enlisted in a "college opt" program with a delayed enlistment.

Given branches of the Army from which to select, I chose in order of preference (1) Intelligence, (2) Adjutant General, (3) Artillery. The third selection had to be one of the three combat arms: Armor, Artillery, or Infantry. From those options, I would begin, as every soldier began, with Basic Combat Training (BCT), followed by Advanced Individual Training (AIT). The next step would be to attend Officer Candidate School (OCS), be commissioned a 2nd lieutenant, and thereafter have a two-year military commitment. At any time prior to receiving a commission, the contract stated, I had the alternative to "opt out" of attending OCS and to have my enlistment revert to what remained of a two-year commitment, same as conscription (being drafted).

Therefore, I was able to graduate in December 1967 before my enlistment date. Meanwhile, in early 1968 I was employed in Camden by the

Kershaw County School District, first as a substitute teacher, then as an assistant to the director of federal programs, specifically to inventory equipment provided under Title 1 of the federal Elementary and Secondary Education Act (ESEA) in a system working toward full racial desegregation. At the time, I was not sure whether my future would ever involve teaching or working in education.

The war 10,000 miles distant became much closer in March. I learned that a high school classmate and friend of mine, Richard (Dickie) Kapp, a Marine lieutenant, had been killed in Vietnam. Joan's brother Robert Anderson (Robbie, or Rob to us), who himself planned to enlist in June, accompanied me to the funeral in Orangeburg. It was a solemn experience. Dickie was the first of my friends to become a casualty of Vietnam.

As scheduled, on my enlistment date in September—ironically on Friday the 13th—Joan and I left our apartment early and drove to Columbia so that I could report at my designated time of 0600 hours (6:00 a.m.), an immediate switch to military time. We had prepared ourselves for this day and said hurried goodbyes in front of the recruitment office on the first floor of the Wade Hampton Hotel on Main Street, within sight of the South Carolina State House. Joan drove away tearfully to teach her classes at Camden High School, expecting to see me soon.

I walked inside the office and joined nearly a dozen other recruits. We were sworn in, then transported by van to Columbia's nearby Fort Jackson for physical examinations and further processing along with numerous other men brought there from other recruiting centers. Hundreds of us stood in rows in a large gym, stripped to our boxers or briefs, as doctors strode in front of and behind us to examine the raw material assembled there. A doctor briefly stopped before me to ask if my flat feet bothered me. I replied in the negative. He marked something on the sheet on his clipboard and moved on down the line.

We were there all day experiencing the time-honored Army ritual of "hurry up and wait," a rite I would continue to practice throughout my military experience. I also got my first taste of two other Army rituals—"police call" (spreading out across a designated area and picking up cigarette butts and other trash) and "mess call" (what civilians refer to in a meal as *food*, in the military quickly seemed more appropriately called *mess*). By late afternoon we queued up for a final time and received orders. With Camden located only 30 miles from Fort Jackson, Columbia, one of the largest Basic Combat Training centers in the nation, I and others had assumed I would spend the next eight or nine weeks there, and with luck might wrangle a weekend pass to go home. Uncle Sam had other plans for me.

I looked unbelievingly at the papers in my hand—SPECIAL ORDERS

NUMBER 181, EXTRACT. Was I stunned! I was booked that night on a flight out of Columbia with a final destination about 850 miles away, traveling halfway across the country to faraway St. Louis, the nearest commercial airport to Fort Leonard Wood, Missouri.

Right after receiving those papers, I was transported to the Columbia airport. There I found a pay phone and called our apartment to relay the unexpected news to Joan. While waiting for my flight, I began my first letter home to her at 6:35 p.m., providing the information I had just learned. I was to depart on a Piedmont Airlines flight for Atlanta at 9:11 p.m. I would have a long layover in Atlanta until my "red eye" Trans World Airlines departure at 4:00 a.m. (The regular world was still on standard time.)

I wrote also that, according to the unexpected news in my orders, my BCT was to begin in Missouri on September 23, and my AIT was to begin November 18 at Fort Sill, Oklahoma. I was thinking to myself, not writing, what a long way that was from home and observing curiously that no other recruits were being sent along with me. I would be traveling alone among civilian passengers.

It was a miserable night trying to sleep in the Atlanta terminal until time to depart. All that I recall about my arrival in St. Louis was viewing the Mississippi River and the relatively new Gateway Arch for the first time and marveling at the suspended replica of Charles A. Lindbergh's *Spirit of St. Louis* in the terminal. After a lengthy wait, I departed Lambert Field on an Ozark Airlines twin-prop craft that would transport me to Fort Leonard Wood.

2

Reception

"Responsibilities which Americans inherit"

After a bumpy flight from St. Louis on a cargo plane that made a rough landing on Fort Leonard Wood's airstrip about midafternoon Saturday, September 14, I disembarked and stood around a bit, uncertain what I should do. Someone in uniform finally drove up, looked at my orders, and told me to hop into the Jeep. He put me out in front of a wooden building.

I entered and showed my orders to a company clerk who told me to wait outside. It was as hot as a late afternoon in South Carolina. I began to hear a distant sound which, as it grew closer and louder, could be identified as troops marching in cadence. As they came into view, I could see their sweat-stained faces and shirts.

The clerk came out and led me across the street to a company area to join other civilian-attired recruits like me. We were assembled into a formation, then yelled at and belittled by several cadre (military persons in charge). I discovered that I was at the Reception Station. The two-story wooden barracks was similar, if not identical, to those I had seen the day before at Fort Jackson. I was assigned to a bunk on the first floor of Building 2173, Company A, for a one-week stay there.

At the beginning of processing, I was given a pre-printed slip of paper onto which I filled in "Joan" after Dear__, "1300" hours [1 p.m.] arrival time, and "14 [Saturday] September," adding "68" after 19__. The slip stated that I had arrived safely at Fort Leonard Wood, would be involved in processing approximately five days, after which I would be transferred to a Basic Combat Training Brigade. It advised that the recipient not write until the trainee sent his "permanent address," but in an emergency could contact him through a local American Red Cross chapter. The slip was to be inserted inside two pre-folded form letters from the fort's commander, "Maj. Gen. Geo. H. Walker."

One letter explained that the trainee would spend his first few days processing, after which "the initial phase of a new soldier's service career is designed to introduce him to another facet of good citizenship." It stated that one goal of basic training was "to help him gain a more realistic appreciation of the responsibilities which Americans inherit along with the many privileges of our way of life."

Expressing the hope that the trainee's "adjustment to military life is not too difficult and that he learns to appreciate and take pride in the traditions and the responsibilities of the service," the letter continued: "The training and development of our young men is very vital to the strength of our nation," and expressed confidence that "the training they will receive will benefit them immeasurably." The letter concluded that the Army was proud to have the recruit as a new member of the Army and was sure that the "parent, spouse or other relative" shared in that "feeling of pride in him" and would "encourage him in his endeavors."

The second letter warned about solicitations directed toward the next-of-kin of persons entering the military. All three papers were to be placed in a postage-paid envelope on which were printed the return address for the fort's Reception Station and "OFFICIAL BUSINESS." I hand-addressed the envelope to Joan. It would be about six more days before I would receive the information to address an OFFICIAL BUSINESS postcard to her, filling in my full name, prefaced by my rank "PVT," and followed by my service number and my "permanent" (for then) mailing address: Company C, 2nd Battalion, 3rd Brigade, Fort Leonard Wood, Missouri 65473.

That first day at the reception area, for supper we were marched to a mess hall and fed. I do not recall what we ate, but it was one of the quickest meals I ever gulped down, as NCOs (non-commissioned officers) moved among us shouting for us to hurry. We scraped our metal trays and stacked them by the sink, then were marched back to the barracks. An NCO approached my bunk and ordered me to dump out the contents of my bag. He proceeded to pick out items that he said I would not need. Those he threw into the trash. Other cadre were doing the same throughout the barracks.

We were assembled outside in formation for a roll call, followed by a police call, picking up butts and trash. We were called back in formation and dismissed. Finally we were able to converse among ourselves a bit until two NCOs stormed in and called us to attention. We stood in a long hall, two files facing one another. The NCOs strutted between our ranks and proceeded to tell us how worthless we were. Each of them picked individuals at random, got up in their faces, and yelled insults.

We were at last dismissed to resume conversations with newly made acquaintances until Taps sounded and lights were extinguished. The guys

2. Reception

on my floor were from Washington, Oregon, Kansas, Missouri, Pennsylvania, and one or two more from South Carolina. There was even one familiar face there—Don Vik, a friend and Alpha Phi Omega brother from USC.

I borrowed Vik's razor to shave for my first time since Thursday night. Before lights out I wrote Joan that as soon as they allowed us to mail home our civilian clothing, I would send back my shaver since there were no electrical outlets in the barracks. Vik had found a Post Exchange (PX) branch nearby and bought each of us flip flops for the shower. I went to that same PX and bought a Coke and a razor. Such freedom of movement and luxuries would be short-lived.

In life and in letters, I found myself jolted into military time usage and thus I employed "hours" when writing to train myself to think that way rather than in a.m. or p.m. time, although later when writing home, I would for a while randomly alternate back and forth with standard time, before eventually converting mostly to writing letters in "home time" for ease of civilian reading. Use of military time in letters not only gave practice but also conveyed a sense of my daily reality.

When the first Sunday reveille sounded at 0600, processing had been completed. Throughout basic and later in AIT, bugle calls would signal wake-up (0430), retreat, mess, Taps, and other functions. After breakfast Vik and I attended a church service nearby. I wrote Joan that, "The chaplain really didn't have much to say and the service was not very inspiring," adding, "I don't guess you could expect new recruits to be inspired anyway." After church Vik and I went to the area service club for "free coffee and donuts."

The service club hostess was very helpful in showing us a map to indicate the area where we would be moving for basic training. About a month before my unexpected assignment here, Joan's brother Rob had completed his basic at Fort Gordon, Georgia, and had been sent to Fort Leonard Wood to begin Combat Engineering AIT. I gave his address to the hostess, who said Rob's area was two or three miles away from our present site, but it would be about a mile or so closer to me when I got to my basic area. The map also showed us that Fort Leonard Wood itself was quite isolated, "in the boondocks" as we said then, with no town of any size nearby. I began more fully to understand its apt nickname, "Fort Lost-in-the-Woods."

Later that day, continuing my letter to Joan begun the night before, I described our Sunday meal—one boiled frankfurter, a tablespoon of sweet potato, one teaspoon pineapple and lettuce salad, a slice of bread, a pat of butter, and a cup of orange juice. I described the food as "gross," adding that we were told food at basic would be better. I quipped, "It's probably true since it couldn't be worse."

I explained to Joan about time and about fire guard duty. From 2100 hours (9 p.m.) until 0500 (5 a.m.) two exterior fire guards patrolled the area, approaching the door of each barracks "at least once every hour," shouting out "fire guard." The person on duty inside had to walk back and forth from one end of the building to the other. When the exterior guards called out, the interior guard had to answer and make himself visible. He had to be fully dressed. I had been lucky that my duty shift Saturday night was 2200–2300 hours (10–11 p.m.), allowing for more sleep.

My letter also reinforced what Rob's letters home had said about the temperature here. Although the middle of the day was "not so bad," it "gets cold in the evening and stays cold until up in the morning." Having anticipated being sent to Fort Jackson, I had reported to enlistment wearing no jacket, only a pair of trousers and a short sleeve shirt for outerwear. Here even the guys with jackets complained of the cold. Those of us with no sleeves shivered. I hoped the next day for issuance of both fatigues *and field jackets*.

We were abruptly awakened the next morning, Monday, September 16, before dawn. Cadre switched on lights and moved rapidly through the barracks hall, cursing and shouting at recruits scrambling to get dressed, shave, and assemble into formation outside. When given the order to fall out to police the area, we were able to converse in low voices. I recognized a few fellows by their clothing. Like me, they were wearing the same garments as the previous day, the only clothing we had. We were marched to the mess hall for breakfast and marched back to the company for another formation, then another police call.

Afterward we were marched to the supply area, made up of older single-story wooden buildings. We queued up in single file and entered the first building. It was like a super-elongated auto parts store where customers stand on one side of a counter, behind which an employee takes an order and passes through a doorway to fill it from storage. A number of civilian employees stood or milled behind the counter. By individual initiative, they would either ask each recruit his shirt size or eyeball him and hand over the size they thought should fit.

The process was repeated in several buildings until each of us had been issued four sets of fatigues (heavy cotton pants and long-sleeved shirts), a field jacket, seven pairs of socks, and two baseball-type caps—all in OD ("olive drab") color. We were also issued seven boxers and crewneck T-shirts, and four handkerchiefs—all white, and two pairs of black leather combat boots. In addition, we received a heavy cotton duffle bag, on which each man found his name already stenciled. Juggling this stack of clothing articles, we were marched back to our barracks.

Here the cadre demonstrated the procedure for organizing footlockers. There was a place for each item, and each item was to be in its place.

There was also a proper method of folding each item. (Later we would be shown how to roll T-shirts and boxers around soft drink cans, stuffing the edges into open tops and bottoms.) The result was total uniformity—an Army goal! One pair of boots was marked with a paint spot on each heel. We were instructed to alternate pairs. That kept us from spit-shining one pair for inspection and using the other for training activities. Each pair was to be spit-shined.

As we organized footlockers, we were able to chat quietly as we worked. We had donned newly issued uniforms and had been given packages into which we placed our civilian clothing and shoes to be mailed home. Once we were all dressed identically, it was more difficult to recognize people whose names we had learned to match with clothing styles and colors. I had to rely on hair styles and colors for identification. (Later name tags would be sewn above the pocket flaps of shirts and field jackets.) In short order, the cadre descended upon us to inspect footlockers, a number of which were upended because they failed inspection—a procedure to be repeated throughout basic.

We fell out for formation, followed by police call, then were marched to the mess hall. After lunch and another police call, we were marched to the barbers. Civilians who issued clothing may have seemed rude and short-tempered in their hurry, but civilian barbers enjoyed sadistic humor. Anyone with long hair would be asked how he wanted it cut, sometimes even getting a naïve response like "a little off the sides." The barber proceeded in all cases to take off all but a stubble.

Military barbering was an extremely efficient procedure, requiring less than ten seconds per head. Each barber used clippers with a vacuum hose attachment that sucked most of the clippings into a 55-gallon drum. Very few hit the floor. A few recruits who had moles or who flinched during the procedure had bloody spots on their scalps. When we had all assembled outside, no one was recognizable. The only differences were height and girth. We were all bald and dressed identically in OD. It took quite a while to learn individual identities a third time.

In the "zero" days prior to the beginning of our training cycle, the daily schedule was formations, inspections, police calls, exercise, and details. At each post-breakfast formation, cadre would select groups for details like grounds care or inside cleaning. One day I was one of several men detailed to a particular address to sweep and mop the building.

Entering the single-story wooden structure, we noticed that the open center had a number of desks, tables, and chairs. The perimeter was divided by cubicles we were not allowed to enter. As I swept, I could not help overhearing conversations, and I quickly realized what was occurring. An Army recruiter in each cubicle was interviewing a conscript who had been summoned there. The recruiter would tell the young man that he had been drafted to replace a soldier who had been killed in Vietnam, but he could avoid that fate by enlisting. The promise of "a job of your choice" in a "non-combat assignment," despite upping to a three-year enlistment, was quite an enticement to retain an inexperienced 18-or 19-year-old kid who had been drafted for a two-year hitch.

In a brief note to Joan Tuesday, September 17, I said that there had been little time to write. I had been up since 0430 and been kept on the go all day. I had been given "a typhoid shot, blood test, & polio vaccine." I had also been on three details. In fact, I was still at one site, sweeping, waxing, and buffing an office. We began cleaning at 1700 and had just finished at 2035 hours. The five of us on that detail learned on return to barracks that while we were away working we had missed PX privileges given to the rest of our company.

I was able to write Joan again that night while I was on duty from 2300 to midnight. My duty happened to be at the same office I had cleaned earlier. My job was to keep company with the sergeant on duty, answer the phone if it rang, and "serve as a runner if any messages are to be delivered." The bonus was that lights were on, and I could write. I told Joan that in the reception area I had seen Neil Allman, a friend I had known since high school. In the Army Reserve, he was at Fort Leonard Wood to take BCT and AIT and was to spend the rest of his six months active duty here.

Going on to discuss family budget matters, I requested that Joan, as soon as she got my address, send a notarized copy of our marriage license so I could complete the paperwork for her allotment payments. I said that since I would be earning such a pittance, I had chosen to claim no exemption for myself. She was to claim both of us on her tax returns. I mentioned we were supposed to receive a partial payment of $25 on Thursday. I had just $1.10 remaining from the $7.00 I had leaving home, as we had been instructed to bring little money.

Lamenting again the mess hall food and cooks "cursing us and telling us to eat and get out," I wrote as a person who delights in a leisurely meal and eats slowly. "You should see me now," I said, "eating a full meal (such as it is) in 7–10 minutes. The only thing that keeps me going is the milk. I generally drink 2–3 glasses per meal."

I explained too my inability to telephone her so far. Although there were three pay phones at the PX and six more within 300 yards of my barracks, we could use the phones only when the company had PX privileges, which my company had been given just twice—Saturday night when lines were very long with waiting recruits, and the other time when I was on detail. I wrote that she should get my mailing address next week, adding, "It really will be good to hear from you." My duty relief had arrived at

2. Reception

midnight, but I remained a few minutes longer to finish the letter. "I really hate to stop writing but as it is I'll only get 4 hours of sleep."

It was Thursday, September 19, when I wrote Joan next, with an hour and 15 minutes free. My only task was to work on my combat boots, shining them to satisfaction. I had pulled kitchen police (KP) duty Wednesday afternoon for a couple hours. About the KP, I said, "We didn't have so terribly much to do so it wasn't too bad." We had taken a battery of paper tests lasting four and one-half hours Wednesday, with another battery from 0645 to 1030 Thursday morning. We had just returned from visiting the dentist for teeth exams. We were scheduled for counseling by a "career counselor" that afternoon and would get "shots in the morning."

Tomorrow we were to "ship out" to our basic training area. I had attempted telephoning Joan again last night, waiting in line at the pay phone one and a half hours. When I finally got a phone, it was malfunctioning. Just as I attempted to dial a second time, an announcement came over the intercom that our company was to return to the barracks, so I had to abandon my efforts. However, I had a promising plan I related in the letter.

Allman and I had concocted a scheme. *If we could get a weekend pass*, we could fly to Atlanta and meet Joan and Margaret, Allman's wife, a friend of hers from Winthrop College who was nearby in graduate school at USC. I added, "It only takes 35 min. to fly from here to St. Louis and then 60 min. (by jet) from St. Louis to Atlanta. We'll have to try to work it out." I reported that I had gotten $25 "initial advanced pay" that day. I mentioned as soon as I received the marriage license copy, Joan could begin receiving her allotment as well as a form to apply for her dependent's PX card.

Friday, September 20, I wrote Joan on a Service Club one-page letter-envelope. I said I had mailed her earlier that day a package of my civilian clothes and my electric shaver. We had been issued our dog tags and instructed to wear them from then on until out of service. We were packed and ready to ship out for basic training, reportedly at 1430 hours.

Our dog tags were two slightly oval metal plates onto which a typewriter-type machine had impressed last name, first name, and middle initial, with serial number, blood type, Social Security number, and religious preference. Each tag had one hole through which ran a chain similar to the type used for pull-type lights. One chain was long enough that, when clasped, it would easily slip over one's head. One tag was attached to it. The other tag was attached to a separate chain only a couple of inches long. This chain was closed around the longer one. We were to wear these around our necks at all times, even in the shower.

We realized, should we be wounded or injured, the dog tags would provide doctors or medics with basic identification. We also understood, should we be killed, a comrade would break the tag from the short chain to turn over to the appropriate authorities. The other tag, still attached, he would place in the victim's mouth.

I told Joan that, uncharacteristically, our sergeant was in a good mood. We had all shined our boots satisfactorily, and he had commented that "our barracks looked beautiful this a.m." I remarked to her, "It sure was great to talk to you last night." The night before I had finally reached her by telephone.

After we talked, I had gone to the PX where a guy in my roster told me that my brother-in-law was looking for me. I quickly returned to the barracks. "There was Old Rob," I wrote. "I think he was as glad to see me as I was to see him. We had a family reunion for a couple of hours." Rob told me that there was a pretty good steak house on post, and we made tentative plans to meet there whenever I was allowed to leave the company area. It would be about a month, as it turned out, before we were able to get together, while the more elaborate plan that Allman and I had made would never prove possible.

3

Basic Combat Training

"In 8 weeks ... teach you how to kill"

We were marched to the Basic Combat Training area Friday afternoon, September 20, about 1700 hours. Fort Leonard Wood, as I had learned, was a sprawling post covering more than 96 square miles in central Missouri. Having been at Fort Jackson, South Carolina, with its wooden World War II barracks and having seen similar ones in Reception here, I was surprised to discover that we were now to be billeted in modern, air-conditioned brick structures.

My initial pleasure was mitigated for we quickly discovered how our barracks remained so sparkling in appearance. The building was patrolled during the night by trainees serving two-hour shifts as fire guards. Wearing basic duty fatigues and a yellow helmet liner with a large "FG" on the front, each guard operated an electric buffer as he walked the hallways. Thus, the tile floors of the downstairs common areas were highly polished. The floors of our sleeping areas—the two upper stories—were slightly less polished, but their sheen resulted from manual buffing.

Our sleeping area consisted of a long hall with iron cots lining each side. Between each cot was an upright steel wall locker for hanging our dress uniforms, issued later. Most of our clothing was stored in the ubiquitous footlocker at the foot of each cot. Our civilian clothing and shoes having been sent home, we had nothing but our military issue. We were expected to organize both storage lockers and to make our beds "the Army way," as we had already learned. All were subject to being "disarranged" if the cadre deemed them unacceptable.

We were not allowed to leave the barracks or the immediate company area without permission. Although there was a branch PX across the street from our barracks, it was off limits. Several trainees attempted to sneak over. Anyone caught with cigarettes was made to put the entire pack in his mouth and smoke them all at once. Anyone caught with candy or gum was made to chew the entire pack. Pushups intensified the penalties.

The names of Glen's company, battalion and brigade and his graduation date stamped at top right of his *Basic Combat Training Cycle Book*.

The mess hall, about a block away, was a modern brick structure and was huge. It was a battalion mess hall, built to serve 1,000 men at each meal. We marched as a unit from our barracks, then peeled off into one line outside a door. When each man entered the mess hall, he yelled out his

3. Basic Combat Training

New barracks in which Glen's company lived (*BCT Cycle Book*).

serial number, prefaced by NG, RA or U.S., thus designating whether he was National Guard, Regular Army (enlistee), or United States (conscript or draftee). Enlistees like me were treated with only slightly less indignity than guardsmen or draftees.

All basic duty uniforms designated as "fatigues" were long-sleeved shirts and trousers, 100 percent cotton, and OD in color. If the weather was especially hot, we were ordered to take off our shirts and train in our white T-shirts. This would normally occur during physical training (PT). The uniform of the day was determined by calendar date, not temperature. Field jackets were to be donned only when the calendar dictated or if specific orders overrode the calendar.

Two types of dress uniforms were issued. The summer type was a pair of cotton poplin trousers and a short-sleeve poplin shirt, both light tan in color. The winter uniform consisted of a long-sleeve light tan cotton poplin shirt and a narrow black necktie, with dark green wool trousers and matching brass-buttoned wool coat. Completing either uniform was a navy-blue nylon fabric belt with a brass slide buckle, black low-quarter leather dress shoes, thin black nylon socks, and an overseas cap that could be folded flat and inserted between the belt and trouser waist. Accompanying the summer uniform was a long raincoat. Supplementing the winter one was an overcoat.

Sunday afternoon, September 22, on U.S. Army stationery I wrote Joan when we finally had a little bit of time off. I had been on detail as a server in the mess hall and was to serve at lunchtime all week. I commented about all the things we had to do in our "spare" time: "keep our rooms immaculate, shine (and I do mean shine) our shoes—2 pairs of combat boots and 1 pair of dress shoes, polish our brass—collar brass and belt buckle, and any 200,000 other things."

I wrote that the beds were comfortable, but we really did not get a chance to enjoy them. Using civilian time designations for Joan's ease of comparison to routines we had established at home, I explained: "We get up at 4:15 a.m. each day except Sunday when we get a chance to sleep until 6 a.m. We have until 5:00 to dress, make our beds (army style), straighten our lockers, sweep, mop, and buff our floors and the hallway outside, and of course shave etc." I described the way beds must be made—"tight enough to bounce a quarter." I drew one sketch indicating the bed with a tight blanket and another sketch showing a tent pole and pup tent pulled tight, shielding one corner to form a "sneeze sheet" for flu season.

Our company being restricted to the barracks, the few times we were allowed to sit, it had to be on the floor or on the footlocker. An inspection could occur at any time, so beds were off limits for sitting. I closed the letter, stating that I had "to clean the barracks & then shower before 9 p.m. Go to sleep at 9, wake up at 12 and be a CQ [charge of quarters] runner until 2 a.m., then up at 4:15, clean up room again & start our day." We had to run and yell to and from the mess hall. I had recently made the mistake of *walking* back to the barracks "and the sergeant was standing in the doorway watching. When I got there I had to pump out 20 pushups." I closed the letter with a postscript, "Do not mail me anything but letters. We cannot have cookies, candy etc. Anything else I have no place to put."

Writing on Wednesday, September 25, I was euphoric because that day I had received a letter from my parents and 12 letters from Joan. It was the first mail to reach me since my arrival. She had been writing a letter each day and saving them to mail when she got my address. One letter included the marriage license copy I had requested to set up her allotment.

We were working now in hectic training, and my letters described a number of activities. We had started marching and drilling before receiving weapons. The exercises were not alien to me as I had been in Boy Scouts, in my high school marching band, and had taken ROTC in college. Some of the recruits had difficulty differentiating left foot from right, and when ordered "right face" would turn the opposite direction. The previous day we had been issued our "weapon" (not "gun"), had all of our field gear, and were "wearing pistol belts with canteens, and poncho rolled on the back. We started today wearing our helmet liners."

The 7.62 mm M14 rifle with its wooden stock weighed, empty, 9.2 pounds and was then the Army's standard weapon. With the rifle in hand, we marched and drilled, practicing the positions of the Manual of Arms.

3. Basic Combat Training

We also practiced disassembly and reassembly, taking the weapon apart and putting it back together. My drill instructor was a firm believer in the merits of spray lubricant WD-40 for cleaning it.

I hastened to reassure Joan that we would not be issued ammunition until we went to the rifle range, adding, "If we had already been given live ammo I would be worried too. Most of these people have been 'playing with' their M14—something they are definitely not supposed to do." I emphasized that the penalty for any infraction was pushups: "My DI (drill instructor) loves pushups." An infraction "costs 30 pushups this week, 40 next week, and on up to 100" by the eighth week of basic.

Each morning there was a barracks inspection. The platoon that won went to the chow line first, and therefore earned a little time to rest or write letters. That was an incentive to clean the barracks well. "Around here each day is like a lifetime and 10 or 15 extra minutes is heaven-sent." I was always glad to have extra time to write. That evening we were supposed to have a test on "military courtesy." We had had classes on "guard duty, malaria control, cold weather preparation, etc." and had seen many "army propaganda films."

During all of our training it was made clear that we were being prepared to go to tropical Vietnam. To that end, I joked that "cold weather preparation" for our current needs was "wasted training." I re-emphasized my address for Joan to write Rob where to find me: "I'm in C-2-3 (that's Charlie Co., 2nd Battalion, 3rd Training Brigade) building P-651, room 111." Some rooms in the barracks housed four, six, or eight persons. I was in a room with two beds "much like the dorm at USC."

My roommate was Paul Holley from Florence, Alabama. I knew him from my same barracks at Reception, so our having been the only ones from there to be in the same squad here at BCT, we had chosen to room together. A Florence State graduate, just two courses from a master's in business management from Memphis State, Holley was single and an Army Reservist, serving six-months active duty like Allman. Allman and Vik were both in my company, but not in my squad.

Physical Training (PT) had been stressed from the beginning. We had PT exercises each morning and each afternoon, learning "movements of execution for Dismounted Drill (DD)." (I inwardly chuckled at the anachronism of the term from an era when soldiers had to dismount horses to drill.) Rain or shine, we drilled. My September 29 letter cited that we had drilled in the rain without raincoats. "When they finally let us put on raincoats we were all soaked."

A passing score on the all-important PT Proficiency Test (PTPT) was essential to graduate from basic training. We would run a mile before breakfast and practice various components of the

Kenneth Herweck
Orian Hinshaw
Paul Holley
Joseph Holliday
Larry Holt

Johnny Homer
Patrick Hull
Louie Inabinet
Joseph Inmon
Norman Jackson

The photograph of Glen (bottom right) is identified by his formal name "Louie Inabinet." The photograph directly about him is his roommate Paul Holley (*BCT Cycle Book*).

test—Run-Dodge-and-Jump, 40-Yard Low Crawl, Horizontal Bars, 120-Yard Man-Carry, and One-Mile Run. Although we did the mile run each morning, we concentrated on one other component each week, and after week five concentrated on all. Each goal had to be satisfied within a set time.

The first PTPT component was a figure 8 obstacle course of barricades to be jumped, scaled, or dodged, and water-filled trenches to be hurdled. The low crawl was a straight course with arms extended and a rifle cradled horizontally, chest on the ground, using elbows, hips, and knees to wiggle the distance. Repetitive usage of the course had worn shallow trenches the cadre exulted in putting trainees through after a rain, even using it after hours as punishment for an infraction.

I especially disliked monkey bars, swinging from bar to bar, alternating hands so never to have both on the same bar at the same time. The 120-yard carry seemed simple, in any fashion carrying another trainee of my same weight, but the timing made it grueling. These events were executed consecutively, culminating with the mile run with scarcely a rest between components.

3. Basic Combat Training 27

Glen at the end of the line during training activity (*BCT Cycle Book*).

While my age (I would be 25 in less than two months) gave me a mental advantage over many of the other trainees, it definitely put me at a disadvantage in physical training. I had been a college student spending most of my time sitting and studying, and I had been married almost two years to a good cook. I was competing here with guys who only months earlier had engaged in rigors like football, basketball, baseball, or track.

My letter Saturday morning, September 28, reported having awakened an hour earlier than usual to prepare for "a big inspection—foot lockers and wall lockers open—by the company commander." I was hoping not to have a PT test today as "almost all of us have colds (myself included) and we're all exhausted physically. We had to run a mile this morning before breakfast at 5 a.m. We'll have to run another mile for the PT test, too."

Finishing the letter later that evening, I reported that we did have the PT test and we had scored 93 percent on the inspection. However, we were told afterward that the test would not count and were "pretty chapped after working so hard and getting up so early but that's just part of the daily harassment here." I sketched in my letter a guidon (flag on a pole) that had "C 2 3" above a big capital "F" with the word "troop" below. I explained the platoon with the lowest score on the day's inspection had to carry the F Troop guidon until the next day's inspection. My platoon had gotten it the previous day because several guys had not shaved. Since today's good score was not counted, we had to stay humiliated with the guidon over the weekend.

In daily informational training, outside or inside, we sat on bleachers listening to monotone lectures on everything from military law and discipline to STDs. Humdrum discourses were interspersed with physical exercises like pull-ups, sit-ups, jumping-jacks, and push-ups—lots and lots of push-ups. Our DIs were quite skilled at pushing us to the limits of our physical capabilities. A trainee who got out of step during a march would be ordered to drop out of formation, knock out 20 or 25 push-ups, then double-time to catch up with the company. Another punishment was making a recruit double-time around the entire formation as it marched in normal cadence. Once when we were transported to a remote area of the post in a rainstorm, I dropped my weapon exiting the bus. The DI ordered me to drop and do 20 push-ups right there in the mud, with my rifle resting on the tops of my hands. I had to kiss my weapon each time my body touched the ground.

Monday evening, September 30, in a letter begun while I was "chewing to death" a piece of contraband gum Joan had sent me, I described a helpful aspect of training. I finished the letter the next day with a negative concern about training.

"I enjoyed the instruction we had this morning," the letter began. It was four hours of first aid, beginning with a "rather gory 30 min. movie on combat injury which showed head wounds, sucking chest wounds, arm & leg wounds, stomach wounds with intestines hanging out, and fractures with bones sticking through the skin." The last two hours, we were put into pairs to practice bandaging one another and administering shock treatments. I recognized, although this was geared to combat situations, "the knowledge could come in handy in any emergency."

My negative reflection on training referred to my DI's calling me aside later that day during bayonet practice. We had begun the training using pugil sticks, poles about five feet long. To each end was attached a gourd-shaped bag filled with some substance. We wore football-type helmets and face guards, padded gloves, and a padded groin protector. A trainee who was stabbed with the "barrel" end or clubbed with the "butt" end of the pugil stick, would suffer the effect of a boxing glove—unpleasant but not lethal.

3. Basic Combat Training

Our training advanced to fixing bayonets on our rifles and practicing different moves on man-sized dummies. We were supposed to scream "Kill" as we plunged our bayonets into the effigy. When the DI asked me if I was angry, I couldn't help but grin and say no. He said, "You will be when I get through with you!" I wrote, "The whole system here—the confinement of the trainees, the discipline, the harassment, and the brutality of the DIs—is for one purpose and one purpose only—to teach us hate—hate intensive enough to make us want to kill."

Continuing I said, "I know I'm not weak or squeamish about death or about my defending myself, and I know that I could kill a man in hand-to-hand combat if it were necessary." However, I continued, "I hate to think of the influence this will have on some of these people 17–19 years of age. These are people who don't even know what life is and they must already be so entrenched in death." I recalled to Joan that Rob and his friend Garrett Milner, both 21, had each written home from their respective training that "all they are interested in doing here in 8 weeks is teach you how to kill."

I was pretty upbeat in my October 2 letter. This had been detail day for our company. Four other guys, Allman, and I had been assigned duty at the Bivouac Pool, the building from which all supplies and equipment were issued to units which were going on bivouac, the one-week outdoor encampment that would be the pinnacle of our training.

Being on detail at the Bivouac Pool was not a tough assignment. We were allowed to work at a leisurely pace organizing equipment during the morning. From 1300 to 1430, we worked only 45 minutes. The rest of the time we napped or watched some of the World Series on a portable TV. That evening after chow we were marched about three-fourths mile to get a shot for yellow fever. It was the eighth shot we had been given since arrival, and, of course, we were "double-timed back after our shots."

The next morning, we performed normal activities despite torrential rains with lightning. "Naturally," I wrote October 3, we had to ground our ponchos and field jackets so that we were soaked as we did push-ups and other physical exercises on the slippery ground. The rain began about 0515 while we were in line to go into the mess hall, and "it must have rained close to 2 inches by 0930," I said, adding, "We marched through low places where water was 1 to 2 feet deep." I reckoned that was training for Vietnam's monsoons.

That afternoon we had "3 hrs. of map & compass reading" and then put that knowledge to practical application on a "pace course" in the hilly and rocky woods. We paired up to "find a point 175 meters into the boondocks using a given azimuth [direction of a compass bearing]. Then we had to return to the starting point using the back azimuth." I described the terrain as similar to that of northern Kershaw County at home, where we had trekked Joan's family woodlands together many times. She would know how muddy the rain made soil like that.

I began a second letter later the night of October 3. Most of my company was on detail but somehow, I had gotten skipped, so I sat on my footlocker, writing more and adding details about the day. Besides "2 hours of DD" there had been two hours of excruciatingly boring classroom instruction on "our American Heritage taught on about a third-grade level." There was a rifle inspection in the evening because the next day was to be our first trip to the rifle range.

Friday, October 4, was rather easy in comparison for me, but I took it seriously. There was "no PT, no DD. We had four hours of Trainfire instruction, introduction to weapon training. I was more at ease than guys who were less exposed to woods, camping, game hunting, and target-practice experiences. Some of the trainees had never touched a firearm until Basic and were initially intimidated."

At the range those of us scheduled to attend Officers Candidate School were also introduced to the M16 that would be used exclusively in Vietnam, and we were taught to dismantle and reassemble it. In the afternoon we had four more hours of first aid.

The weekend of October 5 and 6 I wrote of failures and successes telephoning home: two unsuccessful attempts Saturday evening and a successful one Sunday morning. In between the two, I had fire guard duty (0100–0230 hours) and a "pretty good" breakfast of eggs, ham, toast, coffee, and Rice Krispies. It was cold and rainy, so a more relaxed morning was welcomed. After polishing boots and shoes, I donned my dress uniform, and Allman and I attended church service.

News had come that the U.S. Army Chief of Staff, General William Westmoreland, was to visit Fort Leonard Wood Thursday. "We have to wear freshly ironed fatigues and our low quarters & both pairs of combat boots have to be spit shined," I wrote Sunday. "Even our rubber overshoes have to be polished." I remarked that two weeks of training were down with six more to go, and that during our seventh week we would have tests on "everything we have been exposed to—PT, DD, bayonet, first aid, guard duty, etc."

I began another letter Sunday night which I finished Monday, October 7. The weather was getting colder, and I surmised that Leonard Wood would live up to another nickname, "Little Korea." I was scheduled to take care of allotment papers tomorrow. Allman had brought his portable radio and we were listening to music as I wrote. He mailed the letter for me.

Shortly thereafter, I discovered that I was to be CQ runner from 2200 to 2400. That enabled me to begin another letter October 7 during times

3. Basic Combat Training

I had no duties. I continued my reporting of various activities and family business. Next week we were to march to a distant rifle range, "a nine-mile march so we've been told." We had learned too that our sixth week we would be on the all-important bivouac. Tuesday night I added another page to the letter. I had taken care of the allotment paperwork and application for Joan's PX service card, told her that later next month she should begin receiving $100 monthly, $40 from my pay and $60 from Uncle Sam.

Saturday, October 12, I began a letter after lunch intending to share good news. We had been told we would have post privileges Saturday and Sunday. At a 1300 formation the Platoon Sergeant had reiterated that we would have post privileges, and he warned us to be back on time.

"We were all in a line to sign out and leave," I wrote Joan. "Allman and I were making plans to get a cab and go see Rob and then go to a movie and maybe eat a steak tonight." Just then, our platoon was called out in formation. The sergeant came out, reporting, "The company commander called and said that too many people were going on post privileges and that some were not going to be able to get them." Both Allman and I were among the latter. To add insult to our injury, we who remained behind were assigned details.

I wrote as well about another annoyance—foot blisters. The previous day we had marched a couple of miles and then were trucked to one of the ranges. "However, we marched all the way back double-timing at all-too-frequent intervals," thus the blisters. There was no firing at the range. The purpose of the trip, I thought, was to subject us to a lengthy march and to indoctrinate us to going there.

The next day, "a dreary wet" Sunday, I wrote that my company was scheduled to march to the rifle range on Monday morning, but I would be missing that experience since I had been assigned KP duty. I was to report to mess that night to find out what to do. KP duty was to last from 0315 to 2030. I was not sad about missing a long march and firing from the prone position in what was certain to be soggy mud after today's rain. I added, "We'll be marching out to different firing ranges for the next week and a half, so I guess I'll get my share of marching anyway." Each of those days we were to leave our company area at 0600 and not return until 2000 or 2030.

Various letters over the next ten days included details describing the firing range procedures. A range had perhaps eight to twelve firing lanes. We fired from standing, seated, and prone positions. Only when a trainee was in position in his lane would he be given ammunition. Each round was carefully counted out. The trainee would load it into his magazine, fire on command, police (pick up) his spent brass, and return it to a member of the cadre who ascertained that the number matched that of the live rounds that had been issued. No one would be allowed to leave the range if a discrepancy was discovered.

On Tuesday, October 15, we went to the range and remained later than usual. "We had a nighttime tactical march back to the barracks with ambushes by members of the cadre," I said. "I had not eaten my orange at lunch. I put it in my pocket, thinking it might make a nice snack later. I ate it that night as I lay on the edge of the road hidden from cadre who intended to ambush us. I think that was the best orange I have ever eaten." We were out until 2200 hours.

Wednesday morning we got up at the usual time but had to clean our weapons before departing, so we did not leave for the range until nearly 0900. On the previous day I had successfully zeroed my weapon, that is, adjusted my rifle sights for accuracy. Therefore, with others who had also accomplished this necessary step, I was given the easy detail of stapling targets onto man-sized silhouettes while the others worked to zero their weapons. I was able to write Joan a letter that day by jotting portions at different times on my pocket notepad, which we were required to carry at all times for notetaking.

While firing, I was among only 40 of the 210 in our company who gained the proficiency score that day to "qualify," meaning we met or exceeded the required score. I was cautiously optimistic that my achievement might result in long-awaited post privileges next weekend. The time was 1925 when I began the last of five segments of writing in my notepad, saying we had just returned from the range, having marched the seven miles back in one hour and 35 minutes.

My long-anticipated hope for post privileges finally materialized the weekend of October 19 and 20. My letter, begun early Saturday afternoon stated that as soon as I could sign out, I was going over "to F-3-1" to try to get together with Rob. I explained I would probably take a cab since I was nursing a blister "about the size of a half-dollar on my right heel" from the week's trek to and from the range—about seven and a half miles each way. I was in hopes that it would heal by Monday, when we were scheduled for two more days marching to that same range.

I resumed the letter about five hours later with "Guess who's here in the room with me now?" On the next page was a note to Joan written by Rob while I went to the CQ to sign back in from our outing. "Don't worry about Glen because he is fine," Rob penned. We had gone to the steak house for a T-bone where the food was good, but the best was being able to consume it in leisurely style without anyone yelling, "Get out of this damn mess hall, this here ain't no social hall." Did Rob and I enjoy talking and catching up as we ate!

Rob came back to my barracks and visited until nearly 2100 hours.

He returned Sunday about 1100, and I described him "reading the funnies" in a newspaper belonging to a friend of mine, Paul Martin from Illinois. Enjoying Sunday comics was a long tradition in Joan's family. I asked her to pass on to her family that "Rob is fine. He looks well and seems in good spirits."

In the rest of the letter, I described the "field fire ranges" where we had been Thursday and Friday. Each lane had three targets at distances of 75, 175, and 300 meters. Targets popped up for five, seven, or ten seconds, respectively. I was one of the 12 men out of 70 in my platoon who shot above average on all three. For that reason, I had earned those post privileges I had enjoyed this weekend.

The coming week we were scheduled for field fire practice Monday and Tuesday, with Wednesday being "record range" firing to qualify with the M14, as was required to complete BCT. Tuesday, October 22, I wrote at 0500 that I had gone on sick call for "my blistered feet and my cold." Thus, spared a march to and from the range on "a cold windy day," uncomfortable even with field jackets and gloves, I was hopeful of ridding myself of both my miserable cold and my painful blisters before Sunday. That day we were to begin camping outdoors on bivouac. I was guardedly optimistic that once we returned from bivouac, "all else should be downhill."

The next day, Wednesday, October 23, was the important day. On the way to the firing record range, a fellow trainee accidently knocked my rifle from my grasp, and it hit the ground. Apparently, it slightly moved my sights because I did not shoot as well as I had consistently done in practice and knew that I was capable of doing. I qualified as a Marksman, second to an Expert rating. At least I did not BOLO ("fail to qualify"). Our DIs had threatened us not to BOLO.

In a brief letter that night, I lamented "a long day" when "I just could not seem to do anything right. I ended up barely qualifying." I did not mention in the letter the "accident" of the rifle sights, but passed the mediocre score off as, "Maybe I was trying too hard," adding, "Oh, well at least I'm glad it's over." That's exactly how I felt, for I was ready to move ahead with a major requirement met.

Early the next day I wrote that we were heading to another range for "quick kill" exercises, "shooting at targets for speed and without using the rifle's sights." We were to return later than usual as we were to remain out to "fire on the night-fire range." There we huddled into a small unlighted building to adjust our eyes to "night vision," I wrote later. Then in the dark we were led to a nearby open field (not a range) where we were given BB rifles. Instructors would throw a small metal disc about the size of a nickel into the air for each shooter to hit. I was surprised, but with night vision we were able to hit perhaps half of them.

I concluded the Thursday letter the next morning, with an addition from my pocket notepad. In a boring class on "character guidance," we were getting ready to evaluate "our platoon guides, squad leaders, and each individual member of each squad." Afterwards, recruiters tried again to encourage draftees to re-enlist.

Unlike most Fridays when we trainees anticipated a more leisurely weekend, on October 25 we felt apprehensive. Saturday was preparation day, and Sunday we would march out to bivouac. In preparation for our week of camping, we had been issued shelter halves, sleeping bags, and long johns. It had been getting colder—28° Friday morning and mid-40's for afternoon. We did not know exactly where we were going, but we knew it was a higher elevation on the edge of the Ozark Mountains, with temperatures predicted to continue dropping.

I wrote a postcard Saturday, October 26. We had arisen at 0400 and laid out all of our bivouac gear on our cots for inspection. A letter written Saturday afternoon and a quick note the next morning indicated that I had been able to reach Joan on the telephone, that we were being served lunch early in order to depart at noon Sunday, and that we would each be carrying an extra 55 pounds of gear on our seven-mile march. I had learned too that Rob and I would not both be going home for Christmas at the same time as we had hoped. He would be home on leave in November after AIT and then go on before Christmas to his new assignment—in Korea.

Normally during bivouac, two trainees would put together the shelter halves they were issued and create a crude pup tent as shelter. Unfortunately for us, we were told our shelter halves would be used only as ground cloths to be laid beneath our sleeping bags. Apparently, we heard, on his visit to Fort Leonard Wood, General Westmoreland had mentioned that troops in the field in Vietnam did not sleep in tents. Since we were training to fight in Vietnam, as we were told again, we were not going to use tents either.

Someone forgot to consider that our training that week was on the fringe of the Ozarks in freezing weather.

4

Bivouac

"Really a mess ... completely exhausted"

AT NOON SUNDAY, OCTOBER 27, our training company, with each man weighted with heavy packs and weapons, marched from our barracks for three and one-half hours to reach a hilly and rocky site, the base camp from which we would operate for the week of bivouac. Standing there was one large canvas tent over a wooden floor, centered with a pot-bellied woodburning stove. The tent was for exclusive use of the cadre. Also onsite for use of all was one primitive, partially enclosed wooden latrine that smelled as if it had been used non-stop since World War II.

As I recall, one of our first activities was to put into practice what we learned about navigating a compass course. Each trainee was given a sheet of coordinates and was told to find his way from an individual starting point through a wooded area to a designated spot. Late in the afternoon we were instructed to use our entrenching tools to dig foxholes there.

Our entire company was paired off to tackle the repetitive foxhole task. My partner was Paul Holley. The cadre moved us several times, during which time it became completely dark as we continued working. We chipped and hacked vigorously in the hard, rocky Ozark soil at each site for the goal of "a hole 4 ft. long 2 ft. wide and 4 ft. deep." Despite our futilely struggling for hours, the best example among us might have held a helmet. The cadre delighted in watching us in our frustration.

The already cold temperature continued dropping. Finally, we were allowed to cease hacking and were issued supper. This was my first experience with C-rations ("combat" rations, categorically in Army-logic nomenclature: "Meal, Combat, Individual [MCI]"). Each meal was a small brown rectangular box packed with small cans of (mostly) edible items. Each case had varieties labeled *B1A*, or such. Nearly everything was canned to provide maximum longevity. For opening the cans, each box contained a tiny folding metal opener, a "P-38."

The opener proved a marvelous device once we figured out in the pitch dark how to use it. We were allowed no lighting and had been given no tutelage in the operation of the P-38. This was, I am certain, an oversight as we were given instruction *ad nauseum* in the operation of every other object with an acronym that the Army possessed.

Following a quick supper, we were given guard duty assignments for the night. Holley and I both had duty 2130 to 2300. In military theory, one could sleep one and a half hours, stand guard for one and a half hours, and repeat the pattern until daybreak. I found the least rocky, most level spot possible in the darkness, spread my shelter half and unrolled the sleeping bag so that it would be ready for me when I was relieved at 2300.

I was then posted to my assigned spot. The night was very cold and windy, and about 2200 it began raining and sleeting. I was elated an hour later to be relieved from duty. My heavy, waterproof sleeping bag was the insulated cold-weather mummy type, and I began to feel comfortable fairly quickly. After the speediest one and a half hours I had ever experienced, someone was tapping me on my head to get up for my next shift. The weather was absolutely miserable.

Equally dismal was having to shave at 0430 the next (and every other) morning. We used cold water in our steel helmet pots to wet our razors. We had no lather, nor do I recall soap. "It was so dark it wasn't possible to even see the razor," I wrote, "so one could only drag and pray for the best." If anyone was not clean shaved for reveille, the DIs "would dry shave him with an old razor blade." I never had to endure that.

Monday, November 4, we went to the hand grenade range. We had been given considerable hand grenade training using dummy grenades, but this was the only occasion when we actually threw live grenades.

Each trainee entered the area with a cadre member and was issued, and then threw, a grenade over a wall as he dropped to a prone position. Some of the cadre were sadistic individuals, but every one of them earned his pay that day. The survival of each trainer and his trainee was dependent upon the trainee's ability to perform with an explosive device what he had practiced with a dummy grenade.

Some in our company hurled further than others, but each man heaved his grenade beyond the wall and there were no accidents. We were allowed to keep the pull ring from the grenade "so we could send it to our girlfriends and impress them." I told Joan I would send it to impress her.

The most wretched experience during bivouac was the infiltration course which we endured Monday night. It was supposed to give the trainee experience maneuvering while under live fire. The distance was 120 meters which, I wrote, "must be covered by the low crawl (weapon cradled in arms, with chest and stomach touching ground at all times) over logs, under barbed wire etc. while machine gun rounds are fired over your head, flares are set off overhead, and demolition pits are exploded around you."

We were putting to use our vast experience practicing in the low crawl pit. We went through it twice. The first time was a "dry run" without live fire. The worst part was entering the course, which was anything but dry. At the starting end of the course was a concrete trench filled with one to two feet of water which "was putrid and smelled as if it had been standing there for months."

We double-timed, single file, into the trench. "After the first couple of steps you could feel it seeping into your boots and soaking your feet," I said. The course itself was dry and dusty. At a signal, we climbed "over the top" to maneuver across a replica of a World War I "no man's land."

When we reached barbed wire, we would roll to our backs, use our rifle to push up the wire as we wiggled under it, propelling ourselves forward "by kicking frog style with the feet and pulling with the elbows. Naturally the dry dusty [red clay] soil got all down our backs and in our hair." By the time we reached the end of the course, we were a bunch of filthy, stinking trainees. Of course, we did not shower during the entire week we were on bivouac.

In addition to the special training, we also had PT and DD. Tuesday we spent the whole day, from 0800 to 2330 on ITT (Individual Tactical Training). I wrote, "We ran an obstacle course in pairs—one person firing from cover while the other moved forward and vice versa. We had to go over, under, and around earth mounds, trenches, logs, barbed wire and walk a log over a waterfilled trench. We then assaulted a bunker tossing our hand grenade (dummies that sounded like firecrackers when they exploded) and then rushing the position using cyclic firing."

The whole platoon went out Wednesday afternoon on a search-and-destroy mission and marched about three hours. The weather had changed considerably in the other direction with the temperature near 70°. We had to "hit it," I wrote—dropping to the ground—each time we encountered "any other troops or any time a plane flew over or a vehicle came near." We once hid alongside the road and ambushed another platoon. That same night one squad from each platoon had to go out on a reconnaissance mission. "Naturally my squad was chosen so I had to march for 2½ more hours that night."

Thursday morning, we went to a range for instruction in rifle squad drill. We marched back "at a much-too-rapid pace" that afternoon for more PT and DD. Then we "moved out, packing our bedrolls on our weary backs once more, to another site. We marched 2½-3 hours frequently 'hitting it' as enemy elements (some of our DIs) fired at us with blanks and set off flares overhead." We finally reached our site and set up our perimeter defense.

Friday morning, we went to Close Combat Range "where we were 'hailed' upon our arrival. It was quite a freak hailstorm; the stones were about half the size of golf balls. It was really an experience standing there while the stones bounced off our helmets with a thud."

It then rained pretty hard for about an hour. We were supposed to run through the live-fire course which was similar to the ITT course, except we were to go in two three-man teams, "firing live ammo and throwing a live grenade." The storm prevented that from happening. Pop-up targets could not operate because electricity was out, and "telephone communications with the post were dead and we could not get safety clearance to fire live so we just ran through it without live ammo." In the mud we had to crawl through sloppy puddles under barbed wire obstacles. We also had to cross by way of a "foot log" over a moat about four feet deep. Allman was among several men who fell in.

We additionally had classroom training on various subjects, one of which was gas warfare. As I recall, there were two types: one would burn skin on contact; the other, if ingested, would burn internal organs. Covering skin with proper clothing and using a gas mask were the means of protection. After considerable training, we experienced the gas chamber Friday afternoon. There were two chambers, "one with a tear agent present and the other a choking agent."

We entered the tear agent room where we sat on benches and cadre gave some final instruction before we donned the masks. Tear gas was released into the room. Cadre would approach each trainee who would stand, remove his mask, yell out his name, rank, serial number, and date of birth. Then he was allowed to rapidly exit the building where outside he joined a group of crying and gasping individuals. The gas stung and burned the eyes and exposed skin.

Since this was the last activity of our bivouac, we marched to our barracks from the gas chamber with the backpacks we had carried all week, arriving at 1800 hours. Soap and hot water and clean fatigues were much welcomed. The first opportunity I had to write anything was a postcard just before noon Saturday, November 2. We had gotten up at 0400 and had cleaned all of our field gear used during the past week, now in a condition I described as "really a mess." I myself was "completely exhausted." Bivouac had been an ordeal. We had averaged maybe four hours sleep at night.

"I only brushed my teeth twice," I wrote. "I wanted to but there was just not time." No one showered all week. "I guess the gas chamber was used to fumigate us before we came back."

5

Training Post-Bivouac

"Keeping us occupied and allowing us no sleep"

AFTER BIVOUAC, I BEGAN MY FIRST LETTER at 1630 hours Saturday, November 2. I had post privileges and had crossed the street to get some M&Ms, postcards, comic Army stationery, and a bar of soap. It was raining, and I was not interested in going out in the rain when I could choose not to do so. With BCT's end in realistic sight, I thought I might go eat a steak or go watch a movie Sunday if the weather was nice. I really was "too tired to want to do anything except relax."

Monday, November 4, we had rifle PT with our M14s and then a PT test. The ground was soaked from rain, the 40-yard low-crawl pit was a quagmire, and "all the running events became slipping and sliding exercises." When we returned to the barracks for chow, all OCS candidates and all others going to a combat arms AIT were picked out to fire the M16.

We went to classes from 1230 to 1430 hours, practicing the dismantling and reassembling of the weapon, and how to clean and care for it. The M16, a 5.56 mm rifle with a plastic-like stock, weighed a mere 6.37 pounds unloaded. It had become the standard weapon in Vietnam.

Wednesday, November 6, I wrote, "A group of us zeroed in with the M16 this morning (after an hour of PT in the rain) and then fired on record range for qualification this afternoon. I qualified expert." We sure were glad to return to the heated barracks after being in the cold rain all day. The weather forecast was for low 20s with chances for snow. I added, "Our final PT test is Friday; I surely hope the weather is better by then."

We were being pressed to clean everything for an IG (Inspector General's) inspection, and everything had to be clean to turn in to supply before we left basic. I explained, "Tomorrow we go out to the range and fire the M16 again—only this time we fire it fully automatic." The M14s were not adjusted to fire fully automatic, so this would be our first such experience. I added, "I think tomorrow will be the last time we fire any type of weapon in BCT. It will suit me ok. I would much prefer being at home firing my fully manual single shot 22 rifle at cans."

Saturday was to be a full workday for us because we had Monday off for Veterans Day. I was glad for the break because I had been detailed on KP Sunday. I received a letter from Joan postmarked November 4. Earlier on the morning she wrote it, we had had a phone conversation, some of which concerned OCS.

I had mentioned to her the possibility that I might opt out of going to Officers Candidate School, but she had not understood that the contract I had entered allowed me to do that. She had been worried that I was going to encounter trouble by opting out. Her letter indicated that she now understood that I was allowed to drop OCS, and that she understood as well why I would choose to do so. I knew that continuing OCS would give me rank and opportunity to continue a military career path. However, I was choosing to accept the probability of going straight to Vietnam to fulfill my responsibility and to get back home more quickly to pursue our interrupted civilian goals. I would do my duty, but I did not desire a military career.

The two-page letter I mailed Friday, November 8, I had begun the previous night 15 minutes before lights out, with the first page having been finished in the latrine, the only place that was not dark. We had spent much of the day "cleaning everything," a never-ending chore exacerbated by the coming end of BCT. "It never got above 35° all day today and it misted a good portion of the time," I wrote. "The sun has not been out since we returned from bivouac." We had fired the M16 on automatic in the morning and had a review of DD and bayonet drill, followed by PT in the afternoon.

The second page of the letter I began at "6:10 a.m." (thinking civilian time) and commented on Joan's weekend plans, that she and our friend Libby Williams, whose husband Bob was in National Guard training, were to attend the wedding of another one of my college roommates. Afterwards Joan's brother Rob, now home on leave, was going to drop her off for a visit at my parents' home in Orangeburg on his way down to visit a girl in Charleston.

I told Joan not to write me after Monday because Thursday would be "the last day we'll get mail here." I conjectured that I might be shipped out next Friday, November 15, after graduation that day. I mentioned that one last big thing—the G3 Proficiency Test—would be given the day before graduation. Meanwhile, a more imminent event awaited now, the Physical Training Proficiency Test. I said, "I'll be glad when today is over and that PTPT is out of the way."

I favorably recall with much credit our PT (physical training)

5. Training Post-Bivouac

instructors. They were experienced and knew how far they could push us to the limits of our abilities. When it seemed we were at the end of our endurance, they would stop and give us a break. One DI had a sense of humor. During pushups, he would remark that we looked like we needed a rest so he would put us in the front leaning rest position. As arms began trembling, he would lean over by a recruit and tell a joke. Everyone would collapse laughing, and we would finally have our break.

Most of the cadre gave us ill treatment without regard to color, race, religion, or other factors. All of us were treated equally as sub-humans. I recall only two racially tinged incidents. An African American sergeant from North Carolina seemed to go out of the way to hassle any white southerner among us, particularly my friend Allman from Myrtle Beach, a predominantly white popular resort area in South Carolina. The sergeant would get up in Allman's face and make comments in a low voice indecipherable to the rest of us. While it was custom for trainees to be addressed by last names, this sergeant regularly called Allman "Myrtle Beach," pronounced with a sneer scarcely disguising antagonism.

Just once, in a separate brief incident, I recall feeling like an overt racial target. From a distance only, I had observed our training officer, an African American. He, like the white company commander, did not interact directly with trainees. My initial assessments were that the commander with his swagger stick appeared a jerk, but that the TO was a "stand-up" guy. We trainees were too busy to focus on the three-ring political circus (Humphrey, Nixon, and Wallace) that dominated civilians and presidential elections in November 1968. Therefore, I was startled the day at the rifle range that the TO walked up to me, making some mild, ordinary military comment before ending with the out-of-place utterance, "I guess I know who *you* voted for." I had never before conversed with him and could only think that he presumed because I was a white southerner, I had voted for segregationist George Wallace. I had voted, but *not* for Wallace. I will never know why the TO made that comment, but it changed my previous opinion. A reply was not expected of me, and I made none.

The stationery on which I began a letter to Joan Friday night, November 8, had a cartoon on the bottom depicting a recruit about to face off against a hulking judo instructor. I commented that the image was "quite appropriate since we have 4 hrs. of hand-to-hand combat tomorrow." That day we had completed the final PT test, the required passing score being 300, and "My score today was 348—nothing outstanding but not that bad either." Continuing to write that night during fire guard, I reported that we had started our out-processing procedure: "Our military files must be complete and up-to-date before we ship out of here."

On November 10 I sent a postcard picturing the post hospital, writing on the other side that my friend Vik had been admitted there with "flu or something." Later that same Sunday afternoon, I wrote again during detail as a CQ runner from 1500 to 1700 hours. I was glad I had not had to pull KP instead because, "I'm so sore I can hardly move. I think this soreness is partially because of my cold (flu or whatever it is), partially because of the PT test, and partially because of yesterday's four hours of being kicked, choked, and strangled during hand-to-hand combat."

Not having had KP, Holley and I had gone to church Sunday, after which I relaxed with a couple of other guys browsing the main PX. I had decided after my CQ detail, I would get a hamburger from the PX and go to bed early to try to get rid of my sore throat. However, just as I was being replaced as CQ runner, I overheard some useful information: "The supply sgt. came in and told the guy in charge that he needed 5 men for a detail to clean the supply room at 1800." I knew if I returned to the barracks to stay there I would end up on that detail. I wrote later, "I figured I'd feel worse sweeping, mopping, waxing, and dusting that dirty supply room" than I would going out in the nasty weather (rain and snow). Two other guys and I made a hasty exit. We went to The Steak House and had "a delicious T-bone and then strawberry shortcake for dessert," followed by a movie.

On the next day, Veterans Day, the rain and snow that had started the previous night had changed over to just snow. I wrote Joan that I had ordered a Cycle Book that would be mailed in a couple weeks, "like an annual [yearbook] of our BCT cycle." A postcard on Tuesday, November 12, mentioned that I had gone on sick call and now had inside duty. Writing a letter the following day, marking two full months I had spent in the Army, I was still pretty sick in spite of all the medicine I had taken. "My throat has never been so sore," I said. "I am going to bed now in hopes that I'll be better tomorrow." We were scheduled to take the Proficiency Test then.

Trainees approaching the completion of basic were apprehensive about what would follow. Not much was told us individually. Advanced Individual Training (AIT) was based on one's MOS (Military Occupational Specialty). Men with an infantry MOS expected to be sent to Fort Polk, Louisiana, and those in field artillery to Fort Sill, Oklahoma. By the time I wrote home November 14, I had my orders in hand for Artillery AIT at Fort Sill. Some of the guys had gotten orders changing them from artillery to combat engineering or to infantry. Vik had not received his orders yet.

Once we marched through the graduation ceremony, if we had surmised that ill treatment at the hands of Fort Leonard Wood's cadre would end, it was a false assumption. Our last task was to clean our M14 weapons to pass inspection and turn them in. Having been cleaning those rifles for

5. Training Post-Bivouac

six weeks or longer and knowing the cadre to be critical, when we got out all the cleaning materials and stripped down the weapons after supper, we anticipated some harassment before being permitted to turn in the weapons. However, one after another, as we cleaned and presented our weapons, each was rejected and had to be recleaned. This continued many hours.

Around midnight one of the cadre told us we needed to set up an assembly line and specialize. At his suggestion, we scrambled the rifle parts in different piles: barrels here, trigger mechanisms there, and so on. A group of men would concentrate on cleaning each part. Even that level of "specialization" did not produce satisfaction from the cadre.

Finally, near 0300, we were told to grab our duffle bags as our buses had arrived. We left everything as it was. We were perplexed, but gladly left. Later at AIT, we learned that the Army had replaced the M14s with M16s for training. Some of us who had endured this "cleaning" ordeal conjectured that we were among the last cycles to train with the M14. The cadre had no intention of reassembling those weapons, but had every intention of keeping us occupied and allowing us no sleep our last night of Basic Combat Training.

6

Advanced Individual Training

"Different post, same Army"

I WAS SO EXHAUSTED THAT WHEN THOSE OF US with orders for Fort Sill, Oklahoma, boarded the buses after 0300 hours that morning, I recall nothing until we stopped for breakfast. Our driver pulled into a parking area, and everyone stumbled off into the morning chill. We climbed the stairs to a pedestrian bridge that led to a restaurant on the other side of the interstate. I do not remember its name. Its fare was welcomed if not remarkable.

We were somewhere on the Oklahoma Turnpike, I learned. Continuing our journey after breakfast, we rode through an area of Oklahoma City with residential lots about a quarter of an acre in size. I was amazed to see oil wells behind some of the small houses. These became common sights along with an occasional derrick as we traveled through the countryside.

The trip between forts took about seven hours. I wrote my first letter from Fort Sill Monday evening, November 18, to announce my new address—Battery E, 4th Battalion, 1st AIT Brigade, U.S. Advanced Training Center, Fort Sill, Oklahoma. I was to be in building T 4309 and be assigned to the 1st Platoon, which occupied the first floor. My platoon I would find included around 25 men, and with four platoons being in a battery (the artillery equivalent to an infantry company), I would train in "Echo" Battery with about 100–125 men.

Fort Sill was a sprawling establishment covering 94,000 acres of rolling terrain. During my nearly three months there in the winter of 1968–1969, I often recalled the line from the Rodgers and Hammerstein hit song, "Oklahoma, where the wind blows sweepin' down the plain." There were few trees to form windbreaks and the chill factor could be fierce. In the weeks I would spend there in training, I would experience more snowfall than I had ever experienced in the whole of my life in the Carolinas. I would also find both similarities and contrasts with the Basic Combat Training I had left behind.

6. Advanced Individual Training 45

Glen outside E-4 barracks during AIT at Fort Sill, Oklahoma (Pat McReynolds).

Shortly after arrival for AIT, we were issued additional clothing besides what we had brought from BCT—rubber boots to wear over our combat boots, woolen pants and shirts as over-garments (OGs), cotton and wool-blend "long john" underwear, liners for field jackets with button-on hoods to use in addition to attached nylon hoods, normally rolled and concealed in the jackets' collars, and woolen scarves. Except for underwear and black rubber boots, all items were OD. Instead of modern brick barracks like those at Fort Leonard Wood, at Fort Sill we trainees were billeted in two-story, wooden World War II-era structures with wood floors that we had to mop and scrub manually. There were rows of these buildings with small open sections between them where we assembled for formations.

In the barracks we slept on metal frame beds, also old-styled. Lighting

Jim Brown (center) with Glen (right) and friend, outside of Fort Sill barracks (Pat McReynolds).

was provided by bare bulbs hanging from the ceiling, some directly over bunks. Our drill sergeant would turn on the lights each morning to awaken us. *Who knew how loud a 100-watt bulb could be?*

There was no running water in our barracks, only in the latrine, a separate wooden building about 150 yards behind it. We made jokes about the "150-yard dash to the outhouse." It was quite an experience to hasten outside in the cold night air. Latrines were heated with steam radiators, as were barracks, and were usually warm, but plumbing was old and often backed up and flooded the latrines.

My November 19 letter mentioned that there were two washers and one big dryer in our latrine, and it also had lights on all night. Sometimes I would write letters there while washing and drying my clothes. I wrote from there that some men of questionable upbringing were living upstairs in our barracks. Rather than dress to go outside to the latrine at night, they would urinate in their rubber overboots and dump the contents out the windows.

On the bright side, my early letters noted I was looking forward to

6. Advanced Individual Training

Glen demonstrating the long dash to the separate latrine building at Fort Sill (Pat McReynolds).

going home for holiday leave in about a month—my first visit home since I started basic training in September. My battery was to go as a group at the end of the month to arrange individually for transportation home for Christmas. I had decided I would be paying to make a reservation and would not take the risk of flying standby. Meanwhile, I was still trying to work through the paperwork maze to establish Joan's military dependent's ID card, which continued to be tied up in red tape.

I described my residence as an "old typical Army barracks." Floors were to be "waxed & glossy at all times." Therefore, we had to take our boots off outside the door each time we entered. I conjectured, "That will really be funny when there's snow or ice on the ground."

Although most other batteries allowed the off duty wearing of civilian clothes on base, Echo Battery did not. However, we had the convenience of a snack shop across the street, and as I wrote, "The PX, barber shop, laundry, and a post office are within a couple of blocks." Once we were settled in, as long as we did not have duty we could go anywhere on post after 1800 hours. We still had to get up at 0430 and lights were out at 2100, but we didn't have to be in the barracks until 2300. Our hair had to be cut short. Our daily-wear boots had to be highly shined, and our boots and dress shoes displayed under our bunks were to be spit-shined.

The platoon which was awarded the highest score on the daily inspection got to be first in line at mess, so having a little free time after eating chow was an effective incentive. I reported November 19 that "my platoon won today so we ate dinner and supper first and will eat breakfast first in the morning." We had classes that morning on first aid and land mine warfare and were to have afternoon classes on "nomenclature of the 105 mm howitzer—our chief weapon here." However, another guy and I had been picked instead for a detail in the supply room, where we filled out some forms and then "sat around doing nothing." I later went to the latrine for light and wrote Joan a card—one of several left over from Fort Leonard Wood. Other information I provided was that the mail went off once a day, at 0730 hours, and the weather was "cold and windy."

The mess hall where Echo Battery ate was another World War II old-type wooden building, and it was much smaller than the battalion mess hall at Fort Leonard Wood. Although it served fewer men, there were also fewer trainees on KP, so the workload was not noticeably better than it had been in basic. As I recall, when we were assigned mess hall duty, we got up at 0300 hours and, if all went well, got off about 2100.

As AIT trainees, we still marched everywhere and performed police call, but were not issued rifles. We had classes on various topics, a few being interesting, some extremely boring like those at BCT. I described one of the latter in a November 21 letter. The whole battalion had assembled in one of the theaters for an all-day class. The lights were dim "and people were falling asleep all over the place," I wrote. "At one point the instructor pointed to a certain section and said for the person with the glasses on who was sleeping to stand up to answer a question. Five people stood up at one time. The instructor was completely bewildered."

In the letter I mailed another set of forms I had received to fill out for Joan's PX card. I told her she would need to take them in person to Fort Jackson to have her photo taken and a card made. As it turned out, the process would require her to make several trips to the fort. Pursuing errant paperwork proved a civilian as well as a military ordeal.

Good news in the letter was that our battery had met with a representative of the Transportation Center. I had booked a first-class flight from Dallas to Columbia leaving December 19 and returning from Columbia to

6. Advanced Individual Training 49

Dallas on January 5, 1969. The cost was $86.10 round trip. The round-trip bus fare to-and-from Fort Sill and Dallas (four hours each way) was an additional $18.00. By the time I got home, I would have been away for more than three months.

Other encouraging news was that, although we had been told that the week before we left for Christmas, we would have a four-day bivouac, we were also told that, unlike conditions of the bivouac at BCT, we were to sleep in big, heated tents. That sounded good to me. My Friday, November 22, letter was also upbeat, mentioning that I had received for my birthday (the next day) cards from my parents, my brother Byron, Joan's brother Rob, a letter from Joan's mother, and two cards, a letter, and a package from Joan: "Pretty good for an old man of 25, huh?"

Sunday, November 24, I wrote optimistically about conditions at AIT. We were told we would be trucked when training at long distances instead of marching there. I pointed out that our field gear was simplified with "no field pack to carry, no weapon (like the M14 at basic) to lug around, sleep with, and keep clean." When we had to clean the howitzers (group-fired field weapons), I figured they would be easier to clean than the M14s, joking "at least the parts will be larger."

Gradually some of the guys and I were getting to learn a bit about each other, having casual conversations and griping or joking around as we endured common training ordeals. Last name large-letter nametags sewn visibly above fatigue shirt pockets helped associate faces and names, except for problems with pronunciation. My surname Inabinet (*en-NAB-eye-net*, sounding like *cabinet*) was so often variously mispronounced that one day when one of the lifers loudly stuttered out "Rabbit," everyone including me was so amused by the gaff that they all started calling me Rabbit, even those who had learned that I went by my middle name "Glen" instead of the first name "Louie" on my official records. The nickname Rabbit followed me throughout the Army.

For travel on the post, Fort Sill had free bus service, "old small school-type buses" that followed routes and stopped at any designated stop where someone was waiting. That Sunday I had ridden all over the post, getting off at various points to investigate interesting sites with a friend from BCT, Jim Brown from Missouri, also married and a social studies teacher. Brown and I visited the main PX, and I commented in my letter on items and prices there. Because of time, we splurged—45¢—and took a taxi back to our barracks.

The cleaning, straightening, and boot-shining were similar in AIT to BCT, but we had two-hour security guard (SG) shifts instead of basic's fire guard which had required walking the hall operating a buffer for an hour. At Fort Sill the SG could sit and read or write during his shift. I had just

Glen (facing camera) with other trainees learning to operate a 105 mm howitzer during AIT (Pat McReynolds).

begun my midnight-to-0200 shift when I remarked in my letter that it had begun snowing hard. The wind was howling and shaking the windows and doors in that old barracks.

Monday, November 25, was cold and windy when we were outdoors to begin learning about the powerful field artillery weapon, the howitzer. We went through commands and drill exercises with that two-and-a-half-ton, 105 mm cannon, covering "how to set it up for firing and how to get it ready to move out." The howitzer was 5'8" high, 7'3" wide, 19'6" in length with a barrel 7'7" long, and it had a firing range of up to seven miles. In the afternoon, we spent the last two hours of training learning to disassemble and reassemble the firing mechanism and its 91-pound breech block.

My less cheerful Tuesday, November 26, letter could be titled, "different post, same Army." Our training today had been scheduled to continue outside, but since it was pouring rain, we were to be moved inside. However, first, we had to stand for a time outside in formation and had gotten soaked before we were allowed to put on ponchos. We were allowed to put on overshoes at dinnertime, but by then our feet were already wet.

Friday, November 29, found me tired after having spent from 0300 to 2015 hours the previous day, Thanksgiving, on KP, but I was pleased to have received four letters, including one forwarded from Fort Leonard Wood. Joan updated me on events at home. Her family had gathered for a meal celebrating the 74th birthday of her lively grandfather Smyrl, a World War I veteran, who had taken up woodcarving as a new hobby. Everyone had enjoyed Rob's being home on leave, and all had celebrated Thanksgiving early to have him with them, although they were sad to see him leave for Korea. Her sister Mary Ann had a new boyfriend, Dickie. Imagining friends and homefolk on Thanksgiving made me determined to deal with what I had to do now so that I could be with them myself on the next holiday.

In the meanwhile, training proceeded in the howitzer park, the large gravel and asphalted area where the guns were parked. Some of our guard duty consisted of two-hour shifts patrolling that area during hours of darkness. After we had been given sufficient training in the park, we were ready to transport the howitzers to the field and fire them.

Sunday, December 1, I informed Joan that we were to go to the field Monday and stay until 2300 hours to practice section drills and "laying the piece." To combat the cold, we would don extra-weight underwear, OGs, field jackets with liners, and additional woolen socks, scarves, and pullover caps. We covered our hands with leather gloves with woolen liners.

The howitzer had two wheels to be towed by a deuce and a half (a two-and-a-half-ton truck), then unhitched and maneuvered into position by a gun crew of six men, who were also in charge of assembling its projectile. The maneuver "laying the piece" described placing the gun in a correct firing position in regard to the aiming posts. Section drills were maneuvers that the crew went through to operate the fieldpiece. The howitzer was "jacked up" so that its wheels cleared the ground to allow it to be pivoted. In combat, gun crews usually fired at distant targets they could not see. A forward observer (FO) team in the field would spot the target and radio in compass readings for aiming. Those readings would be translated into settings for the gun. The crew would aim the howitzer by rotating it 360° to fire in any direction and by adjusting the barrel or tube for elevation. For mass effect, howitzers were prominent and powerful field artillery weapons for both attack and defense. They were essential in Vietnam.

I missed the first day of firing the howitzers because I was assigned to be barracks orderly at that time. My task was to guard the building.

Ready for towing to the range, 105 mm howitzer hitched to a M35 deuce and a half truck.

We had no wall lockers, so all of our hanging clothing hung on the walls by our bunks. I also had to "get the barracks ready for inspection—sweep floors and buff with buffer, dust with dust mop, align beds and footlockers, empty trash, dust everything, make sure bunks are tight, and in general keep everything in good order." This had to be done upstairs and downstairs. It was necessary to dust about every 20 minutes. I fumed, "I have never seen so much dust."

We took our first Proficiency Test December 6. I scored 48 of 50 possible points "on the practical part—identifying parts of the 105 mm howitzer, going through the motions of firing etc." We had been given the questions and answers in advance. (How did I miss 2 points?)

It had been a beautiful day reaching the upper 60s but was supposed to drop into the 20s that night. I was assigned a schedule of guard duty from noon Saturday until noon Sunday, December 8. "I will have to walk a post for 2 hours and then I'll be off for 4 hours, then on for 2, off for 4 etc. So I'll have to walk a post four times during the 24 hours," I wrote. "We walk guard using M14s. Because there have been a number of incidents involving muggings, beatings, and robberies in this area, we will have bayonets fixed with orders to stab anyone who refuses to halt." We were not issued ammunition.

6. Advanced Individual Training 53

In another detail, I was the sentinel for the 2nd Battalion Howitzer Park, where I guarded "24 105 mm howitzers, about 30 trucks, and a latrine." The guards on my shift (3rd relief) got "messed over," I said. Since replacements were not always posted on time, my shift had been three hours long, and another one nearly that long.

In a letter I began Saturday, December 7, and finished the following day, I generalized the schedule over the next 12 days before leave, which showed solid attention being given to concentrated training on a number of weapons. "This week," I wrote, "we will study and then fire the 155 mm howitzer, the M60 machine gun, the .50 cal. machine gun, the grenade launcher, and the rocket launcher. Next week we have bivouac Monday and Tuesday, another proficiency test Wednesday, and then HOME THURSDAY." The leaving date I was looking forward to was December 19. Until then training would be intense.

For example, Wednesday, December 11, I wrote that we were inside all day "for an 8-hour block of training on the nomenclature, operation, assembly and disassembly, adjusting and cleaning of the M60 7.62 mm machine gun (4 hours in the morning) and the Browning M2 .50 cal. machine gun (4 hours in the afternoon)." Thursday we were to go to the field and fire the 155 mm howitzer. Saturday was supposed to be a big footlocker inspection. I was glad mine was in good shape, I said, because I would be on KP Saturday and have no time to work on it.

On days we went to the range, we marched to the howitzer park and hitched a howitzer behind each assigned truck. We climbed into the canvas-covered truck bed and huddled onto jump seats on each side. Although we could not see where we were going, the rear was open. We would watch the buildings disappear as we ventured through the rolling terrain of Oklahoma. Water in ditches and small creeks was frozen. Inside the truck bed, we were miserably cold despite our many layers of clothing.

When we reached the firing range, we unhitched the howitzers and moved them into place. We then proceeded to practice fire. There were more men than needed for each gun crew, so we rotated positions. That offered some down time, which we welcomed. By mid-morning we were allowed to remove our over boots and outer garments, which by then we were eager to do.

The week we received field training on the 155 mm howitzer, we trained at a different range. The area, like most of the fort, had few trees. Most days it was windy and quite cold. Near this range was a cemetery. During our lunch break, some of us walked among the graves. One grave marked the resting place of Indian warrior Geronimo, who had died of pneumonia, a captive at Fort Sill, on February 17, 1909. I later learned

Trainees inside bed of M35 truck in convoy carrying howitzers to firing range.

the name was Beef Creek Apache Cemetery. The history I found quite interesting.

Tuesday, December 17, I wrote my last letter of 1968 from Fort Sill. Bivouac was over. "What a breeze!" I said. We went out early Monday morning and fired all day and into the night until about 2130. We returned to the howitzer park about 2200. We were allowed to sleep until 0545 Tuesday morning, went back to the field, and fired until 1630. "And that was bivouac. No resemblance to that of BCT, right?" I wrote.

While I was on SG that last night from 1800 to 2000 hours, the officer of the day, a lieutenant, came in to inspect the barracks, and I had to report to him. All trainees departed on leave December 19, the day after Joan's and my second wedding anniversary, another timely observation I made.

My route from Lawton took me to Love Field in Dallas, to Atlanta, and then to Columbia. What a wonderful sight to see Joan standing there waiting for me! In addition to once again being together and happily communicating face-to-face, we followed timely custom, going to the

6. Advanced Individual Training

familiar family woods and selecting a cedar tree to cut and bring home to our apartment to decorate for Christmas. We drove to Orangeburg to see my parents and my brother Byron and his family, saw family and friends in Camden, enjoyed holiday services and festivities with all, but spent most of our time alone together. Days passed in a pleasant blur. It was a much-needed, much-enjoyed leave that ended much too quickly.

7

1969, a New Year

*"What I will be, I'm not sure;
they haven't told us yet"*

O<small>N MY RETURN TO TRAINING</small>, I <small>WROTE</small> my first letter of 1969 on Monday, January 6, between duties as barracks orderly, listening to music on a portable radio, a Christmas gift from my parents. I commented numerous times about the wonderful Christmas leave.

I had spent "many hours in the Atlanta airport" before my connecting flight back to Fort Sill left at its scheduled time, 4:30 p.m. I slept a couple hours and had a hot dog and a Coke. As it remained daylight flying west, I was able to view sights from the window. In fact, from the airplane I was able to snap some photographs with Joan's and my Kodak Instamatic camera I was taking back to Fort Sill with me. I had had to leave it and my photography hobby behind on entering service, along with my treasured 35 mm Nikon Nikkormat which I had also left in Joan's care and use. Being able at this point of my training to keep with me a personal item like a camera, even a simple one, was an important compensation on my return.

Flying over Atlanta, I spotted Stone Mountain and Grant Park. From our cruising altitude even superhighways were not distinguishable, but when we crossed the Mississippi River (somewhere between Memphis, Tennessee, and Greenville, Mississippi), "it stood out as though it were a mile wide." The sun was just beginning to set when we arrived at Love Field in Dallas, Texas. I waited outside the terminal for about two hours before my bus arrived, and I slept most of the way to Fort Sill.

We were in the field all day Tuesday, January 7. It was quite cold. At 10 a.m. "there was still ice in the ditches and puddles." On Wednesday, Fort Sill was in a stir celebrating its 100th anniversary and making a big deal of it. There was even a new cancellation U.S. postage stamp, "Fort Sill Centennial, 100 Years of Service, 1869–1969." I wrote Joan that while I was less personally interested in this anniversary than our own recent second

7. 1969, a New Year 57

Just-received letters filling his pocket, Glen entering howitzer park with barracks in the background (Jim Brown).

A letter home displaying the Fort Sill 100th Anniversary cancellation over a six-cent stamp.

one, I would benefit from the occasion here because the day was declared a training holiday. We did not go to the field, although we still had details.

One of my details was at the howitzer park, cleaning the field pieces we had fired the previous day. Everyone left in the barracks was polishing boots and straightening footlockers in preparation for a big inspection Saturday morning—personal, barracks, and footlocker. "We have to wear our dress greens and stand inspection in ranks," I said.

Thursday, January 9, preparing for our final proficiency test the next day, we went to the field for direct fire—shooting at a target we could see at close range, in contrast to the ones we had been shooting at out of sight. "The temperature did not get above 25°, and the ice never melted," I remarked.

More significantly, I told Joan I had signed the "official withdrawal from OCS tonight so I should not have to wait too long for new orders." I repeated, having at home discussed with her my intended decision: "I'm pretty sure that I'll be sent to Vietnam.... I don't think either of us should be surprised.... I expected to end up there eventually—whether I went to OCS or not. At least now I won't be in the Army but 2 years, and I can be with you again sooner."

I wrote Saturday night and Sunday afternoon, describing the weekend. The big inspection the barracks had worked hard for turned out to be "a big farce." We had been told we were to wear our dress greens and be inspected by a lieutenant colonel. Instead "a 2nd lieutenant walked in our barracks and kinda half-way looked around and—yep, we dressed out in fatigues."

The good news was my platoon came in first in the inspection, which qualified us for a weekend pass. I splurged—$15 for a room at the Ramada Inn in Lawton, which I shared with Vincent Anders from Illinois and Joel Baum from New Jersey. "It has been pleasant getting away from the post for a little while," I wrote. "It's very unusual to be able to relax like this on a Sunday morning—to sit in a cushioned chair and watch TV (color even)." Lunch was a cheeseburger deluxe with coleslaw, French fries, and coffee for $1.10.

We had gone to a club Saturday night and walked around the downtown area. The bars were seedy with scantily clad females dancing in cages suspended from the ceiling. The section we saw of the city reminded me of a typical Hollywood depiction of an Army town. It made me consider in my home state how Fort Jackson soldiers must view the areas of Columbia where they and their money were welcomed. Sunday afternoon as we walked down one of the Lawton streets, we passed a crew cleaning blood from the sidewalk outside the entrance to one of the bars. Asking what had happened, we were told "some Indians" had gotten into a knife fight.

That weekend pass—the only one I had before I finished AIT—was a

7. 1969, a New Year

welcomed respite, although I was dreading an approaching ordeal. Monday, January 16, would be a regular working day, and I was scheduled to pull two two-hour shifts of guard duty between 6 p.m. to 6 a.m., then work a full day January 17.

My letter referred to another military option likely to be available to me, an early discharge (in GI lingo, "early out") for personnel finishing their time in Vietnam with fewer than six months of commitment left to serve. I wrote Joan that if I were sent there and felt relatively safe when my required 12-month tour was up, I would "most likely" voluntarily extend my time there in order to come back a civilian, rather than to return for a lengthier temporary military routine somewhere stateside. However, if I were in "a dangerous zone or I feel unsafe," I would return when my 12 months ended. Knowing Joan's concerns, I promised to take no "foolish or unnecessary chances."

Back at Echo Battery Sunday night, several of us were called out of formation and told we would have KP the next day at the brigade mess hall, rather than the one where we ate. As it turned out, I wrote Monday evening, January 13, "KP today was not nearly as bad as it is in our mess hall. We finished tonight at 6:45. The KP's in our mess hall are still working."

The letter continued the next night, explaining that Tuesday our battery had been selected to go to the "top of a hill at a demonstration area" to fire howitzers in two exercises for about 800 new trainees to watch. The first demonstrated fire power aimed at distant targets, such as discarded military vehicles placed at various ranges for that purpose. That night the second demonstration was especially impressive. We fired phosphorus illumination rounds to float on small parachutes over the dark target landscape. Each lit an area approximately 400 meters in circumference (about the length of four football fields) so that objects could be spotted for purposes of intelligence or direct firing.

The biggest news of Tuesday was that all persons still OCS candidates received the paperwork informing them where they were to be sent next in their training to serve as officers. Of 19 candidates in my battery, only three were assigned Artillery, which choice all had selected and for which we all had been trained. Four other candidates were being sent to Combat Engineers, and all 12 of the rest—myself included—had been assigned Infantry. That is, I wrote, "I would have had infantry OCS" had I not already opted out, with my officially signed paperwork still making its way through the system. I added that "quite a few others" of the OCS candidates who felt let down with anticipated assignments were now considering opting out too.

All day Wednesday in windy and rainy conditions, we were out on a fire mission. That evening, I was on a powder-burning detail from 4:30 to 6:00 to burn all the excess gunpowder we had not used. As I described,

"We arranged the powder bags in a line one foot wide and we had enough powder to stretch out over 100 meters—over the length of a football field." We lit one end and let it burn to the other. "There was so much powder it took forty minutes for it to burn—and you know how fast gunpowder burns." Excess powder accumulated in combat because each box of ammunition for the howitzer included two compartments, each with enough parts and gunpowder to assemble one shell. Each shell was loaded for the target distance at the moment of need with the amount of gunpowder required, with from one to seven pre-measured numbered bags being dropped inside. Troops were trained to destroy leftover powder to prevent its falling into enemy hands.

I wrote Joan while on SG detail from 2–4 a.m., Thursday, January 16. There would be no time to sleep when I finished my shift as it would be nearly our regular wakeup time. We were to return to the same location for what I thought would be "the last time we will fire the howitzer in AIT." Looking ahead, I added that Friday would be our final PT test, followed by details, with the next week being out-processing and details since AIT graduation was Wednesday, less than a week away.

After our Thursday fire mission and related details, we were back in the barracks getting organized for an inspection at the end of the week with full field layout and footlocker, when someone came in and grabbed several of us for a detail. "The 1st sergeant decided that he wanted a new ceiling installed in the battery commander's office and the office painted," I wrote. "Naturally, it couldn't wait until when everyone will be doing details anyway but it had to be 'did' that night." I stayed only two hours, "but one poor guy had to stay over there all night." Our drill sergeant frequently used the expression, "It will be *did*." Another of his expressions was "on your *feets*!" We were expected to move right away.

I wrote Joan on Friday, January 17, at 8 p.m. while Jim Brown and I were in the laundromat washing field jackets for ourselves and a couple of other guys. With our having been in the field every day until now, our jackets were really dirty. After this morning's final PT test, I had been given another howitzer-cleaning detail. I was not happy about getting that assigned me because another guy and I already "had cleaned two guns by ourselves Thursday afternoon—a job usually done by 5 or more people." The howitzers had fired 100 rounds before lunch and were really dirty. After cleaning the guns, I had another detail to clean section equipment, which a whole gun section uses. "All in all, I had been on detail Thursday for about five hours until 6 p.m.," all that after the previous night's extra detail in the battery commander's office.

Friday afternoon, to avoid being assigned a detail, "I more or less assigned myself a detail inside our barracks. I waxed floors all afternoon."

7. 1969, a New Year

It had turned very cold, and I did not want to "stand out in that howitzer park freezing while I cleaned guns. It was nice to be able to spend a relaxing Friday afternoon indoors waxing floors."

The harassment which picked up after we completed our training, when added to the details which were "dealt out quite freely at all hours of the day and night," made conditions "worse than basic in some ways." No one was to be allowed a pass over the weekend for fear some of the guys might go AWOL (persons Absent Without Leave could be disciplined or considered deserters). I asserted that the battery CO (commanding officer) and 1st sergeant talked about AWOL so much that it put ideas into the minds of some and became a challenge to others. "Since Christmas," I wrote, "our platoon alone has had 4 AWOLs and we have the best platoon."

Monday and Tuesday several of us managed to avoid details by becoming busy with other activities. The second day, for example, Barry Kelso and I went to the Quartermaster Sale Store and exchanged our dress coats. His was too small and mine too large. Then we took the shuttle bus and toured around the post, including a quick look at the post museum. When I returned to the barracks, I helped repaint footlockers. We had been given the wrong paint when we painted them about our second week of AIT. The lockers had remained sticky. Now we had to "scrape the old paint off with our mess kit knives" and repaint.

I wrote of the day's activities while on SG from 8 to 10 p.m. and commented, "By this time tomorrow I will no longer be a trainee. What I will be I'm not sure; they haven't told us yet." Without deliberating on it while writing, I had made a profound statement about the Army—a person "was" whatever he was told that he was.

We graduated from Field Artillery Advanced Individual Training the afternoon of Wednesday, January 22. My letters home made only vague references to the event. I do not remember, nor can I find in letters, a description of what should have been the crowning moment of that last week of training and of being promoted to Private First Class (PFC). Instead, promotion and graduation were overshadowed by KP, SG, and "details, details, details." With the ending of training, which was our purpose for being there, the condition and spirit of our battery and diminishing platoon began to deteriorate. My January 24 letter stated, "We have done so many details that by lunch yesterday they had run out of details for us to do," so "they marched us around the battery area all afternoon."

About the only time we were not pulling a detail, we were "out somewhere dodging a detail." Several of us became quite skilled at that. The weather had gotten really cold, only 12 degrees with 18–20 mph winds, and we had been required to turn in our field gear the previous day, including our field jacket liner and wool scarf. "It's bitter without them," I stated.

Glen (right) and two friends in dress greens after AIT graduation (Jim Brown).

The next day, January 25, I described morning howitzer cleaning detail, followed by an in-ranks midday inspection by the 1st Sergeant who kept us at attention for an hour and "complained about every possible thing." Criticism was random. My belt buckle and shoes really did look ragged because I had not had time to prepare them for an inspection, but somehow I managed to slip by. Yet other guys "wearing new 'never-been-used-before' belt buckles" felt his wrath. He ragged on guys about haircuts. Luckily I had shaved and rushed to the barbershop for a haircut right before inspection. Several guys he deemed "unpresentable" were dismissed from the formation and had to stand a second one at 2:30 p.m.

While other batteries "freely" handed out weekend passes, Echo Battery "graciously" allowed post privileges only. I spent about two hours in the latrine doing laundry and writing letters while listening to the radio. After chow Kelso and I changed into our greens, went to a movie, and then ate some Mexican food at the EM Club (on post for enlisted men of rank E-4 and below).

Some of my friends had been sent to SP (self-propelled) training on post. SPs were howitzers on tracks that looked somewhat like tanks. Those friends had no KP, no details, and no harassment, and were allowed privileges like wearing civvies. Paul Martin came by to see me and remarked that the SP battery he was in was "almost like a vacation" compared to our battery, which he said officials at his battery referred to as "a yo-yo outfit" headed by "a lunatic." Thus it seemed we weren't the only ones who thought this had become a "screwed up" battery.

Sunday night, January 26, a quick note 10 minutes before lights out mentioned three others of the half-dozen men from my unit who had not shipped out. I had gone to the EM Club for Mexican food with Brown, Kelso, and Bill Steffens. A previous letter had mentioned seeing Don Vik. In addition, another friend from AIT who had cancelled OCS, Patrick McReynolds, was also still on post.

I began a new week January 27. My letter that Monday evening described continuing drama in Echo Battery. The 4th Platoon (whose unsanitary behavior I had mentioned while they were living upstairs early in AIT) had been moved downstairs, and the barracks looked "ragged." Our 1st sergeant had walked through and, as a result, we were all "supposed to have a GI party tonight." A GI party happens "when a bunch of GIs get together and scrub the floors with soap powder and hand brushes."

The 1st sergeant also gave another lecture on AWOLs before supper. That number had increased to seven, and I figured that number would double "before the week ends" if the harassment continued. We were expected to wax the floors after scrubbing, "but supply has no wax so they say if you don't wax the floors, you'll be GI-ing them every night this week."

Throughout the training cycle everyone in 1st platoon had been chipping in to buy paste wax which did a much better job than the "sorry liquid wax" that supply was supposed to issue but was out of "95% of the time." Earlier we had not minded paying ourselves because "we had pride in being the best platoon and maintaining the cleanest most well-organized barracks. But now, after the way we've been treated, we couldn't care less. Not a one of us is willing to shell out a single penny for wax again. The barracks can go to hell for all we care."

On the positive side, after a morning detail of cleaning howitzers, I was assigned to the motor pool to wash trucks and self-propelled howitzers, and to police the area. The weather was "almost springlike" and no one over there hassled us, so it was a good duty away from E Battery.

Tuesday, January 28, I responded to news in a letter from Korea that Joan's brother Rob, who I knew was thinking about making the military a career, might be in line for a promotion. "I hope he gets it," I said. The reason I would care about getting promotions while I'm in the Army is briefly monetary, but "being promoted would mean being accepted and proving himself to others for Rob, so I really hope something comes of it."

I had been on a detail the previous afternoon, a cold day, cleaning a classroom for the combat engineers, "not a bad job especially since it was inside where it was warm." I was to have SG guard from midnight to 2 a.m. Were current circumstances deliberately Army-geared to make me look forward to moving on to Vietnam?

Little did I know I would remain at Fort Sill for five more weeks.

8

Officially Holdovers

*"The thought that some
of them might not return"*

By January 29 those of us awaiting assignments were officially labeled "holdovers," and life became for us alternatingly annoying and more laid back. Our mess hall had closed at the end of the training cycle, and we were assigned to have chow in A Battery's mess hall. "A lot of our guys were refused service this morning," I wrote, "because the NCO at the door claimed that their boots weren't polished. Even one of our corporals was told that his boots needed shining. I just can't see that the condition of a man's boots should determine whether or not he should eat."

Some of us began to lunch at the EM Club to avoid the harassment at A Battery. As of Wednesday, I had eaten only three meals at the mess hall. "Their food is so gross and sparse it's not worth standing out in the cold for," I said. "We have to go to the end of the line and eat after their whole battery has eaten, and there is never anything left worth eating."

January 31, when we returned from taking lumber to the bivouac area for a building project detail, we lunched at the EM Club. "Scallops, whipped potatoes, beans, salad, hot rolls, coffee, and strawberry shortcake," I wrote home. "Not bad for $1.00, huh? Our mess hall opens back up tonight for supper, so I don't guess I'll be eating at the cafeteria again."

I had gone to another holding battery where Paul Martin was waiting to ship out to Oakland Tuesday for processing for Vietnam. His barracks was "full of guys who are waiting to ship out and they all look like they're at loose ends," I wrote. "I feel sorry for them because they didn't get a leave. Some of them, like Martin, don't have a lot to say, but some others complain all the time. They go out and get drunk every night and come back to the barracks raising hell and disturbing everyone. Their justification is that they have only ____ (blank) number of days before they go to Vietnam."

Then I made sure to tell Joan, "If I have to go even without getting a leave, I surely don't intend to act that way." I knew she would not expect that I would. I wanted her to continue to understand realistic conditions here, as I had explained at home at Christmas, that it was not likely we would see one another again before I shipped out. Traveling over a thousand miles (the one-way distance from post to Lawton to Dallas to Atlanta to Columbia to Camden) plus the same distance for a return trip seemed impossible given her daily teaching schedule and my day-to-day military uncertainty with only brief random leave times.

When I wrote Saturday, February 1, I described an easy new detail, this time at 4th Battalion Training Aids, a place where miscellaneous educational supplies were warehoused and needed to be organized, and where the people in charge had treated us reasonably. After sweeping the floor, I wrote letters to Joan's uncle and aunt, Jak and Betty Smyrl, and to my parents. The detail ended about 10 a.m. and I returned to the barracks for a nap before lunch, went to the main PX, returned to the barracks, "and napped the afternoon away until time to fall out for supper." Afterwards, Jim Brown and I shot pool with a couple of guys for a while and returned to the barracks to play rummy and rat fink. It must have been the easiest day I had experienced in the Army!

Two days later I wrote pleasantries to Joan replying to news that her college roommate, her close friend Ann Funderburk, was getting married. That night at 8:25 p.m. I wrote her another letter expressing sadness because many guys I knew well had just left at 8 p.m. and others were departing between 9 and 11 p.m., all by various routes expecting to go to Vietnam. Some had been good friends since BCT at Fort Leonard Wood, and I had known one or two ever since the Reception Center. I reflected on differences between their departures and those of friends from whom we had separated at the end of college, stating: "There's the thought that some of them might not return. In the Army you're with these people 24 hours a day."

I had KP all day Tuesday, February 4, followed by SG duty from midnight until 2 a.m. Wednesday. I was wiped out and hoping "to get back on my good old training aids detail tomorrow." Wednesday, February 5, I "really hit the jackpot" and cheered up, receiving letters from my parents, Joan's parents, our friend Bill Norris, and Joan. Mother also said she had mailed me a box of goodies. I was sent back to training aids, but then also to battalion headquarters where we spent most of the day "painting all the baseboards." I was beginning to feel like a painter "after painting the mess hall kitchen until 7 p.m. last night and then painting battalion HQ today."

That night I went with several guys to the EM Club for burgers and beer. On our way back to the barracks, as we were passing near the stockade, a guard ran up to ask if we had seen a man running our way. A prisoner had escaped. The other prisoners were milling about in the stockade, cheering and yelling, and guards were running all about searching madly for the escapee. When we reached the barracks, we discovered that someone had come in and stolen all the bath towels on one side, the side I slept on. This was the first time I had had anything stolen since I joined the Army. However, the following Friday someone stole a fatigue shirt of mine from a hanger, but left the pants and another set of fatigues hanging beside it. Was the U.S. Army getting out of control?

The next day I was at training aids on a detail constructing a battalion flag stand. The result I described as "miserable-looking," but said the detail was one of the easiest I had been on. We were to return the next day to take some lumber to the field. Friends and I were even occasionally taking in movies at night—35¢ admission. Friday, February 7, I was again at training aids. "I don't know how long this detail will last but if I can remain on it until I leave here, I will be happy," I said. The details sent us to the bivouac area "to build some things." For the previous three days I had painted poles in the howitzer park. I mused that whenever the Army ran out of things for you to do, "They give you a paint brush and a can of paint and put you to painting something." I pointed out it was not the best quality paint, however. The paint I had been using was $1.85 a gallon.

A new cycle of trainees was supposed to arrive that weekend at Echo Battery. Those of us left there who had opted out of OCS—Jim Brown, David Cole, Pat McReynolds, Maurice Carver, and I—did not know whether we would remain there now or be sent to a holding battery. McReynolds, Brown, and I had talked frequently about our futures after training. Separately, each of us had made the same decision for similar reasons regarding officer candidate training and had given our decisions to the battery 1st sergeant about the same time. While the Army was taking its time to cut new orders for us, our holdover time at Fort Sill counted on our two-year obligation, so we contented ourselves to do details during the week. We swept and mopped buildings, painted 55-gallon barrels, and raked gravel. We performed guard duty and KP. When not on guard duty or KP, we could roam the post, shop in the PX, visit the post museum, or leave the post on weekends. It was a measured freedom, but compared to the rigidity of training, we made it tolerable, even with irritations.

On a weekend, Barry Kelso and I got a pass and caught a bus to Wichita Falls, Texas, about an hour south and a fresh breath of air from the post. I wrote Joan a quick note Sunday, February 9, on stationery from the Marchman Hotel saying we had to catch a bus at 2 p.m. back to Lawton. A letter the next day described more about the weekend. Before we could sign out Saturday, we were told to move all our gear upstairs in our barracks—footlockers, clothing, and bedding—and organize it. Kelso and

A holdover after AIT, Glen on detail painting 55-gallon drum (Jim Brown).

I had already put on our greens to leave, so we were irritated about the last-minute change. But we hurried, moving Brown's stuff as well because his wife Dianne had already driven there to pick him up and he had managed to leave before the orders to move were given.

Coincidentally, Brown and Dianne had driven to Wichita Falls, where Kelso and I had gone on the bus, but we never crossed paths that weekend. We later learned that Kelso and I were eating pizza inside Shakey's Pizza Parlor, where Brown said they had driven by three or four times and started to stop but did not. He and Dianne had driven back to Lawton the next morning, where they thought we were going to be staying, and had checked at several motels in an effort to find us. They had planned to pick up Kentucky Fried Chicken and take us on a picnic out in the country from where we used to fire the howitzers. Brown and his wife, both from Missouri, sympathized with us guys so far from home and the visits of loved ones.

8. Officially Holdovers

Back at the barracks on Monday morning before breakfast, we were told to move all our belongings back downstairs. There was never a reason given for either move. At that time Brown was on detail driving a truck and Kelso had been picked to serve in the chow line, so I moved all their stuff in addition to mine. After lunch there was yet another move.

This time we were ordered to move completely out of Echo-4 barracks and into Delta-4 barracks. Although we were to sleep and eat at Delta, we were still "assigned" to Echo so that our mailing address would not change. As I did not expect us to remain at Delta after the weekend since a new cycle of trainees was arriving there, I did a minimum of unpacking. I anticipated that we would still pull KP and fire guard outside, no better off than we had been at E-4. However, since we would still report to Echo for formations and details, I was hopeful that I could retain the training aids detail. In my February 10 letter, I sketched a map indicating my old barracks at Echo and my new one at Delta, along with the location of the latrine, mess hall, Snack Shop, PX, and training aids.

My security guard duties at Delta barracks, from midnight to 2 a.m. on Wednesday, February 12, were quite different from routine, however, as I described in my letter at that time. Previously able to stay in one spot and write letters during guard, I was now told I had to walk around the barracks and check on things. "It is very important that I check on one particular person and make sure that he is asleep," I wrote, as I was told that he would "rob everyone in the building blind if he had half a chance. As a matter of fact, the platoon he was in during the regular cycle wouldn't even let him pull security guard because they knew it was safer with him asleep." I considered the rest of the holdovers pretty trustworthy, but there were several that I did not know well enough to trust completely. I had become "extremely cautious of almost everyone" since my fatigue shirt had been stolen.

Another detail I described was also very different from previous ones. Sent to the bivouac area, I was assigned to moving stumps with an engineer group. A wrecker came to load and then unload the larger stumps at the dumping site, but those of us working there loaded and unloaded the first load—and subsequently some smaller sections—by hand. I told Joan that some of the stumps were as large as our apartment bathroom at home.

The first afternoon Kelso and I worked there, we cut fallen trees into sections with a two-man crosscut saw. One tree was between four and five feet in diameter. It was warm enough to work in my T-shirt. We holdovers had had to turn in our canteens with our field gear the week we graduated, and whoever was responsible for our detail supplied no water for us. The sergeant said he would make certain we had water the next day and told us we might expect that detail again.

Thursday, February 13, marked five months that I had been in the Army, as I wrote Joan while on detail at training aids. I also ruminated about other significant dates—when we met, got engaged, and married. I noted that all of the Infantry OCS candidates were leaving today. "I really hate to see them go; they're a great bunch of guys." The guys who had received orders for Infantry OCS were getting a seven-day leave (plus three days travel time) before reporting to Fort Benning, Georgia, for their next training. On February 14 we went back to the bivouac area to finish moving the tree Kelso and I had cut, but "the cable on the wrecker's winch got all messed up." By the time we got it fixed, it was 4 p.m. and time for us to head back. Unlike the last time we were there working in T-shirts, it was cold and rainy.

Early Saturday morning, February 15, I wrote acknowledging having received lemon drops and cookies that had arrived "in good shape and ... were delicious." Whenever we received a care package from home "we usually let friends sample some of the contents." I was sampling a lemon drop myself while on detail and writing home. It had rained most of the weekend and was now snowing.

I described my recent KP as "the easiest and best" I had ever had—"only 13 hours and ten minutes. I was on side sink—washing all the silverware, trays, cups, glasses and bowls. We could go out into the dining room, sit down, and take a break whenever we finished our work." I estimated that we had sat three or four hours all together. Furthermore, when supper was over, "the cooks were working as hard as we were to finish so we could leave. It was the first time I ever saw cooks cleaning the stove, floor etc. Usually they just tip around telling the KPs what to do. It really wasn't bad at all."

My attention turned to Joan's newspaper and magazine articles she was writing and illustrating freelance outside of her classroom teaching. Even before I enlisted, we had begun imagining both of us combining writing and photography, perhaps with travel and teaching careers. I told her that I wished I were home to take photographs for her. "I really miss my photography," I said. "I have enjoyed the Kodak Instamatic.... I wish I had had it during basic." Since bringing the small camera back from Christmas, I was keeping it in my pocket when I could and had been snapping candid shots of friends and activities around the post.

"Well, it *has been did* again" began a second letter dated Saturday, February 15, and written on stationery imprinted "Holiday Inn of Wichita Falls–Downtown." Dianne had driven down for the weekend, and the Browns had asked me to get a pass so we could get together some time. McReynolds and Andy Helms got passes too, and I planned to stay with them. Brown suggested we all go to Wichita Falls. We five rode together

8. Officially Holdovers

and got two rooms at the motel—one for the couple and the other for us three. We enjoyed eating together at a steak house and then Helms, McReynolds, and I went off to "leave Dianne and Jim alone." It snowed again Sunday night, enough to cover the ground.

Writing Tuesday, February 18, on a 4–6 a.m. SG shift, I reported that yesterday morning it had snowed about an inch. Then the sun came out after lunch, and it was gone by 3 p.m. I reflected on the contrasts of the exactitude of BCT and its specific eight weeks with the uncertainty of the present stretch of time and activity. "Now, all we can do is plan one day at a time. We could get orders in late this afternoon and be processed out and ready to leave by 10 a.m. tomorrow." I continued, "I expected it [going to Vietnam] before I enlisted so I haven't really been shocked or surprised by anything that has happened." For now, what I could hope for was only something simple, like getting back on the TA detail. Yesterday's duty at the engineers had not been bad, just monotonous: "We stayed inside all day cleaning, sanding, and painting tools."

I very much wanted to see Joan before I shipped out, despite the feelings of impossibility. A window of chance for a weekend leave opened at the end of February. Almost instantly that window seemed to close when I also saw my name on the KP list that Saturday. I will always remember the kindness of another holdover in the barracks, an African American buddy that I knew slightly but whose name I cannot now recall, although I was ever deeply grateful to him. Hearing my situation, he offered to take my KP, saying, "Go home and see your family."

Hastily I threw a few items in a small travel bag, and with no further planning I grabbed a ride to Lawton Airport. It was Friday afternoon, February 21. Snow had begun to fall with a forecast of accumulations. The airlines serving the small airport had cancelled flights. There were two other soldiers and a civilian—a local woman perhaps in her forties—who were also anxious to get to Dallas. We investigated whether there were smaller, independent carriers who would fly, but none would.

The woman told us she had a car in the garage at her home. She offered its use if someone would drive it and help pay for gas to Dallas. We three soldiers quickly agreed and the four of us caught a taxi to her house. I rode 200 miles through a snowstorm with total strangers to get to Dallas. As we drew nearer Love Field, the snow lessened, and we discovered no flights from there had been cancelled.

By military standby I flew to Atlanta, then to Columbia, and hitchhiked the rest of the way to Camden. I arrived at our apartment in the dark of night to find the car gone and the doors locked. I got the landlady to open the door, I went inside, went upstairs, and fell on the bed exhausted and immediately went to sleep. I had no idea where Joan was, and she had no idea I was coming home. I had not called—not so much to surprise her, but rather not to get her hopes up if I could not get there. With the snowstorm and the uncertainty of flying standby, chances were good that I might not be able to make the distance home and would remain stuck in an airport.

Meanwhile, some fellow teachers and Joan had gone that evening to Rock Hill, 65 miles away, to a traveling cultural performance at Winthrop College, her alma mater—ironically the musical about comic hero Don Quixote, *The Man of La Mancha*. When she drove home, parked, and approached our back door, a snoopy neighbor who kept her eye on everyone called out from her door to ask if I was home. Apparently, she had seen the landlady open up for the door for a man in uniform.

Joan rushed inside, did not see me nor did I, sleeping soundly upstairs, hear her calls. She ran upstairs and found me in a deep slumber. I had not had enough sleep, but that was the best awakening I had had in quite a while. Except for being with Joan, everything else that weekend was a blur. It was a surreal time and I do not recall who else I saw. It is difficult to refer to that as a weekend pass because so much of it was spent in transit.

Sunday afternoon February 23, I drove our car with Joan to the Columbia Airport. As we approached the Alpine Road exit, the sun was about to begin its slide behind the horizon. It was a huge reddish ball that seemed like a tunnel into which Interstate 20 would disappear. To this day, Joan and I think about that poignant time if we are in that vicinity under similar conditions. At the airport we said our faith-filled goodbyes and she slid to the driver's side to return home. I went inside and began the ordeal of a night-long return to Oklahoma.

9

RVN Training

"Charlie has some really nasty booby traps"

MONDAY NIGHT, FEBRUARY 24, I BEGAN A LETTER that I continued early the next morning. I referred to a phone call earlier that evening and also to the "wonderful weekend" I had enjoyed at home. "It was short but maybe that helped because we didn't have enough time to feel sad or sorry that I would have to leave Sunday," I wrote. We had, in fact, felt blessed with the unexpected time we had together.

My activities told more than I put into words in my letters about what was now happening, or would happen next. Those words of explanation had already been spoken at home. An envelope, obviously hastily mailed and uncharacteristic with no return address and postmarked "Lawton, OK, Feb 27," contained segments of letters I wrote Tuesday (25th), Wednesday (26th), and Thursday (27th).

We were in training again, required to finish a 16-hour block of RVN (Republic of Vietnam) training. It consisted of an orientation; classes and films on Vietnam, its government, and its history; and a visit to a mock Vietnamese village. There was considerable emphasis on booby traps. "Charlie has some really nasty booby traps," I commented. I provided a description and sketches of one type called a "spider hole." The military alphabet that rendered the enemy's name "Viet Cong" (initialed "VC") as "Victor Charlie" gave rise to the widely used nickname simply "Charlie," or to spinoffs like "Charles" or "Chuck."

The final segment of my letter described Wednesday's "classes and films on jungle survival, disease, reptiles, ambush and counter ambush." One film was entitled "Your Year of Opportunity." I commented, "Only the Army can come up with something like that." Thursday we completed RVN training: "We went out in open trucks today and naturally today was the first cold day we've had this week." We were "ambushed" and had to jump off the trucks and charge the aggressors. We were supposed to move to another area by helicopter, but for some reason we went by truck instead. We had to get off the trucks and charge an enemy area "in an infantry sweep attack." We crossed a creek while smoke bombs went off above and explosives below "sent streams of water 30–40 feet into the air."

After that we toured two mock villages—a typical Vietnamese village and a Viet Cong village. We also got vaccinations for cholera and other maladies I never thought I might face. I had my first experience with pneumatic guns. On one occasion, we got four shots at one time with two medics on each side of the recruit, a gun in each hand. Before getting the shots, we were instructed to relax our arms. Trainees who flinched ended up with cuts rather than sticks and had streams of blood running down their arms.

Much of a letter dated Saturday, March 1, described a continuing ordeal in which I had begun trying to exchange a pair of my boots that had warped on the inside. The repairman at Clothing and Equipment Repair had filled out paperwork for me to take to Echo Battery's supply sergeant. He in turn had to fill out more papers for me to take to Quartermaster Sales to exchange the boots. "An unbelievable amount of red tape," I remarked.

I went on to report that McReynolds and I had gone on another weekend jaunt with the Browns. This time we traveled Interstate 44 and spent Saturday night at the Holiday Inn of Chickasha, about 45 miles northeast of Fort Sill. We had to drive through a snowstorm on the return trip. From Lawton I mailed Joan a Chickasha Holiday Inn postcard with a Fort Sill postmark. Writing at 5 p.m. Sunday, March 2, I reported us back at Fort Sill, covered with five inches of snow. Brown, McReynolds, and I were in the Service Club writing letters and contemplating going to a movie for fear of being put on a detail if we returned to the barracks.

My follow-up letter a short time later that night, dated Sunday 6:15 p.m., had "Holding Battery" written in place of "Echo" in the return address, indicating that an obvious change had taken place that I did not need to explain—that I had been moved again to a new place. Instead, I described the weekend outing. We had first driven south toward Wichita Falls and picked up burgers for a picnic along the road. After eating, we rode back toward Lawton and stopped at a discount place called Surplus City, where I bought a pair of Levis for $3.25 and a shirt for $2.98. Both Brown and McReynolds already had civvies. Not only were civilian clothes good for the weekend, but I was now allowed to wear them in a holding battery after duty hours, and, instead of dress greens, wear them to the Service Club, movies, or the EM Club where fatigues were not allowed. I closed my letter with thoughts about the "faith and belief" Joan and I both shared and how fortunate we were.

Monday, March 3, I began a letter at 9:30 p.m. Instead of the 9 p.m. lights-out I had been used to, lights did not have to be out in the holding

9. RVN Training

battery until 10 p.m. I did not like that as well because "usually by 9 we are ready to go to bed and it's practically impossible to go to sleep while the lights are on and 26 other people in the same room are awake." Wake-up time in the holding battery was 5 a.m., instead of 5:30 or 5:45, to which I was accustomed. On the other hand, I wrote, holdovers had "no KP, no fire guard, no security guard, and we didn't even have to wait in line for chow; we just walked right on in ahead of the trainees." The downside was that we had to walk three-fourths of a mile to chow—a consolidated mess hall that served 1,000 men per meal.

Since all of the pre–OCS AIT batteries ate in the same mess hall that I did now, I ran into my University of South Carolina friend Don Vik again that night at supper. He had been delayed in finishing his training because of having been hospitalized, but was graduating that week. He had been assigned Artillery OCS, was still planning to go, and was getting married as soon as he finished OCS. Another coincidence was that on the way to chow, I had run into another old USC friend, Jimmy Alderson, whom I had not previously seen at Fort Sill. He had lived on my college dorm hall where his nickname was "White Owl" for his very light blond hair. He had also enlisted for OCS but was considering dropping it.

An unnecessarily time-consuming saga finally ended. My warped boots at long last had been replaced with a "brand-spanking-new" pair. After a detail spent sanding tools, I received mail that had accumulated since Friday back at Echo Battery—a letter from brother Byron, one from Joan's mother, and three from Joan. I had speculated earlier that the worst of winter had passed, but at 5:30 the next morning, March 4, I wrote, "It has turned real cold here since Sunday's snow. I wore my long johns yesterday for the first time in a month. Brrr!" I remarked that I did not relish the long walk to breakfast in the cold, but a consolation was that the food was better there.

My March 5 card related that Brown, McReynolds, and I had been given the day off for donating blood, so we had taken our passes and gone into town. We walked the Lawton streets, looked in pawn shops "and in general just goofed off." We ate lunch and supper there and went to the USO and played pool. The United Service Organizations did a commendable job providing refreshments and recreation, but their efforts could provide us only so much. "We all were miserable," I said. "We couldn't help but think how we could have enjoyed such a day off in civilian life. But we were not at all happy even having time off here.... I realize all GIs feel this way and the only thing that can cure the feeling is a discharge." In the meantime, I indicated a temporary remedy: "I'll be in a better mood tomorrow because I'll talk to you tomorrow night. I can hardly wait to hear your sweet voice." Telephone calls, by necessity, were infrequent, but were cherished.

10

Oakland Departure

*"So much to be thankful for
and so much to return to"*

AFTER I HAD BEEN A HOLDOVER FOR SIX WEEKS, our group got new orders issued March 3 and delivered to us Thursday, March 6. I called Joan right away. We talked seriously and calmly as I related the facts, but we could not speak long. Everything was moving quickly. Pat McReynolds received orders to go to Korea, and Jim Brown to Fort Leavenworth, Kansas. I was to report to Oakland Army Depot for deployment to the Republic of South Vietnam. Both my friends consoled me, but I imagine were thankful they had been spared Vietnam. I was happy for them—especially for Brown. Kansas was adjacent to Missouri and his home and family. Dianne would still be close enough to visit him. I was prepared and not surprised to have gotten the assignment I had expected.

Thursday, March 6, I also scribbled a quick note to Joan that I was mailing her things "that I won't be needing until I get home." At 7:30 the next morning, I wrote her a card stating, "I'm writing this from the Lawton Airport. We fly out of here at 8 a.m. by jet non-stop to Oakland. We'll be there at 9:30 Pacific time. They're not wasting any time getting us there, are they?" I also told her regarding the hasty phone call I had made to her, "I appreciate your taking the news as you did. It's not easy thinking about the coming year but it will pass and then all will be well once more."

Saturday, March 8, I wrote a postcard at 7:30 a.m. and mailed it from Oakland Army Base in California. On the front was a montage of the Golden Gate Bridge, state capital, two mountain scenes, and the message "Hello from California." My flight, I said, had made a brief fuel stop in Albuquerque, New Mexico, and had arrived in Oakland at 10:30 a.m. We ate lunch and then "began processing about 12:30 and didn't stop until 11:30 p.m. I have my jungle fatigues and jungle boots etc. & could ship at any minute."

During the processing, we were given plain postcards to address to

10. Oakland Departure

our next-of-kin (NOK). The reverse side was a printed message telling the recipient what to do should he or she require financial assistance "during my absence overseas." I had filled in the three blanks (date) "*8 March 69*," (Dear) "*Joan*," and at the end of the printed message on the signatory line, "*Love, Glen*."

A letter dated 4 p.m. on Saturday, March 8, proclaims about Oakland, "Boy this place reeks of details." Commenting that I had only one sheet of paper, I stated we had mandatory formations at 7:30 a.m., 12:30 p.m., and 3:30 p.m. At these formations, names were called for those manifested for a flight out and those men would step out of formation and were led away. Those remaining would be randomly selected in small groups for details— "KP, guard duty (both of these run 24 hrs. a day), clean-up, etc."

I revealed that "I did something this morning I normally never do." When one of the sergeants had asked for six volunteers, I had a "gut feeling" that it might not be too bad, and I stepped forward. Two went somewhere; the other three and I went "to a small bay that sleeps about 28 people."

From my detail site, I could see the San Francisco skyline and the Golden Gate Bridge. I continued, "We swept the floors & straightened up a bit and then we lay down on the bunks and napped the rest of the morning. This afternoon we waxed and buffed the floor. The sgt. was impressed with the job we did and so I am on the same detail as long as I'm here. He also keeps us off night details. This sgt. has the theory that a guy who volunteers will do a better job than one who is picked.... I really was lucky 'cause two of the guys who came here with me from Echo-4 had KP today."

Not only were men shipping in and out, but every day troops were returning from Vietnam. I observed, "They must come straight from the field because they arrive in jungle fatigues & boots. They're dirty and unshaven but they all look happy." I requested Joan not to worry about me because I was in a good mood and "as ready mentally to go to Vietnam as I can expect to get," adding, "I've got so much to be thankful for and so much to return to that I'm not worried at all."

In a United States Army envelope with my old Fort Sill return address but bearing an Oakland postmark stamped March 10, I again wrote a letter in segments. I began at 6:45 a.m. Sunday, March 9, stating that I had wanted to go into San Francisco last night (they issued passes only from 6 to 12 p.m.) just to see it and take some photographs, but I did not want to go alone or with someone I did not know. Instead, I stayed around the barracks, called Joan, and then took a shower and went to bed. I began another segment Sunday at 5:30 p.m. Joan and I had spoken on the phone that morning. I lamented that I would "surely miss hearing your sweet voice for the next 13 months." I had learned that Vietnam time was 20 hours ahead of Eastern Standard Time.

My letter recalled a few observations about my flight to Oakland. "Most of Arizona and New Mexico was covered in snow ... the Grand Canyon, Death Valley, and Lake Mead were really impressive from the air," I said, and "the snow-capped peaks around Albuquerque ... were beautiful." I regretted I did not have my camera out then, but resolved to have it available on the way to Vietnam in case I might be able to get a shot or two.

Over the next page and a half, I expressed some of my feelings and thoughts. I was not scared, "at least not yet. I am apprehensive, I suppose. I can't help but wonder where I'll be, what it will be like, whether or not I'll ever be confronted by Charlie etc. I guess if I really wanted to worry, I could drive myself crazy but I see no need to worry yet. I'll worry if and when the need arises. So far I've managed to keep in good spirits and I intend to continue throughout the next 13 months ... we've learned from experience that all things pass and so we'll just do the best we can and pray that everything will happen for the best."

I concluded this letter assuring Joan that "should anything happen to me," I loved her "more than I ever thought I could possibly love someone," and that she had brought me immense happiness ... and "I could never have found a wife more suited for me." I added, "We'll be together again before you know it. Just wait, I'll be back at your side. I love you with all my heart."

Sunday, March 10, at 10 a.m. I wrote news factually on a postcard picturing the Jack London Square on the estuary in Oakland. I said, "Bob Carey (who came from E-4 with me) & I had been called out at the morning's formation. We leave at 8:50 a.m. tomorrow. We have now moved from the Transient Company to Bldg. 790 where we will stay until we ship. As a matter of fact, we're restricted to this bldg."

Indeed, we were *locked* in Building 790 which resembled a huge gym that had been converted into an emergency shelter. There were several hundred cots in rows in the center. There were latrine and shower facilities, and along the walls there were banks of vending machines and, most importantly, pay telephones. We were divided into small groups. At mealtimes each group was escorted out, under guard, and marched in a file to the mess hall where the group sat together. When we had eaten, we were marched back to Building 790.

Great precautions were taken to prevent desertions. Monday morning after breakfast those on my manifest were bused to adjacent Oakland International Airport where we boarded a World Airways commercial aircraft. Besides Carey, there was not a single person that I knew on the flight.

On a postcard picturing the Golden Gate Bridge and the San Francisco skyline, postmarked from Anchorage, Alaska, I wrote at 11:30 a.m. Monday, March 10, that we had flown over the Oakland Bridge about 25

10. Oakland Departure

minutes ago and were now in flight over the Pacific. We were flying World Airways at a speed of about 550 mph at an altitude of 35,000 feet. Two stops were scheduled, at Anchorage (where I mailed the card) and in Japan. Our flight time would be about 18 hours and our final destination was Bien Hoa, Vietnam. "So I don't guess I'll be in Da Nang or in the Delta," I presumed. I had taken a few slides from the plane. I offered assurances, "I am fine so don't worry."

A second postcard picturing a caribou in the rays of the midnight sun and postmarked at Anchorage was written that afternoon 3:30 p.m. (1:30 Alaska time) during our layover there. The runway had recently been scraped of snow, but its edges were piled high. "Boy, I've never seen so much snow in my life," I remarked, and then quipped, "It's warm here—34°—good weather for jungle fatigues." A third postcard also postmarked Anchorage on March 10 and depicting grazing caribou in Mt. McKinley National Park, stated, "This is the way it looks here except I haven't seen any caribou yet."

A fourth postcard with a Japanese scene bore a Yokota Air Base cancellation stamp and was dated Monday 12 p.m. (Pacific). When we stepped off the plane on its stop to refuel and change crews in Japan, we encountered weather colder than in Alaska. We were to remain there about an hour before our next stop. Thus far the overall mood on the plane had been remarkably upbeat with excitement over seeing Alaska and then viewing Mt. Fuji as we flew into Japan. Leaving there, on the last leg of our journey, the disposition of the passengers changed dramatically. Jet lag, exhaustion, and the anxiety of what lay ahead brought on a quiet gloomy temperament.

Landing at our destination, Bien Hoa, little did I realize how many of the hours of classroom instruction and the days spent on the windswept plains of Oklahoma would be of limited preparation for assignments I would encounter in Vietnam.

11

Vietnam In-Country

"A stench then unrecognized"

THE APPREHENSIVE FLIGHT FROM JAPAN grew more tense when the pilot announced we had entered air space over Vietnam. I strained to see through the darkness below. Occasionally I glimpsed what appeared to be fires and explosions. The latter were likely the results of fire missions, as we would soon learn, since the bulk of the artillery's work was done at night when the Viet Cong were most active. It was a somber group who followed the prompts from the flight crew to prepare for descent.

My plane landed at Bien Hoa Air Base at about 11:30 p.m., Tuesday, March 11. When the plane taxied to a stop, an officer came aboard to announce that we would remain on board until we were debriefed. The plane's engines were shut down during refueling. This meant that the air conditioning and circulation system also ceased. The temperature began to rise inside the tightly packed cabin. By the time another officer came aboard to debrief us, we were profusely sweating. I do not recall specifically what information he gave us other than to be alert, probably warnings similar to those given at commercial airports today: to be aware of anyone leaving a backpack, bag, or other item and walking away, or of any other suspicious activity. As we deplaned, each man was given a number. I was "86."

The cool midnight air I anticipated stepping into was instead nearly 90 degrees, still and stifling. My eyes scanned a hodge-podge of personnel and vehicles on the tarmac. Closest to our plane was a Jeep with a .50 caliber machine gun mounted in the back. My olfactory senses detected a stench then unrecognized, but one that would become omnipresent during my experience in-country—the smell of diesel fuel burning GI excrement.

Latrines in American camps, I would learn, were basically outhouses or privies with modifications. Because of the heat and humidity, solid walls extended only about halfway upward, with the top half being screen wire. In time I would observe that most latrines were multi-seat, often as many as half-a-dozen. Because of the country's high-water table, it was folly to dig a toilet hole in the soil. Instead, a half of a 55-gallon barrel would be placed under each elevated toilet seat. Latrine duty, colloquially "shit burning," involved a GI lifting a hinged door on the outside and sliding the receptacle a distance from the latrine, pouring in some diesel, lighting the mix, and occasionally stirring it with a board to assist its burning. When burning was completed, the GI would then replace the half-barrel under the seat. Pervasive odors lingered.

Most of the Bien Hoa terminal where we landed the night of March 11 was a covered but open structure that had some concession stands with tables and chairs where travelers could sit and eat while they waited. I do not know that I purchased anything to eat or drink, but I recall sitting in that section while listening for my number. I felt movement under the table around my feet—young children were "polishing" boots and then asking for money. This was my introduction to a prevalent practice among the Vietnamese—unsolicited services demanding payment.

When I heard my number 86 called, I joined other men clambering aboard several passenger buses. These were air-conditioned, their closed windows protectively covered with metal grating. We were warned to stay alert on the bus and to shout out if we observed anyone outside attempting to attach anything to the window grating where VC were known for attaching grenades. The convoy was escorted by machine gun–equipped Jeeps. We went through several checkpoints on the eight-mile journey to reach the 90th Replacement Battalion at Long Binh. Here in the night we immediately began in-processing, which continued until 4 a.m., the process, of course, interspersed with standing around and waiting.

Finally assigned to barracks, we had about an hour to try to grab a nap. Our 6:30 a.m. formation was followed by the first command, a police call to clean up the area. Names were called for men with orders. The rest of us were assigned details—KP, motor pool, and the like. My first detail was to help build a sandbag bunker for a transportation company. While a corporal in faded jungle fatigues was leading us to the detail location, I was able to observe part of the post. There were soldiers everywhere, most busy on various details. Walking along the road were numerous Vietnamese females in native dresses and cone-shaped straw hats. I would learn that the women worked in the barracks, sweeping floors, shining boots, and doing laundry.

We returned to the replacement camp area for lunch and a repeat of the morning's formation, with more names being called with orders and the rest of us sent out on afternoon details. When I came in for a pre-supper formation, my name was called, as was that of just one acquaintance. Carey received orders to Pleiku, mid-country in the Central Highlands.

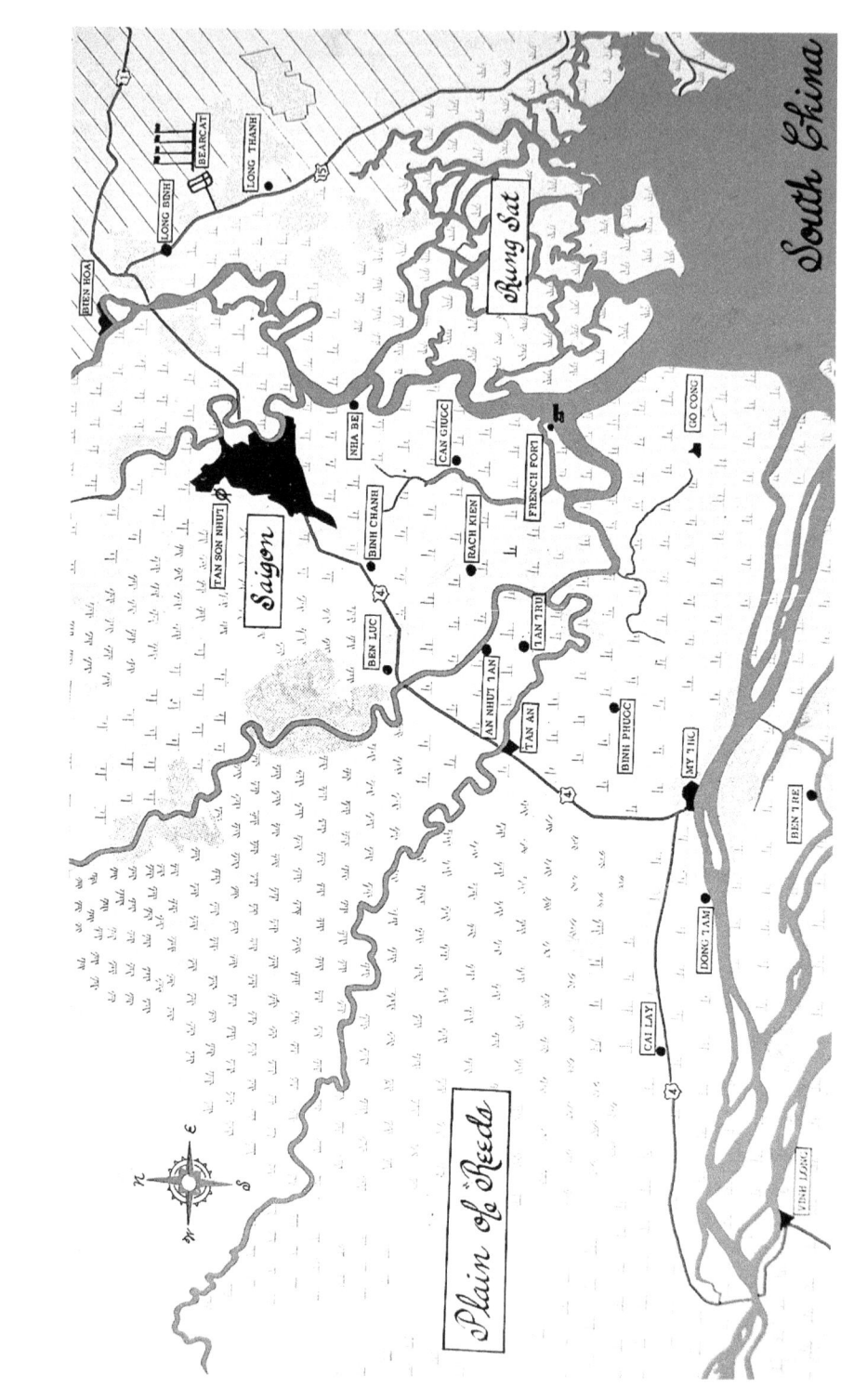

11. Vietnam In-Country

I was assigned to the 9th Infantry Division at Dong Tam, a place I would soon hear GIs more easily pronounce "Dog Town." It was then I learned that I would be going south to the Mekong Delta.

Carey and I ate, took what passed for a quick shower, and reported back to the formation area with our baggage. In a typical Army "hurry and wait," we waited there until 10 p.m., then were ordered to stack our gear and were sent to an empty barracks to sleep. I would later write that "In Long Binh we heard artillery fire, occasional machine gun or light weapons fire but nothing happened real close to us. The area was pretty well guarded and choppers flew over all during the night, shining search lights around the outer perimeter. As we were about to enter the barracks, we saw Charlie try to shoot down one of our copters. He must have taken about 6 or 8 shots but each one exploded right behind the chopper. It finally flew out of range."

We had barely settled down in the barracks before a siren alerted us of a mortar attack. The VC preferred this muzzle-loading weapon for its portability. For the first time the feeling flashed over me that I did not write about—that *people* were trying to *kill me*. We hurriedly took action rushing downstairs because the bottom floor was protected on all sides by sandbags. We lay on the floor, pulling mattresses on top of us. We heard mortar rounds hitting, but not too close. I remained there on the floor until about 3 a.m. One hour later they called a large group out to pick up tickets to our destinations. About 18 other guys and I were put on a detail loading all the baggage on a truck. We GIs were then put on a bus that returned us to Bien Hoa Air Base. Carey would go north and I would go south. Waiting at Bien Hoa, I wrote my first letter home to Joan on March 13, telling her of my arrival and my first two days in Vietnam.

Although it would go unmentioned in the busy time when I would be writing my second letter on March 15, an episode occurred in the interim which remains vivid in my memory. To leave Bien Hoa, six or eight of us were sent aboard a Caribou, a twin prop plane with short takeoff and landing capability. The plane landed on an unimproved and desolate landing strip, the location of which remains unknown to me. The pilot told us he could not proceed to Dong Tam because of turbulent winds in the area. The plane promptly flew off. We saw no one around. We new-arrivals, strangers to one another and having no leader, were left with our gear on the edge of that crude, unmanned strip in the scorching sun, with no knowledge of our location nor information about when or how we were to be transported to Dong Tam, wherever that was.

After a while, still alone, we saw a young Vietnamese boy riding a

Opposite: **Map of the Mekong Delta (9th Division brochure).**

bicycle towards us. As he slowly came near, we watchers noticed he had a container filled with soft drinks attached to the rack behind his seat. He stopped and, in broken English, offered to sell us drinks. He was asking $1 per bottle. Perplexed as we were, we were so thirsty that we eagerly pulled out MPC to give him. Military Payment Certificates were the paper scrip we had been given in exchange for the U.S. currency we had brought with us, the use of which was forbidden in-country. We were to use either MPC or local currency, with metal coins being called *dong* and paper called *piasters*, 100 of which being worth almost $1 U.S.

At the point of thirsty exchange of drinks and MPC, an officer pulled up in a Jeep and halted the transaction. He explained that "gooks" (the regularly used slang name for the local people) would try to overcharge for anything they sold. The "going rate" for soft drinks was 50¢ and if we exceeded that, he said, we would "mess up things for everyone." Although annoyed about the lieutenant's intervention, the young entrepreneur quickly took our 50¢ MPCs and handed us lukewarm colas.

Eventually, following that bizarre episode, a deuce-and-a-half showed up to transport us four miles away to Dong Tam. We were handed M16s and bandoliers of magazines and instructed to "lock and load" and be ready if we encountered any Viet Cong on our journey. There was no canvas on the truck bed, so we had a panoramic view of our surroundings as we traveled along, gazing at farmers and water buffalo in the rice paddies, and pedestrians and motorists—most on bicycles or motor scooters—on the road. We entered the compound and were delivered, without further incident, to Reliable Camp (the 9th Division being nicknamed the "Old Reliables"). We processed in that afternoon and the next morning, and then began our jungle training.

On March 15 I wrote Joan from Reliable Camp, having completed day one of a five-day jungle school. We had been issued and had zeroed in our own M16s "which we will live with for the next 12 months." We had classes on the M16, the M60 machine gun, the M79 grenade launcher, two different types of hand grenades, and demolitions. In addition to firing our M16s, we also fired the M60 and the M79. We set off a one-fourth pound charge of C4, the Army's standard demolitions material "which is 1½ times as powerful as TNT."

At a cost of $8 million, Dong Tam had been established on 600 acres of swampland which had been reclaimed by U.S. Army engineers dredging soil out of the Mekong River. Dong Tam was now a large helicopter base and a deep river harbor on the northern bank, handling many ships and gunboats. Because of those factors and its status as 9th Division Headquarters, Dong Tam was a frequent target of Viet Cong mortar, rocket, and ground attacks. I reported, "Last night Charles hit us with two separate mortar attacks—one at 10 p.m., the other at about 1:30 a.m." The VC attack "also probed our perimeter but was repelled." I assured Joan that there were "excellent bunkers right beside our hooches," the small buildings that sufficed for barracks in Vietnam.

I wrote in a long letter March 19 that I had had little sleep the previous night, for I had guarded the ammo bunker from 11 p.m. to 3 a.m., and then "Charlie hit us with a mortar attack at about 4:45." Practically all of my jungle classes that day had been "out in the boondocks." I explained, "We go out in the mornings and stay until supper. We eat C-rations for dinner and sometimes for supper too if we stay out late enough." I added, "Many of our classes have been out in a banana grove which has numerous canals running throughout. The patrol we went on yesterday consisted of wading through these canals which are waist to chest deep and contain all kinds of vegetation. So far I've contacted no leeches and have seen only one snake. Hope things remain that way."

Our training had included a class on swimming which entailed jumping into the river where it was 10–12 feet deep. We had on jungle fatigues and boots. I was surprised that, unlike regular combat boots, the jungle boots "don't weigh one down." We were taught when treading water to take off the wet fatigue shirt, trap air inside, and use it as a flotation device. It worked!

When I got my first in-country haircut (40¢) and a shave (20¢), I said I was uneasy because the barbers were Vietnamese. Even though it was broad daylight in an Army compound with many people around, since our allies and our enemies looked the same, it was an unsettling experience watching the barber sharpen and put his straight razor near my throat to shave me.

I described the area around Dong Tam feeling "like being at the beach but back off front beach in the dunes. The sun beams down upon us all the time, and it's dry and dusty—not sandy but just loose dirt that blows everywhere." Everything got covered with dust and dirt. Except for the bunkers, most buildings were walled up about four feet with the remainder screened for ventilation, as the air was hot year-round. There was no hot water and limited potable water. We had to put just a little water in our steel pot to shave.

The next morning, my letter continued, we were set to "graduate" from jungle training. Afterwards I expected to ship out to my yet-to-be-announced unit. Until then, I had no address to send home, and thus could expect no mail. Once I arrived at my unit and had an address, I surmised it would take about a week for Joan and other family members and friends to get my address and then another week before I could receive mail from home. I declared I would "certainly be glad when my year over here is over and I can come home to you. Living under these conditions … really makes one think and stop to appreciate all he has at home. We are so fortunate, Joan, and we have so much to be thankful for. I love you so very dearly."

I related an incident from Reliable Academy that I had not previously mentioned: "Charlie hit us with a mortar attack while we were out in the banana grove eating dinner. You don't have to pretend there's an enemy out there; he most assuredly is out there and he won't let you forget it." Before I closed my letter, I was able to include my much-anticipated mailing address, although I had to send a postcard the following day to make a correction to it.

On March 20 at the end of jungle school, which variously dispersed us, I was driven in a Jeep about 17 miles on Highway 4 north to 2nd Battalion headquarters at Tan An City to receive my next assignment. I would later learn that the Mekong Delta in southern Vietnam covered over 15,600 square miles of villages surrounded by rice paddies and a labyrinth of rivers, canals, swamps, and islands. My Jeep trip through a small

A typical farmer's hooch constructed of palm fronds, as seen from a road in Long An Province.

11. Vietnam In-Country

The tidewater creek having receded, a papa-san storing his catch in the basket and removing his net as his family watches.

portion of the area afforded me a snapshot preview of the land and its people.

I described some typical scenes: "Most of the land is rice paddies or banana groves. Once in a while one sees a swamp filled with banana trees, coconut palms, mango trees, and other vegetation." The banks along all of the canals were also covered with vegetation. "Most of the people live in thatched huts with dirt floors. Most of them live on a canal or else they have a scum pond in the yard," I said. "They own water buffalos, goats, ducks, cows, and sorry-looking dogs." Highway 4, the main highway in South Vietnam, was "unbelievably crowded. People on bicycles, motorcycles, scooters, walking, in autos, trucks—people everywhere."

Since it was nearly 5 p.m. when I arrived at battalion headquarters just outside Tan An City, I had to wait until the next morning to process. Meanwhile I had time to observe my surroundings. Protecting the compound, spiraling coils of barbed wire called concertina, were stretched between metal posts that spanned the flooded rice paddies between the military compound and the city. Metal cans with pebbles inside were hung along the wires to create a primitive but effective alarm system. Wired claymore mines attached to other metal stakes were aimed outward to deter potential attackers. I learned the mines required frequent inspection

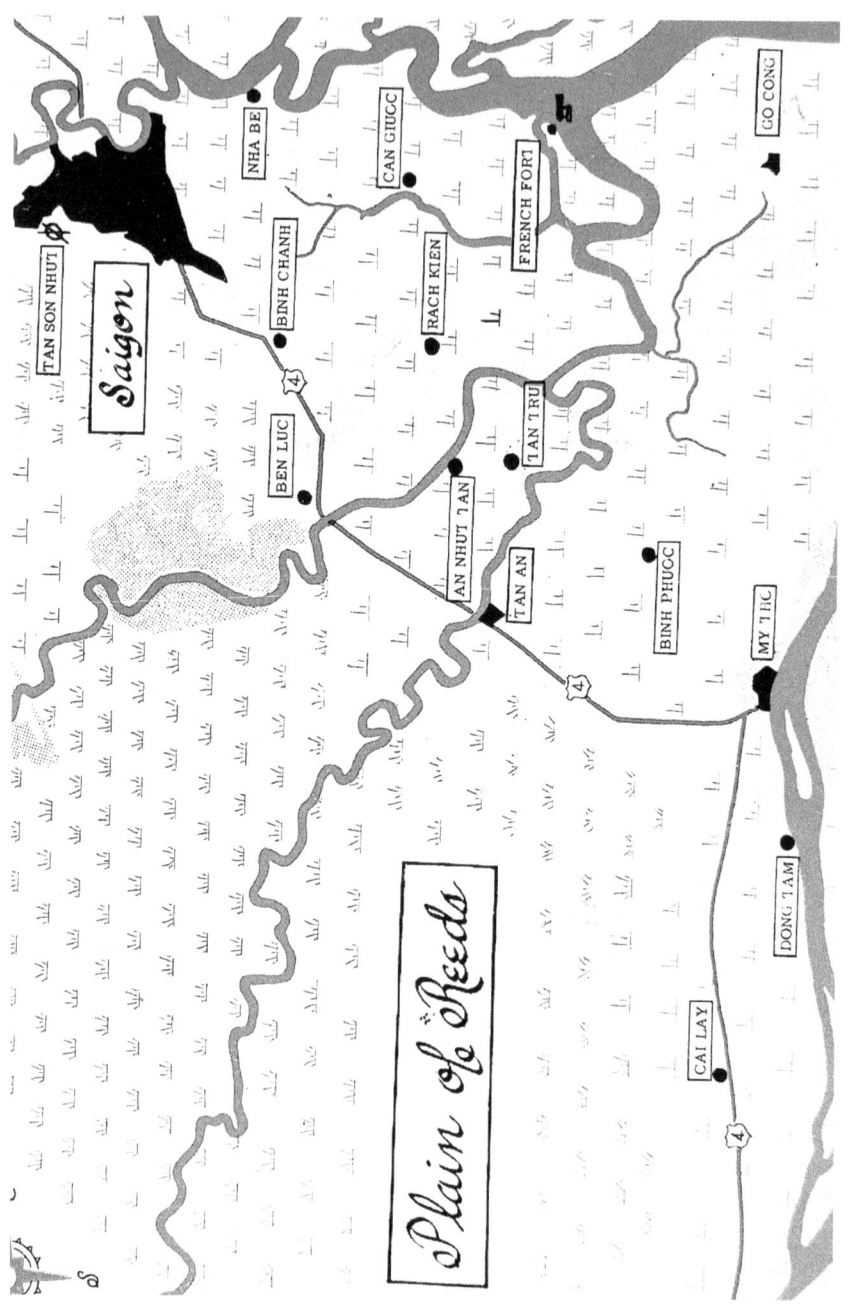

Enlarged section of Mekong Delta map indicating Tan Tru, Tan An, Ben Luc, the Plain of Reeds, and Highway 4 (9th Division brochure).

to ensure that no saboteur turned them inward to explode toward the compound. With evening approaching when I arrived, I saw guards being posted to bunkers located about every 50 yards along the perimeter of the camp.

Processing the next morning, I received assignment to Charlie Battery, 2nd Battalion, 4th Field Artillery Regiment at a firebase seven miles away called Tan Tru. It was so named because of its location about a mile from the Long An Province village of the same name. The compound was reached by vehicle by turning off main Highway 4 and traveling eastward on a narrow clay and dirt road dissecting rice paddies, small villages, and hamlets. I would learn that GIs called the highway "Thunder Road," and in time I would become familiar with its varying features.

On each side of Thunder Road rice paddies extended until broken by dense areas of vegetation we called "tree lines." Because these areas flanked various waterways that meandered through the Delta, they remained dense and lush even during the dry season when the rice paddies were arid and inactive. The deep mud in the paddies then became as hard as concrete with splits over a foot deep. Thunder Road would likewise become like concrete. Travelers would reach their destinations covered with dust. That was its condition when I arrived.

In contrast, during the monsoon season the paddies would fill with

A dry-season cloud of dust, raised by a M35 truck approaching Tan Tru firebase on "Thunder Road."

water, a natural cycle that allowed local farmers to engage in the labors of rice cultivation. During the monsoon, April through October, Thunder Road would become a quagmire, at times impassable. The road's pliability then allowed the VC to bury land mines. The condition would necessitate a team to "sweep" the length of Thunder Road to Highway 4 each morning before any military vehicles were permitted to travel. The numerous bridges over creeks and rivers also required daily inspection to detect explosive devices that might have been attached during the night. Thunder Road's safety was essential as it was our sole land connection to main Highway 4, which to the south led to our battalion headquarters in Tan An, and to the north led to our maintenance battalion at Ben Luc and from there onward to the South Vietnamese capital city Saigon, about 40 miles from Tan Tru.

Each day our battery sent a vehicle on a "distribution run" taking Thunder Road to Highway 4, first going north to Ben Luc carrying equipment requiring repair or replacement, and then going south to Tan An carrying outgoing mail. The vehicle would return to base with parts or equipment and with the most important commodity for us GIs, mail from home, handed out at the end of the day at mail call. An enlisted man with a military driver's license usually drove the supply sergeant on the run in an M38 or M151 Jeep, an M37 three-quarter-ton truck, or an M35 deuce-and-a-half truck, dependent upon transport need. Thunder Road led to the main entrance of our compound, which looked somewhat like the entrance to an old Army fort in classic western movies.

As I learned the importance of Thunder Road to Tan Tru Firebase, I would come to recognize the firebase's role in the defense of its region of the Delta. My battery, Charlie, was just one of a number of units located within that compound, but it was the only one assigned to the 105 mm howitzers on which I had trained at Fort Sill. On arrival at the firebase, I was assigned to a specific one of Charlie's six 105s, so I was also given a bunk in a hooch near that cannon.

This hooch was constructed protectively with a wooden floor and a double-board wall bottom filled with dirt and clay, above which was stacked an upper wall of protective bags and ammo boxes also filled with dirt and clay. It had a tin roof on which there were other layers of filled sandbags. There were no windows, only a few small openings like gun ports that provided scant ventilation. There were no doors to hinder rapid exit for fire missions. Signs at entrances reminded us that weapons were to be unloaded and cleared before entering. We slept with our ammo bandoliers and weapons beside us, but unloaded. There were walkways or ramps to the entrance of most of the hooches. I would later learn that because the compound had been established in rice paddies, when the monsoon rains

11. Vietnam In-Country

Left side of hooch "duplex" constructed of sandbags.

Right side of hooch "duplex" where Glen first lived upon arrival at C Battery.

came there would be standing water throughout low areas and surrounding the hooches.

When I arrived, the military was constructing new bunkers to live in.

The walls were to be double walls of 2 × 12 boards with a foot or more of dirt and clay between them. The roofs were of heavy timbers as well, with clay between the layers, and with tin on top to repel rain. These structures had doorways at both ends, but about three feet from each opening was a wall section identical to the structure's walls. Personnel could enter or exit quickly, but bullets or shrapnel could not enter. These were well designed for protection, but not for comfort. Little air circulated and the hooches were very hot. The new constructions were expected to be in use soon.

We worked on building these new bunkers, filled sandbags, or performed other details during the day. Most of our fire missions were at night when the VC were most active. My first fire mission was the night of March 21, followed by another the next day. Due to the flat terrain and dense vegetation, we never saw our targets. Fortunately, while I was there, we never had a full-scale ground attack requiring us to lower our tubes and fire anti-personnel "beehive" rounds, each of which spread 10,000 stainless steel darts in an arc of destruction. We had mortar attacks and, less frequently, rocket attacks. During my first few nights there, we had alerts for ground attacks by North Vietnamese Army (NVA) regulars, but they turned out to

More protective bunkers replacing ammo box and sandbag hooches as living quarters.

be probes of our perimeter by sapper squads, small groups carrying satchel explosives. Our berm guards took care of them before they could breach the perimeter.

Even when we had no fire mission, there were duties. Each night every gun section of eight men supplied one man for berm guard to occupy the bunkers on the perimeter. Each bunker there had three or four men taking shifts to watch or sleep.

The rest of the crew took shifts standing with the phone by the howitzer. The person on phone duty had the responsibility to alert the gun crew if a fire mission came in. At times when we received intelligence of unusual enemy activity, we would be placed on 50 percent alert or on full alert. For the former, two men, in addition to the one monitoring the phone, had to be outside by the fieldpiece; for the latter, it was "all hands on deck" with flak vest, steel pot, and locked-and-loaded weapon.

I wrote to Joan Saturday night, March 22, while we were on 50 percent alert. I did attempt to assuage her concerns by informing her that "No one has been killed here within the battery in almost a year and only a few have been wounded." Had I known then what was soon to occur, I would not have added the following statement: "Several recon sgts. and RTOs (radio-telephone operators) have been killed, but they go out in the boondocks—right in Chuck's back yard."

The next day I happily reported, "Nothing happened last night. No ground attack, no rockets, no mortars, nothing." I related, "The last time Charles tried a ground attack was in December and Charlie Battery really brought smoke on Chuck. They fired several bee-hive rounds direct fire. The next morning a recon patrol made a VC body count of 37 and found 7 mortars set up that Chuck had never had a chance to fire. Since then the VC haven't tried another ground attack. I'm probably as safe here as I would be anywhere else in Vietnam."

A major general had visited our battery that day and "my section fired a fire power demonstration for him," I said. "All in all I think we did a pretty good job and we were commended by the battery commander." I mentioned that the officers and senior NCOs had been nervous about the general's visit, so we had a police call that morning from 8:00 to 10:00. That night my gun section was "firing radar." I explained that meant "We fire at anything the radar picks up that's moving outside our perimeter."

Because of our good performance for the general, we were to have the following day off (except for the morning formation, gun maintenance, "police call etc., etc., etc."). I summarized, "Otherwise we have the day off." I commented the following day about our "quasi-free" day. In addition to the duties and details previously mentioned, we "had to take turns overseeing a detail of Vietnamese women who were digging a ditch outside

"Sandbag dollars" cleaning the ditch along C Battery's "main street" in Tan Tru firebase.

of our hooch. They are called 'sandbag dollars' because they fill sandbags and work for a dollar a day." Vietnamese women also worked in our camp as KPs, relieving GIs of a commonly despised detail. I sarcastically stated how much I was looking forward to "s—t" burning duty.

On March 26 I reflected on "how wonderful our life together has been" and my anticipation that our relationship would continue to deepen in the years ahead. I commented that "Things have been pretty quiet around. I probably should not even have mentioned to you those intelligence reports…. I haven't even heard a mortar round drop since I left Dong Tam." Nevertheless, we were constantly aware of VC presence. We frequently observed helicopter gunships bringing heat on Charlie, and that afternoon we had been watching Air Force Phantom jets "dive bomb a wooded area" less than one mile away.

11. Vietnam In-Country

A Vietnamese worker and C Battery members watch an F-105 bombing the enemy in a tree line near Tan Tru fire base, with guard bunkers along the berm and the river in the upper right corner.

In a letter begun March 30, I acknowledged the fact that Joan—like other homefolks—quickly received news happening in Vietnam, being called "America's first TV war." I reiterated my reasons for writing about mortar attacks in Long Binh and Dong Tam and anticipated ground attacks against Tan Tru: "I didn't want you to hear about something that happened near me and begin to worry—especially if it just happened that I hadn't been able to write you for a couple of days." When I continued writing the following day, I quipped, "I've had my Monday-morning malaria pill and I'm all set to go, I guess. Over here one can almost live on pills—malaria pills, sodium chloride tablets, and water purification pills."

Joan and I continued discussing her life too, including advantages of her interest in taking a leave of absence from her teaching job during my tour so she could enroll fulltime in graduate school at the University of South Carolina, especially if she could get an assistantship. I wrote that I was glad to hear that she had sent in her application to take the Graduate Records Exam for admission eligibility, along with making application for an assistantship teaching freshman English. "I know you'll do fine on the GRE. I'm in your corner pulling for you," I said. "I sure hope you get an assistantship too. That would really be nice." I added should she not receive the aid, "By all means go ahead and borrow the money. It will probably be the best investment we'll ever make."

12

RTO

*"I didn't volunteer for this job
but ... I must ... do my best"*

By the end of March, I was finally receiving mail. Joan had been writing letters to send me even before she had an address. When I started receiving mail, it came in droves. I was also getting letters from other family and friends. I commented to Joan that I had received eight letters from her that day and had gotten another eight from her two days earlier. These letters confirmed to me that a lot of news about action in Vietnam was being reported stateside, some of it similar to and some of it unlike what was happening where I was.

As I write this memoir, rereading the letters I wrote home then, their contents bring to mind specific details and awaken memories of events and aspects that I omitted. My letter Tuesday, April 1, included a map I sketched to indicate where I was and where I had been since my arrival in-country. That letter also gave information I had not told her yet, but told her now, for the same reason I gave her earlier. I did not want her to be uninformed about my whereabouts or more concerned than necessary. I explained that my assignment that I had detailed to her earlier had been changed, and I described the new one I had already begun.

"I have not been with the artillery for a week," I wrote, explaining that the Battery Commander had called me in and said that he was sending me out, along with a forward observer (FO) and a reconnaissance sergeant from Charlie Battery, to supply Alpha Company of the 2nd Battalion 60th Infantry Regiment as an artillery radio telephone operator (RTO). I did not mention in this letter, but regretted that very recently I had made attempts to reassure her about the relative safety of my placement by contrasting it with less encouraging statistics for FOs and RTOs who were out in the field with Charlie.

All the explanation I was given for getting a new assignment I then repeated, telling her that the BC said that "he had looked over my 201 file, which contains all the info the Army has on me, and said that I should be well qualified to take over and call in the artillery should anything happen to the FO." Since I was a college graduate, he said I would have had sufficient training in math to do the job.

I did not mention to Joan that I had never before ridden in a helicopter, although I was promptly sent out on an "Eagle Flight" with its orders to make contact with the enemy. It was the first time I had heard of the term and was just flown off on a Huey helicopter without knowledge at the time of the mission's tactics. The instructions on how to operate the 20-pound radio telephone I had to carry on my back at all times were given to me by the reconnaissance sergeant in a team planning session just before my first take-off. Everything was definitely OJT, on-the-job training.

My immediate reaction to my first Huey ride and Eagle Flight was awe as I viewed the expansive scenery below. The open chopper, while offering much-appreciated natural "air conditioning," also exposed an amazing aerial panorama of the country that I had barely seen from the ground. From my position seated on the floor, my legs dangling over the edge of the completely open side door, my pleasure rapidly changed when the door gunner next to me suddenly began firing. We had dropped into a "hot LZ," a landing zone with return enemy fire.

Sounds of gunfire and explosions of grenades resounded both from

Huey helicopters (slicks) preparing to land outside of Tan Tru compound to transport 2/60 Infantry troops with the 2/4 Artillery FO team for Eagle Flights.

Troops being transported to a landing zone on an Eagle Flight, as viewed from an accompanying slick above the rice paddies and waterways of the Mekong Delta.

nearby choppers and from the ground. I could see our M79 rounds hitting the tree line. Although everything was happening quickly, it was as if I were watching it in slow motion. Someone behind me said something that I could not decipher above the din. Immediately he loudly repeated "JUMP!" and I felt a firm push against my back. I knew nothing about the right way to do it, but instantly I *jumped!* What was probably a height of six to eight feet from the hovering copter appeared much farther. With the heavy, awkward radio on my back adding to my weight, I landed thigh-deep in the muddy rice paddy. Stunned but struggling, my adrenaline flowing, I made haste to reach cover and to contact artillery support.

When I wrote Joan on April 1, I simply described my new assignment: "So for the last week I've been living down the street with Alpha Company which is the infantry company we go out with. We go out nearly every day; some days we stay out all day and all night and then come in the following morning. In such a case we have the rest of that day off as was

Glen "on the horn" in contact with artillery support as the fleet of slicks approaches the landing zone (Robert Evans).

the case today." In the past seven days, two of the times we had been out day-and-night, so twice we had received the reward of time off, known as "standdown."

I gave her the general idea of a typical day, which started early when we went outside the compound gate to await being picked up by helicopters (which we might call helis, copters, choppers, slicks, or a model name like Hueys). Our Charlie Battery artillery team—the FO Lt. Robert Gant, Recon Sgt. Robert Evans, and I as RTO—rode in the chopper with the infantry's CO of A Company and his two RTOs. I recall that about 50 or 60 of us went out on about six to eight helicopters, including transports and gunships, but my letters did not dwell on close contact exposures while inserting and extracting troops in the hostile conditions that Eagle Flights encountered.

A light observation helicopter (LOH), flying low over tree line to inspect damage to a smoking VC bunker attacked by a Cobra gunship, barely visible at top of photograph.

When we were sent out, I explained in the April 1 letter, "We already have usually 12 target areas mapped out ... densely wooded areas where Charlie can hide himself and/or his mortars. We are dropped into a paddy near one of those target areas, sometimes knee-deep in mud when we jump out." Other times the ground might be hard and dry. After easing along to find "the nearest dike or source of concealment," we would call the spotter flying overhead for our exact location, to have accuracy calling in any needed artillery. Meanwhile if helicopter gunships scanning the area "see any VC running, or if our appearance draws sniper fire, they prep the area spraying it with rockets, grenades, and fire from the mini-gun. We then go in and police up the area."

I continued, "If we make an insertion and find nothing, as is some-

During a brief break on a paddy dike, Glen checking his map for pre-set targets at the next destination (Robert Evans).

times the case, we report a negative find and wait in an open area for the choppers to pick us up. Then we are inserted into another target area." Depending on results, we might make only one or as many as four or more insertions in a day's time. Occasionally we might walk from one target area to another, often a considerable distance, an action we called "humping the boonies."

The letter added: "A Co. has 3 platoons. Each day that we go out, one platoon stays in camp as a security element and the other two go out. We, the command element ('the flag'), go out every day (except for stand-downs). The two platoons sweep the area clearing all booby traps, mines, or whatever, and checking out the hooches, and we follow behind.... Sometimes on our night patrols we transfer to boats and go up or down

Amid artillery smoke countering a VC ambush from the tree line, Alpha Company 2/60th grunts spreading out to cross the rice paddy in search of enemy dead or wounded, weapons, equipment, or propaganda.

the river, make a landing and walk inland to whatever point we intend to spend the night. It's really simple—no tents, no sleeping bags, no nothing—you just lie down on the ground and go to sleep until it's your turn to stand guard."

One benefit that I enjoyed was that while we were on standdown, I had no duties or details. I could sleep, go into Tan An or wherever I desired. I had been to Dong Tam the previous week and to Tan An that day. These excursions provided me an opportunity to photograph local scenes. Also during several insertions, I had carried the Kodak Instamatic and had taken color slides. I captured images of the land snapped from the choppers, and images of the land and people snapped from trucks. I wanted "to capture the people both in the city and in the countryside." I looked forward to upgrading my photography equipment for better results.

My letter acknowledged that I was now in more danger, "which is why I hesitated to tell you this. But you are my wife, and you have a right

12. RTO

On a Long An Province street, book-laden students among parasol-carrying women wearing the ao dai.

to know what I am doing and I could not continue to write you without either telling the truth or fibbing.... I didn't volunteer for this job but it was handed to me and I must follow it through and do my best. I'll be extremely careful, so don't you worry about that.... This is just one of those things that neither of us has any control over." I closed this letter expressing my faith that God was in control and would bring me home safe and sound.

On the evening of April 2, my letter related events of that day's insertion, which I described as "the latest episode of man against nature ... battling the muck and mire of the Delta's rice paddies. We made several creek crossings by means of footbridges which would make an acrobat nervous. Most of these consisted of poles laid atop tripods of other poles, extending from the stream's bed." It was a difficult balancing act to cross, and there was always the fear of punji sticks (sharpened bamboo spears) beneath the murky water's surface. Also tricky was finding firm footing as we threaded our way along tangled vegetation overgrowing dikes of the paddies, often hiding places for booby traps. We crossed by wading "one stream which had no bridge and was quite deep. Only my nose and eyes were dry when I reached the other side."

About times like these, I remember well the feeling of holding my

Glen with radio at end of a column of strategically distanced GIs on the narrow dike of a muddy paddy as each man eyes the path for trip wires or booby traps (Robert Evans).

M16, ammo, and radio handset above my head to keep them dry. The only time I was submerged occurred when we were crossing a canal by sliding one foot ahead of the other along a board that was about two feet beneath the surface and was not visible. It was extremely slick, and when one foot slid, I lost balance and disappeared. Several comrades reached down and pulled me up. The handset on my radio went dead, and we used another radio to request a chopper to bring out another handset. It held us up maybe 30 minutes to an hour.

I observed in my April 2 letter that Charlie used tactics like Francis Marion, the South Carolina Revolutionary War guerrilla leader, striking the enemy without warning and then retreating to his haven. Unlike the British using horseback to try to follow "the Swamp Fox" through the muddy mires, we use the helicopter, I pointed out. Our gunships could fly in excess of 135 mph and "pinpoint a barrage of rocket, mortar, and minigun fire in any location at any time." The minigun, a six-barreled rotary machine gun, fired 2,000 to 6,000 rounds per minute. A chopper could

12. RTO

hover over a target to continue fire. "Seeing one of these helicopter gunships 'work out' is something to witness," I marveled. I commented in passing that the dry clay in some of the paddies had cracks extending as deep as two feet, but I was told that the dry season would soon end, and the monsoon rains would begin.

The first page of an April 3 letter headed "Wednesday" had a scratch-through, under which was written "Thursday." That fact accidentally illustrated the validity of some details of a typical day that remained true as long as I served as RTO: "It is almost impossible to keep up with what day of the week or what day of the month it is. Each day is just like the preceding day and so will be the following day. Of course, we go different places, but the scenery is the same—dense jungle-type growth and/or open paddies—and the objective is always the same. Some days the vegetation is denser or the mud is deeper or the river crossings are more treacherous, but nevertheless each day is basically the same."

My growing weariness shows further. I said, "You don't wake up wondering what to wear today, what the weather will be like or what you want for breakfast. You know what you're going to wear, you know what the weather will be—hot and dusty—and the only choice you have concerning breakfast is whether to eat or not to eat, because you know what will be for breakfast."

Those days that we were out in the field, I recall that we usually ate two meals of C-rations, to which we paid careful attention. In the morning before we left the firebase, we would learn the expected length of that mission and would procure the number of Cs appropriate for it. Each meal came packaged in a small cardboard box. For ease of handling, we would take out the individual items, weather-sealed in plastic or small metal cans. We would drop an item into a boot sock, tie a knot, drop another item, tie another knot, and repeat until the meal was secured. Then we would tie the open end of the sock to our belt. The knots were to separate the items to keep them from rubbing together and making a noise to betray our presence. We seldom stopped for lunch, but during the day when possible we would take brief breaks to take out the first item or two and "snack." A person could become inventive stacking the items to have a dessert choice at the bottom of the sock. We were sure to take our empty tins with us. To leave them as trash was an invitation to the VC to use them for booby traps.

Occasionally, we were able to supplement our Cs. We often carried a small bottle of hot sauce to spice things up. Whenever we found some fresh coconuts, both the milk and the "meat" were welcome additions. We often carried gum or candy obtained from the Sundry Pack (SP) each GI unit received monthly, which also contained writing tablets, razor blades,

Recon Sergeant Robert Evans lighting a cigarette while Alpha Company awaits chopper extraction and children from a nearby village display C-rations given them.

lather, soap, and cigarettes. While all of us were individually responsible for the food and water we packed, that was only one of the vital personal preparations we made for each mission. All members of the company packed their own gear and checked their own weapons and ammunition. Those were the kinds of topics I wrote Joan about.

In addition, in advance of a mission, we in the flag (the infantry leadership and our FO team) gathered and studied our plastic-cased copies of the very detailed topo-style map of the areas where our group was to be inserted. Before leaving on a mission, the flag would have made note of locations that would offer the VC cover as the most probable places we were likely to be ambushed. Using durable, but not permanent, markers we would designate these places as targets, and each of us in the flag would label our copies identically: 1A (one alpha), 2B (two bravo), etc. Nearly always Charlie Battery provided the fire support for any artillery fire we called in on the targets.

One responsibility of the RTO was to "get on the horn" to call in the target numbers and their map coordinates to Charlie Battery's Fire Direction Center (FDC), which would enter the coordinates into their Field Artillery Direction and Control (FADAC) computer. The RTO was to maintain telephone communication with the artillery support throughout the whole fire mission. The information in the computer was relayed to the battery's gun crews, who would aim one of the howitzers on the designated target for our first insertion, even before our helicopters entered the area.

If we encountered Charlie at that location, we were quickly able to call in fire. If the enemy was in the target area, we would call for the battery to fire on target "one alpha," for example. The command, "Willie Peter, two hundred up," meant the crew of the pre-aimed howitzer would immediately fire a white phosphorous round set to explode 200 meters above the target. When we in the field observed the location of this puff of white smoke, we would adjust fire if needed. If the smoke was directly above our desired target, we advised the battery to "fire at will." They automatically would lower their tubes to adjust for the air burst and would send as many as six HE (high explosive) rounds screaming our way. All through training at Fort Sill and fire missions in Charlie Battery, I had seen the rounds fired from the battery. It was quite another experience seeing results on the receiving end.

My letters do not elaborate on the goals or results of orders to find and make contact with VC. My memory recalls enough to allow me to summarize those actions I was involved in. Some days, an insertion would yield no enemy, but the next insertion might flush out the enemy and result in a firefight. A typical day might be described as hours of walking (humping) and struggling with nature (mud, thick vegetation, water currents and crossings, and mosquitos) interrupted by moments of terror.

During my time as an RTO, I was never in a sustained battle. The enemy in the Mekong Delta generally was not a battalion of well-armed and uniformed NVA regulars, but rather a small group of VC dressed in black pajamas or shorts and carrying small arms and mortars. They could spring an ambush, conceal their weapons, and blend right in with the farmers working in the fields. From a concealed position in a tree line, two or three VC armed with AK (Soviet-made) rifles could pin down a company of men crossing an open paddy. By the time we were able to return fire or to call in artillery, Charlie was slipping away to morph into a "friendly" civilian. His goal was to keep us on edge and prevent us from taking advantage of our superiority in numbers and equipment. His

A Charlie Battery gun section firing a mission as crew member at the left assembles 105 rounds and discards surplus powder bags while smoke fills the air.

surprise attacks did that even if they claimed no victims. If they succeeded in killing or wounding a GI, they considered it a bonus.

Charlie's other effective method of undermining American morale was the use of booby traps. These include "spider holes," small holes covered with sticks and grass, in the bottom of which were metal or bamboo spikes that might injure a GI who stepped into one. There were also punji pits, larger camouflaged holes with numerous sharpened bamboo stakes that would impale a victim who fell into one. Crude mines, small shallow cans with explosives and glass or nails for shrapnel, were also very dangerous. These booby traps seldom resulted in immediate death or critical injury, even when Charlie poisoned the punji tips with excrement. They created terror and psychological damage, however.

Normally, when a soldier tripped one of these booby traps, there was no "enemy" to be seen, only the "friendly" Vietnamese farmers working in nearby fields. Even a minor injury would likely require calling for a "dust off," a medical evacuation chopper. The platoon would continue its mission, now short a critical member, and with everyone uneasy. I remember when one of our men stepped on one of the mines and was flown out by medevac. We continued on the day's mission, the platoon one man short, but with the nerves of all on edge.

After days of sustaining injuries and losses like the one described above, when we did make contact with the enemy, resulting in their death or injury, most of us felt no compassion. Our medics would render aid and the rest of us might give a cigarette when one of the wounded requested one. They did so through gestures and pidgin English, although it seemed that all Vietnamese were able to crudely pronounce Pall Mall and Salem, their favorites.

I remember an occasion, following a firefight, when we had six or eight captured VC in a muddy clearing in the dense jungle. Some were sitting, others lying on the ground, one or two of them seemingly unresponsive. Our job was to guard them until someone from another group arrived to take them away by chopper. We detached any normal tendency for concern that some were gasping their final breaths. They were enemy; they had tried to kill us. Previously, they may have killed other Americans.

Following another ambush, we watched as a wounded VC walked out of the dense tree line into the rice field. One arm was extended high and clutched a white "flag" of surrender. The other arm hung from his shoulder by a few tendons or ligaments. The only emotion I felt was wondering how he managed to walk that 100 or so yards without collapsing.

Most of us often felt contemptuous of those who surrendered. The act of surrendering joined other oddities of America's war in Vietnam. United States ground troops were required to honor all government directives—American or South Vietnamese. The Chiêu Hôi program stipulated that American troops must not fire at any enemy who raised his arms in surrender. This certainly seems honorable and humane. However, a VC could ambush an American patrol, killing or wounding men in the process. He could continue firing until he exhausted his supply of ammunition, and then yell "Chiêu Hôi" and he was untouchable. It required tremendous restraint from soldiers, who just moments earlier had witnessed this VC kill one of their buddies, not to even the score.

These experiences I did not write home about, nor did Joan ask me about them. She read widely and prayed, having grown up in a family of World War II veterans, her father having been an Army glider pilot and her uncles having served also. Joan had realistic understanding. I did not forget these experiences, but I did not dwell obsessively on them either, and Joan would learn about them in time, some of them only when reading this manuscript. I always told her what I could when I could.

In an April 5 letter I answered questions Joan had asked. I explained that the PX at our firebase in Tan Tru had been torn down ("never open anyway," I quipped), but the one at Tan An battalion headquarters was adequate for purchasing film and getting it processed. If I needed something that was unavailable there, I could hitch a ride to Dong Tam division

Helicopter view of a section of Tan Tru firebase, including C Battery's "main street" and gun sections in foreground, ammo dump in lower left, and Tan Tru Village at end of road in upper right corner.

headquarters on a day off. No, I did not need her to send me film or process it for me.

I described our artillery battery set-up: "Charlie Battery consists of 6 gun sections (8 men per section) plus the executive post, FDC, the ammo section, and of course the cooks. Each gun section lives in a hooch and has a small ammo bunker. There are other buildings such as mess hall, supply room, orderly room, EM Club, and NCO Club. Right down the street is the 2nd Bn of the 60th Infantry, and on the other side is a mortar unit, and over by A Co 2nd/60 is a battery of 155 mm self-propelled howitzers. That makes up Tan Tru." The list neglects to mention the medical aid station, the motor pool, and a small communications (commo) section.

The entire camp had been established in rice paddies and was

Buildings on C Battery's "main street," including NCO Club, EM Club, supply room, and mess hall with banana trees at its entrance.

somewhat oval in shape. The perimeter consisted of a berm, a wide dike two-to-three feet high, atop which were defensive guard bunkers spaced at about 50-yard intervals. Bunkers were of various shapes and sizes, but all were constructed of sandbags and/or earth-filled wooden ammo boxes. PSP (perforated steel planking) formed the base of the structure's top. Sandbags had been laid on the PSP, then sheets of metal roofing to divert rain, with more sandbags on top to hold the roofing in place. There were small openings without doors, and smaller openings for firing ports. Guards would have an M60 machine gun in addition to each man's M16.

Out in front of the berm were coils of concertina wire and strands of barbed wire from which were hung metal cans filled with small pebbles or metal objects that theoretically would sound an alarm if VC attempted to infiltrate. Claymore mines attached to metal posts were set out in front of each bunker, facing outward for protection.

I described a "hooch" as "almost any kind of dwelling someone lives in." The word applied to the huts of the Vietnamese people as well as to the quarters of GIs. The one I slept in when I first arrived at C Battery was

A locked and loaded M60 machine gun atop a bunker guarding C Battery at Tan Tru firebase.

about 16 × 10 feet and slept eight men in metal over-under bunks. My quarters at 2nd/60th housed "an entire platoon (about 43 men)." I slept on "an air mattress placed on a wooden shelf on the wall." I responded to Joan's question about mail service by saying that the letter I had received that day (April 5) was postmarked March 31, so "that's pretty quick service for 10,000 or more miles." I stated that I dropped letters in a box by the door of the orderly room. Collected mail was taken daily to Tan An.

We had gotten a little bit of rain that day—"the first since I've been in-country." As the monsoon season would begin in a couple of weeks, I imagined it would be "raining off and on from now on." I described current conditions as "terribly hot and dusty," to become in monsoon "hot and steamy." I described "heat deflection rising from the earth across the rice paddies as it does from a highway on a hot day back home." I remarked that at present only paddies close to waterways held water, and elsewhere "because of the dryness and tremendous heat of the sun the earth cracks open fissures often going 1½ to 2 feet."

Mekong Delta waterways were also controlled by the tide. The waterways formed the travel routes for commerce and controlled a rhythm of life. One of our days out, I remember we came upon a family taking their produce to market on a small waterway. The tide was going out and the water had become too shallow for them to continue, so they tied their boat to some bushes on the bank, clambered out and positioned themselves under a shady tree to wait until the tide again raised the water level enough to allow them to continue on their way. Mentally, I compared that level of patience with Americans' impatience having to wait at a traffic light or being caught behind another motorist who was committing the cardinal sin of driving the speed limit.

Some days we went into small communities of six or eight dwellings; other days we humped through sparsely populated areas with open rice paddies or through dense vegetation. On April 6 and 7, we traveled to a place unlike any other—the Plain of Reeds, an area of 2,500 square miles stretching to the Cambodian border.

Monday, April 7, I gave Joan my impression of the Plain of Reeds: "It is the most desolate and godforsaken place I have ever seen. It's so bad I wouldn't even wish it on the VC. It's nothing but grass and reeds often waist or chest high—some parts dry and other parts wet and muddy. The dry parts are so dry that tracer rounds fired into the scattered patches of scrub brush (where Charlie hides) often set the dry grass on fire. There were numerous fires all around us and the sky was full of smoke. The Plain of Reeds also contains many booby traps, bunkers, and spider holes—all of which we destroy as we sweep the area." I remarked that from the air, "Some parts of the P of R look like the surface of the moon because of the countless craters and pock marks created by artillery rounds and rockets from air strikes."

The letter continues with plans: "We will be out again tomorrow, but not to the P of R, and will stay out tomorrow night. Consequently day after tomorrow will be a standdown." I said that I hoped to find a ride to Saigon, where I had heard much about their huge PX. "If Nikons are to be found anywhere in Vietnam they certainly should be there," I said, focusing on my ambition to acquire better camera equipment to capture the reality of views around me.

At times I reflected on the sheer madness of the life I was living. One day I would be in a godforsaken place and the next I could be eating a great hamburger and drinking a milkshake in the capital city of South Vietnam, shopping in a well stocked PX. It would seem surreal that one day people

In the remote Plain of Reeds with a folded map ready in his pants pocket, Glen becoming a prime target on the horn with the unwieldy radio antenna extended to maximum height (Robert Evans).

would be dying in front of me and the next day I could be in a store calmly looking for camera accessories. Yet that is the way it was.

Our second day in the Plain of Reeds, we experienced a very dangerous incident of "friendly fire" which could have turned deadly. We began hearing thuds no further than a half mile away but steadily approaching our position. We were maybe 100 yards from a canal where an ally ARVN (Army of the Republic of Vietnam) gunboat was moving our direction, lobbing rounds from grenade launchers as they traveled. The infantry CO hurriedly got on the horn to eventually reach the liaison between the U.S. and RVN forces, who radioed the boat's captain to tell him to cease fire, that he was about to fire on friendly forces. We watched the boat as it came into view and then disappeared from sight, moving on along the canal.

Another day an incident occurred when we called in an airstrike after we were ambushed. A Bell AH-1G helicopter gunship, a Cobra, responded and began firing on the enemy. It was making passes over the VC and then

The Bobo Canal in the Plain of Reeds, its terrain crater-marked over time by artillery fire and airstrikes.

pulling up over our position to circle around to make another pass. The grenade launcher beneath the Cobra swiveled in order that it could fire as it approached its target, passed over its target, and even after it cleared the target. Apparently, there was a glitch of sorts because when the Cobra completed its first pass, one round was coming out as it slung the tube forward in preparation for its next pass. That round came out directly at us, but fortunately caused no casualties. The infantry CO quickly contacted the Cobra to prevent that happening on the next pass.

Depending on where our missions took us, we would have support from an artillery battery (usually Charlie Battery or another battery from 2/4 Artillery), choppers, or occasionally Air Force fighter bombers. On one occasion we were ambushed and were taking heavy fire from a tree line. When we called for support, we got response from a supersonic F-105

Thunderchief, a jet fighter bomber. We were told to put our faces down and hug the earth. When the 500-pound bomb detonated a few hundred yards from me, the ground heaved under me, an overwhelming sensation I never felt before or since.

When we were ready to be picked up at the end of each insertion or mission, we got on the horn and arranged an extraction. As the choppers approached, we "popped a smoke" to provide a visible, colored signal from a smoke grenade to guide helicopters to the open place we had secured for them to fly in to extract us. To prevent the possibility that VC listening on our frequency might discharge the same signal to lure our craft within their firing range, we waited until choppers were almost on us before disclosing the color of our smoke. Usually, we were picked up by a group of Huey helicopters we called "slicks." They would return us to the road outside our compound where they had picked us up.

To create a secure landing zone (LZ) for the extraction, usually a group of soldiers formed and guarded a perimeter. When other men hurriedly boarded the slicks and engines were sufficiently revved to get quickly off the ground, the perimeter guards would rush to the choppers, now hovering above ground, and scramble aboard. I remember the day a CH-47 Chinook flew in to extract us. Since a Chinook was sized like a Greyhound Bus to carry a whole company, only one was required. However, its size made it much slower getting off the ground and required a larger secured LZ. Because of the greater perimeter and the fact that the Chinook utilized closed doors, unlike the Hueys with doors latched in the open position, the troops securing the perimeter could not sprint to the craft and jump aboard as it lurched skyward.

I was unaware of these facts when I was tabbed one of the six men to secure the perimeter. It was with a sinking feeling that I watched the chopper ascend and disappear. I got on the radio which was never off my back, and those of us left behind had to make our own way back, walking across several rice paddies to find a road, which we followed until we reached Tan Tru Village, and continued another mile to our firebase. The total distance was probably no more than five miles, not a daunting distance but certainly one fraught with anxiety. After having done much walking throughout the day, followed by our final trek, we were very happy to go through the checkpoint and enter our firebase.

My lengthy April 9 letter expressed appreciation for letters and packages from family and friends. I mentioned I was trying to reply to everyone who wrote me. I sent a note to Joan's Aunt Lucy Brown, thanking her for a package of homemade fudge. I included three 20 piaster bills for her three children, local currency we were allowed to use although we were paid in military scrip. Hometown friend Summers Till had sent me an issue of *Modern Photography*. A letter from a college friend, National Guardsman Bob ("Bush") Williams, had foolishly suggested I "go to Saigon, rent a Honda and cruise around sightseeing." He also asked if we took "pep pills" to stay alert. I mused, "With Charlie around, who needs <u>anything</u> to stay alert." Comments from people back home reinforced my conviction that most had little understanding of life in a war zone—especially this one. Even when I returned home, when some folk inquired whether I had been "on the front lines," I immediately knew they had little understanding of combat in Vietnam.

I mentioned we had been on an "overnight" and were on a standdown for the remainder of the day. We had been trucked to Ben Luc, where we boarded "tango boats" which took us upriver to our overnight position. The next morning boats picked us up for the trip back to Ben Luc from which we were trucked back to Tan Tru.

The overnight missions on boats were frightening. We boarded them right before dark and traveled up or down the river. The crews were often Vietnamese who spoke little English. The craft's powerful diesel engine rumbled loudly, causing me to think every VC in the province could hear us coming. These vessels resembled the landing craft used during World War II D-Day landings. The bow was a ramp that dropped to allow troops to walk ashore. One very dark night when the boat I was on pulled up to the riverbank and lowered its ramp, the first soldier to step off disappeared. The boat had not pulled up close enough, and the man, expecting to step upon the bank, slipped into the deep, dark water. Fortunately, men behind him were able to rescue him.

Once we were on land, our anxiety did not diminish but rather increased. We walked along paths and across paddies to reach a predetermined area where we would set up an ambush position. Animals would usually slip away as we approached, but one night right after we disembarked from the boat and were still near the river, we must have awakened a troop of monkeys. They raised such a ruckus I was certain we had lost any element of surprise that possibly remained after the noisy boat ride. One night our itinerary took us through a small village. Everyone was inside their hooches, and everything was eerily quiet. We walked right beside these huts, terrified by visions of who was on the other side of the thatched walls just a matter of feet away. I imagine the people inside were even more afraid than we were.

We moved some distance further and set up for the night in a dry paddy, using its dikes as a perimeter. Each of us served guard duty in two-hour shifts along the perimeter. When I was relieved from my last shift in the wee hours of the night, I lay down on the hard-packed clay and fell into a deep sleep from total exhaustion.

I awoke as the sun began rising to transform the warm night to a hot day. I sat up, stretched, and was startled to discover two dead VC lying maybe 20 yards away from me. I learned they had been shot as they approached the other side of our position and had been dragged over where I was with the rest of the flag element. What was really disturbing was that I had heard nothing. I do not think I slept that soundly again as long as I was an RTO.

Everyone looked forward to getting mail that came to camp while we were out on overnights. The mail I picked up after the Ben Luc mission consisted of a card from Summers Till back at home working construction, and a letter from AIT friend Paul Martin, who was "having a rough time and getting little sleep" in Vietnam, serving in a battery of self-propelled 8-inch howitzers firing 200-pound projectiles, and being subjected to wall locker and footlocker inspections. In our battery, no one had wall lockers, and many did not have footlockers.

I also received a package from Joan which included Cracker Jacks, most of which were consumed by my buddy Recon Sgt. Evans, who bunked above me. Although the two of us lived and served with the infantry, we were still assigned to the artillery battery, where our mail was sent and had to be retrieved. The next day was also a standdown, so I hoped to go to Tan An, Dong Tam, or even Saigon, being especially eager to see what the Cholon PX there had available.

I closed the April 9 letter with a report that Tan Tru had received "10 or 12 mortar rounds night before last," but they caused no damage and were "the first taken since I arrived." I added that I had been reading a copy of *To Kill a Mockingbird* that I had found, and I had also been reading the New Testament she had packed for me when I left. I reassured Joan that I was "being extremely careful and I'm taking the best possible care of myself."

On standdown April 10, I caught a ride to bustling, noisy Saigon with Charlie Battery's first sergeant and his driver in a Jeep—"first class" transportation compared to the usual deuce-and-a-half truck. I said, writing the next day's letter: "Saigon is really something. It is so huge and traffic is unbelievable. It's kind of like USC–Clemson football traffic—only worse because of all the various types of vehicles—rickshaws, bicycles, motorcycles, ox carts, pony carts, and cars, trucks, and buses of every type and vintage." I also noted, "The sidewalks are filled with people selling anything from peanuts to women. Walking down one of Saigon's streets is like walking down the midway of a county or state fair—people shouting and pulling at you to buy something."

Many of the buses had racks on top for farm produce and crates of animals. When we pulled into a parking spot, we were surrounded by

Conveyances of every size and description crowding an intersection of one of the tree-lined streets in Saigon.

Saigon street vendors hawking a variety of goods from farm products to electronics, some of them contraband.

A downtown Saigon street congested by a hodge-podge of pedestrians, bicycles, motor scooters, motorcycles, cars, trucks, buses, and military vehicles.

groups of children offering to "watch" our Jeep while we were gone. "Top" gave the leader of one group some money and they quickly "took possession" of our vehicle. Top explained if we ignored them, we likely would return to find missing items, like the 5-gallon fuel can, spare tire, or even the tires themselves. It was, he said similar to purchasing insurance, and the amount of money paid was trivial in comparison. We left nothing in the Jeep that was unattached, carrying our M16s and bandoliers of ammo with us.

As we walked down the street, a local man approached us, offering to sell me a "numba one" wristwatch and pulling up his sleeves to reveal numerous watches from wrist to elbow on both arms. I shook my head and replied as we spoke to the people in our camp, "No, papa-san, I *have* number one watch," and pulled up my own sleeve to display the Seiko I had recently purchased from the PX. The hawker then followed us down the sidewalk trying to negotiate buying *my* watch.

After about half a block of this persistence, I brandished my weapon, shook it, and said in a loud voice, "No, papa-san, didi mau!" which meant "Leave," or "Go away," or, when expressed in a loud voice as I used, "Get the hell away from me." Papa-san got the message and hastily departed.

We went to the USO. "It was quite nice—almost like back in the world. They had Cokes, etc. with *ice* in them, running water, sinks, and toilets that flushed when one pulled the lever. It was the first time in a month that I had enjoyed such luxuries." I also enjoyed a cheeseburger and milkshake for lunch. We left the USO Club for the Cholon PX, which seemed to have everything—except Nikons. Their stock of SLR (single lens reflex) cameras of any kind was nearly depleted. I was told they normally stocked all brands, including Nikons. I ordered a Nikkormat FTN with a 55 mm f:1.2 lens—"the fastest lens on the market," but I was told I would have to wait three months for it to come in.

My letter to Joan listed details about prices of lenses and filters I was interested in, with prices in the PX compared to those in the States. I repeated that I was not foolishly spending on anything, and I considered these purchases as investments. I told her that since I had ordered a new camera, "I guess you can call the F:2 Nikkormat yours now." I referred to the SLR that I had left with her and which she was using. I sounded rather sentimental, reminiscing that after I graduated from college, we had purchased that camera from Luther Adden, with whom I in earlier years had spent much time conversing about cameras and lenses, as his camera shop was next door to Renneker's Men's Shop, where my brother Byron worked. Obviously I was thinking of home, and little did I know that the new camera I so eagerly anticipated having in my hands in three months would actually take *ten* months to arrive.

In my April 13 letter I learned that Joan had been surprised and pleased the previous week to receive a corsage of live flowers which I had ordered when I first arrived in-country, to be wired to her to wear to church on Easter Sunday, a custom of the time. I wanted her to know that "even though I'm 10,000 miles away my thoughts are always with you." I referred to Joan's letters and cartoons that brightened my day, writing that "mail call really is the bright spot in every day." That day was a stand-down after an overnight during which it was "terribly hot," and "mosquitos feasted upon me" despite judicious use of insect repellant. I quipped, "Better the mosquitos than Chuck, however, so I shan't complain."

I did lament the condition Joan and I experienced of being unable to discuss matters together as we were accustomed, stating, "It's so bad to realize that you can be thinking something and I am not aware of it for 5–7 days." Joan continued evaluating her considerations of full-time graduate school attendance, a major decision that was difficult to discuss in letters with long-distance mail delays.

On April 19 I wrote that I was some 30 pages from finishing *To Kill a Mockingbird*. There were a number of paperbacks around and I had been reading another as well. While I was on standdown, I had time to read and write. "It has been fairly comfortable in the shade today with an occasional breeze blowing. I have spent most of my time here by the doorway

Glen displaying one of the squirrel-sized rats which inhabited C Battery (Ernest Brown).

to our hooch," I said, "and it's been quite enjoyable except for the rats running across the floor. They almost drove me crazy running around last night while I was writing." I emphasized sardonically, "They're so huge we'd have to call in artillery to get rid of them." The rats, nearly the size of squirrels back home, made their homes in the ammo box walls of our hooches. They were a great nuisance, but one we just had to tolerate.

Sunday, April 20, we went on Eagle Flights and made three combat insertions. On the last one, "We captured 6 POWs … a VC propaganda team … 5 men and one woman." I reported that we were scheduled for Eagle Flights tomorrow and would stay out overnight. Tuesday should be a standdown. One of Joan's letters had inquired whether I had spent Easter "in the Plain of Reeds." I could not remember. I told her that here "Easter was no different from any other day. However, we were about that time out in the P of R for 3 consecutive days, so I'm sure I must have gone there Easter Sunday."

I also described several days earlier, when our Eagle Flight had taken us further from Tan Tru than I had been before, and we had flown toward the coast. From the slick I could see where a major river I assumed to be the Mekong emptied into the South China Sea. Viewing that part of the Delta from above was breathtaking.

After we were on the ground, I observed that hooches here were smaller than those further inland, likely because of the smaller plots of ground high enough to keep inhabitants dry. The paddies were full of crabs. I recalled, "We passed one hooch where an old woman was dicing crabs to feed her chickens. She was using an instrument that seems a cross between a butcher knife and a machete. All the Vietnamese have them to cut coconuts, pineapples etc." I lamented, "She was so photogenic, but I didn't have my camera."

Occasionally, I said, we saw a hooch made of wood or concrete with a tile roof, but "most of the country people live in thatched huts." However, I explained, "Almost all the hooches contain mud bunkers, and the mud around here is like cement when it hardens. When the shooting etc. starts, the people don't have to leave the house to find protection." I said also of the people, "Most of them only have a table or two and maybe

Tranquil domestic scene of civilians in part of a small village in Long An Province.

A boy-san outside a hooch in Long An Province.

a chair or two for furniture. They sleep either on pallets on the floors or in hammocks. Chickens, ducks, and pigs roam in and out of the hooches as frequently as do the children."

I was "a tad tired" when I wrote Tuesday, April 22. "We were out last night and today have a standdown," I said. "We go out tonight and have another standdown tomorrow." Friday was to be another standdown and I wanted to go to Saigon then. "We walked out to our overnight position last night and then back this a.m., a distance of about 4 miles. Coming back this a.m. wasn't too bad because we could see where we were going, but it was rough walking through the paddies in the total darkness." I added, "At least it was dry, one of the few nights we've been able to stay completely dry."

Another experience that was exactly the opposite: "Yesterday we made 4 insertions. Less than 10 minutes after we made our first insertion, we had to cross a stream. It wasn't very wide but it sure was deep. Only my head stayed dry. About fifteen minutes later we killed a *beeg* snake that tried to cross our path. It was about 7 feet long and almost as big around as one of those 46-ounce grape juice cans."

My letter diverted to a discourse about "what I would like to do when I get out." In a letter I received the previous day, Joan had described a position she had learned about that I told her was "exactly what I have been trying to come up with for us both to work for [a job like the one at the S.C.

Dept. of Wildlife and Tourism]. You know how much we both like to travel around the state to famous places and go to off-the-beaten-path places. And you know how interested we both are in taking pictures and writing. We both like our state and are interested in promoting it. I wish you would look into this more deeply and see what you can find out."

After another paragraph of wishful thinking about the future, I described recent observations of Tan Tru village, through which we had walked going to and coming back from our recent mission. "It is about one-half mile from our base camp," I said. "Walking through it this morning was so interesting. It is not on a major road but rather is kind of off to itself. It has a village marketplace, and all these people were there with their products for sale this morning." I described the village as "so quaint and so colorful." I explained, "All towns and villages are off limits to us, but before I leave here I've got to try to get permission from somewhere to go through there and take pictures. It is so unique. It's right on a river too which makes it even more interesting."

I related a colorful experience told to me by a buddy who was on perimeter guard with a Vietnamese Tiger Scout, an intelligence operative with the infantry: "The scout was grabbing those huge rats by their tails and smashing their heads against the dike. When he had several, he

Two modes of transportation intersecting with reflections of Tan Tru civilians on sampans and along the shoreline beside their village's single bridge crossing the Vàm Cỏ River.

proudly held them high by their tails, saying 'numba one chop-chop'!" My letter explained that, "Chop-chop is slang for food, and anything that is #1 is, well, number 1. The worst in their scale is #10. There's no in-between. Something is either #1 or #10."

That anecdote I followed with an experience of my own when I saw a Vietnamese man "walking through the Tan Tru market place this morning with boo-coo rats [*boo-coo* meaning *much* or *many*, derived from the French word *beaucoup*]." I described him "carrying them by their tails like someone would carry a string of fish. In one hand he had a couple monsters which were still kicking and in the other hand he had several that had already been skinned." I asked Joan if she could imagine eating a rat. My thoughts prompted my comment: *Ugh!*

My April 23 letter began with information about processed slides I had just received from the lab and that I was sending home. I described some interesting local scenes, as if they were verbal photographs that I had not been able to snap. At Ben Luc I had seen a couple of Vietnamese men "bring a full-grown hog tied by its feet to a pole and put him feet up on the back of a pony-drawn cart. Then they drove off nonchalantly with the hog just squealing." Also, I saw standing outside Tan Tru's gate "a woman waiting for a bus, a three-wheeled motor scooter bus. She had been carrying a gunny sack and she put it down. It began to move and grunt." All over,

A farmer in Long An Province laboring in his rice paddy during the growing season.

Using sickles and manual procedures practiced over generations, workers harvesting rice in Long An Province.

"people going to market were carrying chickens, pigs, goats, ducks etc. as well as all their vegetables on motor scooter buses and on motorcycles, bicycles, trucks, etc." I remarked too that "the natives' chickens are the most sorry-looking specimens imaginable. At one hooch I cracked up at a half-grown chicken which had no feathers at all. It was running around looking as if it had jumped out of a stewing pot or something."

My April 24 letter began quite typically. After greeting "my most wonderful wife," I chatted about tomorrow being a standdown and hoping to go to Saigon to check on camera lenses. I mentioned receiving "an amusing letter" from S.W. Caldwell, insurance office manager where my father worked. Today's mission resulted in making two insertions, killing another snake, and spending "a good part of the afternoon just sitting on a dike under the shade. I didn't even get my feet wet today for a change."

I concluded, "All in all, it wasn't a bad day."

13

Back in Charlie Battery
"Mixed feelings leaving the grunts"

I BEGAN THE SECOND PAGE OF MY APRIL 25 LETTER on the following day. After I described the lenses and bag I had purchased in Saigon for my camera that had not yet arrived, I dropped the *big news* about which I myself was still surprised. "As of today I am no longer an RTO with the 'grunts.' I am now back in Charlie Battery," I wrote. "They said they needed someone 'intelligent' to take over the job of TAERS clerk (It stands for The Army Equipment Records System) which would become vacant when the present clerk went home. Anyway, the battery commander had recommended me for the job and they pulled me out of the field. I'll have to pull bunker guard and stand formations in the mornings again." I would no longer be clambering from helicopters on searches for VC, but I certainly was not leaving the war.

Just as quickly and unanticipatedly as I had been assigned to be an RTO, I was reassigned to the battery. I had presumed I would spend the rest of my tour with the grunts, so I was surprised when my FO told me I was to return to my battery the next day. I promptly asked him if the reason for my reassignment was dissatisfaction with my job performance. "Negative," he promptly replied, stating that I had been previously recommended to take a position that was now becoming vacant. The tour of duty was ending for the battery's only TAERS clerk, and I had been assigned to replace him right away.

Once again, the Army had put me in a job which I had not requested and for which I had no training, just their presumptions I had "math skills." My stint as an RTO had been strictly on-the-job training. For the TAERS position, I was sent to battalion headquarters for three days' training and was given a manual on the records procedure. The TAERS clerk, I learned, was responsible for records for all the equipment in the battery. I would have to maintain detailed logbooks, especially for the battery's motor pool. The records there were described to me as "messed up," a

13. Back in Charlie Battery

statement with which I soon agreed, although I hoped that once they were straightened out, what looked like a job of basic bookkeeping shouldn't be too difficult.

I described mixed feelings about leaving the infantry assignment and returning to C Battery. I would surely miss the standdowns, and I did not look forward to the resumption of duties and the everyday harassment that existed with living in the battery. One who usually enjoyed working with others, I would now be the single person working by myself in a crude "office," a small freestanding shack near the motor pool. On the front of the structure there was a door and a "window" which could be propped open for ventilation. A similar window was on a side wall. With the monsoon rains reported coming soon, I would not mind having a roof overhead, and I knew Joan would be happy that I was in a less dangerous situation.

When I returned from TAERS training, I was not assigned to a gun section, but to a separate component of Charlie Battery called the Service Battery. This included men from ammunition, communication, and maintenance—just about everyone in the battery who was not assigned to handling the six howitzers. Since I was not on a gun crew, I would not have to get up for fire missions, most of which occurred at night. I was, however, subject to guard duty.

The two-level bunker manned by the Service Battery was constructed of wood and steel and lots of sandbags. Each night three members of this battery would have rotating guard duty. Each man had an hour of scanning the darkness from the bunker's upper level and then would sleep (or try to sleep) for two hours on the wooden benches on the lower level. Unless it was raining, the guard on duty frequently climbed on the roof, where it was cooler and the visibility better. Often all three of us would sit on top and talk until nearly midnight.

Occasionally I would be assigned guard duty with one or two guys who were smoking pot, illegally of course. Those times, I stayed awake the entire night. I would not go below to sleep and trust my life to someone who might be impaired.

One of the guys I enjoyed being with on guard duty was also married, Stanley Parson from New Jersey. We would talk about how we missed our wives and looked forward to returning to civilian life and home. I do not know whether "Peaches" was her real name or a nickname, but Stanley certainly did like to talk about her. I had more in common with Stanley than I did with most of the single men who were right out of high school or dropouts who were drafted and really had not started a life to which they could anticipate returning.

We each performed bunker guard duty every third night, but when

The bunker Glen usually manned on perimeter guard duty, with barely visible concertina wire to hinder ground attack and a "fence" to detonate incoming rockets.

our compound experienced any type of attack, all members of the Service Battery were to rush to defend assigned spots. One of those was the ammo dump, a half-acre shaped like a square horseshoe. One end was open to allow supply trucks to enter. The other three sides were enclosed by dirt-filled sandbags and ammo boxes that supported structures resembling covered shelves. Most of the ammunition for the six 105 mm howitzers was stored on those shelves. Only a small quantity of ammo was stored near each gun emplacement.

One of the nights when we were hit with incoming Viet Cong mortars, two other men and I were assigned to a bunker on the corner of the battery's ammo dump. Unlike the berm bunkers, the ammo dump structure had no openings through which to place rifles and fire at attackers. It was designed "for protection only," which I considered ironic as we were sitting atop live ammunition. Our orders were to stay inside the bunker during the mortar attack, and in the event of a ground attack, we were to exit the bunker, find cover, and protect the ammo dump.

The VC mortarmen lacked precision aiming. They would drop in a round, make an adjustment, send a second round, make an adjustment, and continue the process until they hit the desired target. We referred to this as "walking rounds in." Unless the VC simply lucked up, the first round usually overshot the mark and the second undershot it, but once they had the target bracketed, each tweak of the mortar tube got them closer to zeroing in.

Inside the bunker, we could see nothing. We heard the muffled sound as each mortar hit. The first one landed beyond us toward the inside of the compound. The second was short of us nearer the berm. We knew we had been bracketed, and the ammo dump was the target. Our quarters were very close and hot. We were sweating and trembling. I do not know about the others, but I was praying hard that God would protect us.

The third round severely shook our bunker and was very loud. After what seemed an eternity, but was only minutes with no additional strikes, we emerged from our bunker and discovered the side of the dump opposite us had taken a direct hit. Unknown to the enemy, but critically fortunate for us, four of our six howitzers had gone on a field mission that day. This meant that approximately two-thirds of our ammo had been removed from the dump. The side that sustained the hit was empty.

There were times, especially as an RTO, that I heard VC bullets whiz past my head, but one of the times I was the most afraid was that night in the ammo dump bunker. Afterward I traveled to our division headquarters at Dong Tam not long after it had sustained a major attack. I saw what little remained from its ammo dump that had received a direct hit. The sight gave me chills. These close-encounter incidents were among ones that I did not relate to Joan, nor to other family or friends, when I wrote home. It was easier to write about cameras, stereo systems, or topics that would affect our future.

With Joan considering her grad school options, I reflected on the GI Bill benefits I would have at the end of my Army stint. I wondered if I would want to use them when first coming home, remarking "It seems I've spent my whole life either in school or in the Army." Actually, except for half a dozen years or so, I had.

I was grumpy writing Joan April 27 and complaining that schedules were especially "screwed up" on Sundays. Breakfast was served from 8 to 10 a.m. with formation at 10:00, and "lunch/dinner/supper or whatever" served from 1 to 5 p.m. We were supposed to work only from 10 a.m. to 1 p.m. on Sundays, but I as TAERS clerk had to work until 5 p.m. Before reporting for guard duty that night, I took a shower. "Sure makes a fellow feel better even if the shower stall is crude and one has to haul his own water," I said.

Our shower was a covered structure with a wooden floor and sides boarded up about four feet. A shower nozzle was attached to a metal drum-half, raised overhead on a wooden platform. To take a shower, I filled a five-gallon bucket with water from the "water buffalo," a trailer

One scene following a major attack against 9th Division headquarters in Dong Tam that left considerable structural damage and numerous casualties.

parked nearby, and carried the bucket up a ladder to pour the water into the drum. When water was limited, a "Navy" shower was necessary: open the showerhead long enough to get wet, close it, lather up with soap, rinse off, and dry. During the dry season, often there was only enough water to shave or brush teeth. I was told that a device above the shower would divert rainwater during monsoon and the drum would stay full then.

On April 29 I wrote Joan from my office. One of the perks of my job was a radio there which I tuned to the Armed Forces Radio Network to listen to news and music. I thanked Joan for the voice tape she sent me. This was the first such tape I had received, and I borrowed a recorder (reel to reel, the only kind) in order to listen to it. Pleased with this new technology, I began planning to buy a recorder of my own on which to send and receive tapes from family and friends.

I had been promoted from Private First Class to Specialist 4 effective April 1 and would receive $40–60 more per month. Including extra "overseas duty" and "combat" pay, "I would now be making $214 a month." I was told Joan's allotment would increase $30 without any additional deduction from my pay. I hoped that was true because "that extra $30 will pay half the rent" on our apartment, which Joan wanted to keep for my coming home.

I wrote the first day of May that I was in another hooch to record a tape to her on a friend's recorder. There was a poker game with boisterous noise and crude language going on there. Frequently I had to stop and erase background outbursts and re-record. I was a bit self-conscious talking "to myself," but I think I got used to the idea toward the end of the tape.

We had taken "quite a few mortars" last night, I wrote, but I didn't think they caused much damage. I mentioned news reports of "an expected Communist offensive this month." In my area, I said, we expected there to be a continuation of rocket and mortar attacks, rather than a "show of power." The only places Charlie had successfully launched ground attacks, I told Joan, were near the DMZ or a "neutral" border like Laos or Cambodia, "into which he can retreat." I launched into a lengthy discourse on long-running, unsuccessful peace talks in Paris.

War zone dangers affected us in other ways, too. May 4 our allies, the ARVN (Army of the Republic of Vietnam) mistakenly dropped a 105 mm round on us. It hit "out by our mess hall about 7:15 this morning," I wrote. "Luckily it is a Sunday morning when no one is stirring that early." There was some damage to the building and two minor injuries. "A piece of shrapnel ... hit one of the cooks in the behind," I said, and "another guy who was nearby got a small piece of shrapnel in his side." Had this happened on any other day, our battery would likely have been moving about preparing for morning formation, and there could have been mass casualties.

I spent most of the day in my office, I said, working on paperwork and then cleaning my M16. It was somewhat cooler there than elsewhere. I drew a diagram of my shack with the "windows" propped open. I asked Joan tongue-in-cheek to determine its architectural style. I quipped that cleaning the office was easy: "I just sweep the dirt through the cracks in the floor (¼ to ½" cracks)."

The following day, "the hottest day since I've been here," made me feel certain that the monsoon rains must be very close at hand. I mentioned packages I had received and requested Joan to advise people to send me no more Kool-Aid, as many well-intended people had been doing so from civilian reports that soft drink powders made canteen water tastier. I had plenty now, and since I was back in the battery, I was eating "3 hot (?) meals (??)" a day and didn't need as much of anything. I had previously asked that anything edible and perishable, like cookies, be sent in small quantities that could be consumed immediately. The environment there was not conducive to preserving food on hand.

I told Joan I was trying to go to Dong Tam for several purposes: I wanted to purchase a small portable tape recorder. I was sending letters requesting advice on stereo systems from brother Byron and my friend Bush, and I had a box to mail Joan of miscellaneous items, including my processed color slides of Vietnam scenes, which would be more safely preserved in the environment at home.

On May 7, having had guard duty the night before, I was entitled to a half-day off. I worked that morning and took the afternoon off to sleep and then write letters. Our battery had generators, some authorized and some not, so my hooch and some others had electricity, although it was not dependable. Many of us had small electric fans which tremendously aided moving air for sleeping. Fatigued from guard duty, I fell into a deep sleep. However, the power went off and I woke up "covered with sweat." I decided to go back to the office to write letters where the temperature was somewhat more tolerable, "only 97° or 98°."

I gave Joan news I had received in letters from AIT friends Jim Brown and Pat McReynolds. Brown was fine but didn't like "all the inspections and spit-and-polish of stateside duty," although he said he "realizes his luck in being there instead of here, so he doesn't complain." McReynolds was about 17 miles from the DMZ, assigned to the 1/31 Artillery (Honest John Missiles) which he tabbed "the softest unit in Korea." They had civilians to do laundry, make beds, shine boots, and perform guard duty. There was a golf course, and they were off at 2:30 for

On a roadside approaching a moving vehicle of GIs, friendly children with a toddler, undiapered by custom, in the care of an older child.

13. Back in Charlie Battery

recreation every Tuesday and Thursday. I appreciated my friends keeping up with me.

On May 8, experiencing a mild side effect of the weekly malaria pill, I was also peeved because two trucks had gone to Dong Tam and I had wanted to go. My immediate supervisor, the motor sergeant, said no, that we were "too busy." The only news was that I had begun using a different wash woman who had been recommended by several guys. One of our KPs, "she washed 2 sets of fatigues, 2 towels, about 4 or 5 pr. of socks and some underwear, and was quite happy to be paid the sum of two bars of soap and six bars of chocolate candy, all of which came to me free in an SP pack. Actually, it's not as 'cheap' as it appears because they cannot obtain soap over here unless they get it from us." When water was in short supply, the women who washed clothing, including ours, drew it by hand from the rice paddies where they drew their household water.

I finally got to Dog Town May 9, but the PX had no tape recorders. I was able to mail two packages to Joan and order lenses. The next night I had ammo dump guard. I stated that I wished I could get another promotion because if I were E-5, I would not have guard and other details. A promotion, however, was quite unlikely: "A lot of guys go home from Nam as Sp. 4. I guess I was lucky to make it so quickly. None of the other guys that I know from Fort Sill who came over right after AIT have made it yet. Oh, well, all I really care about is the money. The rank means nothing." That was not really true; the rank would have meant no details.

A mama-san collecting water for her household.

Water collected for household use being stored in earthen vessels so impurities could settle to the bottom before water to be used was scooped off the top.

My letter referred to two boxes of my boots and clothing that Joan should have received, one from Fort Sill and the other from Oakland. The one from Sill I had entrusted to a battery acquaintance to whom I gave money for postage the day I shipped out, a day when the post office was closed.

Since Joan had never received this package, I had come to the conclusion that likely the guy kept both the items in the box and the postage money. Guess he figured (accurately) that he would never see me again, and I certainly had no recourse. Such situations were not uncommon.

14

Monsoon, Mosquitos, Mortars

*"It don't mean nothing.
It's only temporary."*

IT POURED RAIN THE NIGHT OF MAY 12. The next morning I reported that "the ground was quite muddy everywhere." It was cloudy and had "become cool and windy, which is very refreshing for a change. It looks as if it is going to pour again tonight. I guess the beginning of monsoon is here. The next 5 or 6 months will be wet." Since my arrival in-country, I had heard everyone talk about monsoon season but had yet to experience it for myself.

I knew, from reading and from being told, that in South Vietnam, for approximately half the year, the weather was hot and dry; it never rained. At the beginning of monsoon, rain might pour for a brief time. The sun would come out and it would be oppressively humid. The rain might come again the next day or might skip a day before it again poured. Each successive day the deluge would be of greater duration. At the height of the season, rain might be unceasing for nearly a week. Then the process would reverse until it ceased raining altogether, and a dry six months of no rain would resume.

In addition to rain on May 12, we were hit that night by mortars, "the second night in a row. We also got one 107 mm rocket which hit the mess hall and blew out one side." I suggested that Charlie might be making a last stab at an offensive before the constant rains came. "He has been shelling many different places in the last few days," I said. "Ho Chi Minh's birthday comes this month and there are rumors that Chuck plans to celebrate it appropriately." Whatever the reasons, I expected May to be a bad month. Along with the recent rains, the mosquitos were becoming much more prevalent and active.

The May 13 letter also included bad news. I regretted what I learned from the infantry unit with which I had been serving as RTO until two and a half weeks earlier. "Alpha Company got into quite a bit of trouble yesterday," I soberly reported. When the medevac helicopter arrived, the FO team was helping load casualties into the chopper. The FO Lt. Gant, Recon Sgt. Evans, along with "the guy who took my place as RTO, all got shot by snipers. Gant got hit twice in the back, Evans twice in the thigh, and Finley twice in the shoulder. All three are in Saigon at the 3rd Field Hospital and are being sent to Japan."

I did not state the obvious. Had it not been for my unexpected reassignment, I would have been in the attack. My relief was that all of them were evaluated "not in critical condition." I soon learned that after treatment in Saigon, the lieutenant returned to duty. My friend Evans was evacuated to a military hospital in Japan, and then sent home to Walter Reed Hospital. I had never even met and did not ever learn the outcome of Finley, the GI who replaced me as RTO.

The next afternoon I wrote from my shack while the motor sergeant was away. The day had been extremely hot, but it was cooling off and clouding over as if it were going to rain. "It didn't rain yesterday, and I didn't have guard last night," I said, "but I expect both things tonight." I described an incident from the previous night that had set our camp on edge. About 11 p.m., a soldier from one of the infantry companies came into our area "to get" a sergeant in the battery. "He shot a couple of rounds at the wrong person but luckily missed." No one knew who was responsible for the shooting until this morning when the same guy came back and slugged his intended victim. "They hauled the fool off to LBJ, as Long Binh Jail is called," I said. "I call him a fool not simply because of what he did, but because had he not come back this morning no one would have known it was he who had done the shooting *AND* he was supposed to leave Vietnam for the States today or tomorrow."

On May 16 I wrote that we were on alert to move out on a road march to Thu Thua, a nearby place. "It's 3 p.m. and we haven't left yet so maybe we won't be going. There's a chance I won't have to go anyway," I said. "That's one thing about the Army, you never can tell." Meanwhile, I was elated that I was about to discard the air mattress that was all I had to sleep on since my return to the battery. "I have some friends in the supply room from whom I got an almost new mattress," I explained, adding that I also got "a clean mattress cover, a pillow with a clean pillow case (first pillow I've had since I left Fort Sill), mosquito netting, and a fan no one was using. So as long as the electricity is on, I can remain rather cool and comfy."

There was no road march, but neither did I have electricity. I think I lost the mattress too. The next day I revealed that I had been moved to a new hooch, "a shack that has no lights." I began writing from my office,

14. Monsoon, Mosquitos, Mortars

"where there is one lone light." I drew a diagram to indicate where my "new" hooch was in relation to the one I had been in, but I cut short my letter writing because the mosquitos started "tearing me apart."

Sunday night, May 18, I scribbled a hasty note. I had been working all day and had to report to guard duty in a few minutes. "Tomorrow is Ho Chi Minh's birthday," I said, "and intelligence reports say that we will probably be hit tonight. There are reportedly 200 or more NVA within four miles of our camp so we anticipate a ground attack. Don't worry. I'll stay awake and alert." Monday I reported about the previous night. "We got mortared at about 8:30 pm and things were kinda restless for the rest of the night. I got maybe an hour's sleep." I had the afternoon off and slept past chow.

The next day, Tuesday, brought excitement of a different sort. "A bull got loose in our camp," I wrote. "He was chasing people all over. He chased one guy into a hooch and almost followed him. Finally they chased the bull into a field, and some Vietnamese came for him. It was rather amusing." My interests then turned to discussing cameras and lenses. I was anxious to receive the Nikon Nikkormat I had ordered and said I looked forward to both of us using the equipment I hoped to accumulate, and I even intended to set up a darkroom "when we have our own home."

May 22 began with a bang. We had a mortar attack at 4 a.m. We stayed on alert until 5:00 and then had chow and morning formation an hour earlier than usual in order to have "more time to prepare for the colonel. We policed the area for over an hour." Everyone was hustling to prepare for a battery inspection by our new battalion commander. I had worked late the previous night on the books and on cleaning my office. I cut my letter short to report for the night's guard duty.

I continued writing the next morning. It had rained during guard duty, creating about six inches of mud, and "naturally we had a police call." I remarked, "Picking other people's cigarette butts out of the mud is to me one of the most degrading things I could do." I resumed the letter later that afternoon: "It is really pouring. My office is wet, wet. I can see I am going to have to do a little repair work. Boy, when it rains here it doesn't mess around." The busy day forced me to lament, "I hope to be able to listen to your tape tonight. I can't believe I've had it 24 hours and haven't listened to it yet."

Enjoying letters, lately along with tapes, was the best part of my day, yet at times attention I could pay to my personal life in another world had to be delayed. I remarked, however, on the significance of our consistent communication. I first acknowledged Joan's "sweet letter" I had just received, commenting that it was "amazing how well we have come to know one another." Her saying that from my work habits and my letters

Area behind Glen's office during the monsoon season.

she could visualize "the way I would clean my weapon or write a letter or make an entry in the logbooks etc.," amused me with her descriptions, but they were "so accurate." She certainly had watched me writing when I was at home, but had never observed the other activities. I added, "You know me so well and I know you so well and we are so happy together. We love us, don't we, Joan?"

We had been communicating for some time about two matters, each of which would eventually need to be decided, and both of which involved the finances and schedule constraints of our presently separate lives and our future goals together. For one matter, now that Joan was finalizing plans to attend graduate school, she was considering whether for benefit of her studies and potential work that she should move from our Camden apartment to live on or near the USC campus until I returned home.

In the meantime, a helpful suggestion for lodging was made to her by her uncle Jak Smyrl and his wife Betty. Their close friend and neighbor Gene Sloan, Jak's fellow journalist at *The State* newspaper in Columbia, had recently died unexpectedly. His widow Kathleen (Kitty) and two school-aged daughters lived a mile or so from campus. A career writer and editor, Kitty was willing to rent Joan a room, and Joan asked my advice. Weighing various aspects with her, I summarized, "I'm favorable to the idea but only if it's what you want. If you feel however that you would have more privacy elsewhere, then do what will be best for you. As long as you're happy and content, I am happy too."

I turned to the other pending decision in our communications. I had been gathering realistic information about an R&R, "Rest and Recuperation," option that after a certain point of his time in service a GI with an approved leave could meet his wife to vacation together in exotic Hawaii. Talking to several married men who had taken that option, I heard the same from all—"great but too short." I felt how hard it would be to have just five days together and then have to return to the reality and stresses of separate day-to-day lives for six or more months. Looking into the practical side, I learned that while I could request an R&R date and probably get the month I wanted, I could not be assured ahead of the exact days. For Joan to request leave for a week of traveling and vacation amid school term demands, she would need precise dates well ahead. Besides, I feared her transportation cost ($400–500) would be "depriving yourself of almost everything." I assured her, "When I see you, I want to be able to stay with you forever."

A recent letter reported that Joan had received a box I had sent her containing some of my color slides I had snapped, a Vietnamese dress kimono from a Tan Tru market, and an aged wooden carving, about 10 inches square including a mythical bull-like creature. I wrote an account of finding the latter after we had been flying near the coast where, from our chopper, we could see a big river emptying into the sea. On the ground, as we searched a heavily vegetated area, in a small clearing we came upon partial remains of a decaying structure "destroyed by age and the war. There were no walls and part of the roof was gone." About all that remained were supports and a raised area surrounded by tumbled blocks like the one I sent. I was quite fascinated by this and wished Joan could see it. I picked up one of the scattered carved blocks, "wrapped it in my poncho so it would be protected from water damage and breakage, and then inserted it under the straps on my radio and thus brought it back with me."

My May 27 letter vented frustration, the writing of it having begun at 10 p.m. after I had just returned from a detail. Earlier I had gotten off work and taken a shower, stating that "for once we had water in the tank." I had returned to the hooch to write Joan when "I was summoned to the ammo dump to help unload trucks." The battery had gone out on a road march that day, having loaded heavy ammo into the 2½ ton trucks, hitched up the howitzers, and towed them somewhere to set up for a fire mission. "They had taken boo-coo ammo with them," I said, but had fired only six rounds, "so we had much work to do." Perhaps I might normally have had a different attitude like, *well, I sure am glad they did not have to fire a lot today and I'm glad to help unload*, were it not for other things.

On my mind, aside from usual details and harassment, was a specific incident involving my photography friend Lee Dudley, who had gone along on the mail run at the 1st Sergeant's request. I described the report: "The driver of the vehicle was caught for speeding—26 mph in a 20 mph zone—and got a DR (delinquency report). The BC is going to 'bust' both the driver and Lee to PFC (they're both Sp/4)." I could see the driver being punished but not Lee—especially since he was going on order. I added, "More Article 15s and reductions have been issued to people in this battery than you would believe." While I recognized "the Army just being the Army" and "normally I don't make a big deal of it," I stated, "It seems that some people have completely forgotten that there's a war going on over here." Referring to an upcoming IG (Inspector General) inspection in July, I pointed out, "That means footlocker displays etc. socks rolled etc. Can you believe this when people are dying over here? I really find it hard to grasp."

Looking forward to being back in civilian life again, I assured Joan: "Sweetheart, no matter how bad things seem, I always am able to make a joke out of it. I know how things will be when I return, so I can bear anything until then. We have many expressions in the Army. Over here, when things aren't going right, we say, 'It don't mean nothing. It's only temporary.' As long as I know this is true, I'm fine."

Two days later, on May 29, I wrote that today Dudley had found me a tape recorder in Tan An, and I described it in such detail that it sounded like an advertisement. I had received two letters from Joan, and one from my mom and dad. The previous day I had received a letter from Joan's mother and one from Brown. I reported, "Jim is now Sp/4 too and seems to be a bit happier with his job. I think maybe Dianne might be moving out there near him." It was raining tonight and "quite cool." It had poured last night, "so I just walked outside the hooch and showered. Boy was that a cold shower!"

On June 4 I responded to a letter from Joan in which she had mentioned deaths in Vietnam of two young men she knew. I knew she was concerned for me and the deaths of persons in her acquaintance had heightened that apprehension. The contents of my letter were both an attempt to lessen her anxiety and to express some of my personal feelings

14. Monsoon, Mosquitos, Mortars

In Long An Province, stacked crates of bottled soft drinks in the foreground juxtaposing rows of coffins in the rear building.

about the complexities of the American war in Vietnam. I assured her that I took "all precautions" and knew better than to "put my life in jeopardy."

Referring to what she and my parents had written about people "who didn't want to come to the 'Nam," I said, "I didn't really want to come here either, but I wasn't afraid to face what I had to face. I did have reservations about a situation I knew so little about, but I have never feared dying just because it could happen or because others have. I have every intention of returning to you and I will. I tell you about Vietnam—the unique, interesting things I wish you could see and the things that are ugly and I hope you never have to see. I think the latter is the reason I don't really mind being here, so maybe my family will never have to find out firsthand what war is."

My letters talked about but didn't usually complain about things like "heat, mud, rain, mosquitos etc.," or other things "which neither I, the Dept. of the Army, or anyone else can change." Besides, I said, "I've been hot and sweaty before," recalling Florence, Hampton, Varnville, Crocketville, all humid South Carolina roadsides, "where I worked highway construction the two summers before we married, so this is nothing new to me."

I remarked, "The things I do gripe about are things which could be altered—for instance the stateside-type harassment and spit and polish.

Several people have to be in a change-of-command ceremony for some colonel tomorrow. They must wear spit-shined boots and clean-starched, pressed fatigues. Some of the lifers set up an ironing board and had spray starch for the guys. I can see having polished (but not spit-polished) boots and wearing clean fatigues, but starch etc. in a combat zone where many people are dying each day just doesn't seem right to me." Here we were supposed to think that "It's all right for the peon—the enlisted man— to crawl through the mud and filth, but when a Colonel (Lt. or full bird), Major etc. comes around that same soldier is expected to look like he is ready for his first inspection in basic."

I justified my complaints: "I feel that since I accepted my obligation to my country and am doing my duty here, that I have the right to express my opinions and gripes. I don't think I'll ever be able to say I *enjoyed* the Army, but I do feel a sense of pride in serving my country and of being in Vietnam. I am glad I was able to experience firsthand what it's like in the field, to be under fire, and to face an enemy who is every bit as cunning, ingenious, and determined as any that any other American soldier has ever faced. I don't think the experience will hurt me."

To conclude the lengthy epistle, I said, "It's not pleasant, it's not fun, it's not easy, but it's not impossible either. A person who does a job that must be done even though it may be demanding usually develops into a better person. I try to tell you how it is—the truth. I am well, healthy, and as happy as I can be under the circumstances. I am neither overworked nor underfed and conditions at their worst are not such that I can't endure. Instead of thinking of death I think of and treasure life and I spend my time planning for our future. We have so much to be thankful for."

The following day, I wrote about mundane topics. I mentioned I was enjoying my new tape recorder and asked Joan about the machine her parents had purchased and whether she would be able to use it. I had received from my parents a tape which they recorded in their back yard with background noises of their dog barking at squirrels in the trees. I had received from Joan a letter, a photo magazine, and also my Tel-x-tender attachment from home, as I anticipated arrival of my camera on order. Dudley had received from his folks the Nikon he had left at his home.

After work that day, another guy and I labored until 8 p.m. putting a tin roof over the sandbags covering our hooch so we could stop the water pouring in from rain. I drew a sketch showing a shack surrounded by water, accessible only by a wooden boardwalk since the monsoon rains had already filled the paddy. "As you can see," I said, "we are now living on an island. There are boo-coo dead rats floating in the water around the hooch, some dead from poison we put out, others probably drowned." I closed my letter humorously with "boo-coo love."

14. Monsoon, Mosquitos, Mortars

A dry-season view of the hooch Glen lived in for about six months.

I wrote again on Sunday, June 8, unaware at the time but would learn later that President Nixon met that day with the South Vietnamese president at Midway Island to announce the first of incremental withdrawals of American troops from Vietnam under the policy of Vietnamization. Life would meanwhile go on as normal for us. My letter shows I worked that day at the motor pool until about 6 p.m. and then continued roofing the hooch until about 8:00. I speculated that we were about two-thirds done and could finish tomorrow. Two days later, I reported hearing from AIT friend Barry Kelso, who said he decided he could not take three years of Army life and had quit OCS after nine weeks. He was at home for 30 days' leave and seemed really happy with his decision even though he is coming to Nam after leave. Bill Rabon, another friend from BCT/AIT, also quit, Kelso said. I quipped, "Us dropouts are gaining strength."

Joan's letter I received June 11 told me that she had agreed to teach summer school at Camden High, a half-day program, and would begin graduate school the fall semester. I agreed it seemed a wise choice. I was hopeful this would give her a bit of a break before the rigors of grad school. I did not know that, by the time I received the letter, she had already begun

During the monsoon season, Glen's hooch from an angle showing C Battery's motor pool on the right.

contracting freelance articles to write and was voluntarily assisting with local historical research and writing in her extra time.

I added a postscript: "Had guard duty last night. Tomorrow the Btry (except for me and a few others) will go on an air mobile operation to the Plain of Reeds, so I'll probably have guard duty for the next couple of nights." In an air mobile operation, the gun section with all of their equipment boarded a bus-sized CH-47 Chinook helicopter, with one end of heavy cables attached to a howitzer and the other end to the underside of the chopper. The Chinook would lift off and hover with the howitzer a few feet off the ground, allowing soldiers to attach another cable under it from which was suspended a large net filled with about 100 rounds of 105 mm ammo. The gun section assisted in loading the net and attaching the cables, but since these men were inside when the Chinook began to hover, the attaching of the cables for suspending the howitzer and ammo had to be done by those of us outside on the ground. It was quite a sight to see this operation in flight.

On June 13 I provided more information about the air mobile mission and the harassment of those of us left behind in Charlie Battery. As everyone had left except for about a half-dozen of us, for protection the grunts were to take over our bunker and we were not to pull guard duty. "However," I wrote, "the lifers decided that it wouldn't be Army-ish for us to have the night off, so they were going to make the six of us peons pull guard on top of one of the bunkers—about one hour per person. However, that wasn't tough enough, so they decided to put each of us on two posts pulling 3 hours apiece." These were not normal guard locations, so there was no security value in posting us there, just harassment.

I wrote Friday, June 20, lamenting that I had had so little time to write lately. I had guard duty Tuesday night, worked until 9 p.m. Wednesday on the logbooks, and then "we got hit by the worst rocket and mortar attack I've been through over here." I had expected a ground attack, too, since four of our six howitzers and three of the five infantry companies were in the Plain of Reeds. However, "we were lucky." Thursday two guns returned, and I had to help unload the Chinooks; next I worked on the books until 7 p.m., and then we were hit with rockets and mortars again. As for tonight, I had worked until 8:30 on the books, and "I hope we don't get hit. I'm tired and sleepy."

I explained that we were working to be ready for an IG inspection in about three weeks, at which time "the books have to be perfect (which they never have been)," given the state of figures at the start of my beginning to work with them. "I have to work every night—unless I have guard duty—until they're right," I said, that is, *mathematically correct* or *balanced*. "I am practically having to rewrite each logbook from one cover to the other." I gave an example of one of the situations. One of the Jeeps was deadlined for 22 consecutive days because of an inoperative oil pressure sending unit. A vehicle is supposed to be parked when deadlined and not driven at all. "However, the lifers continued to log it out and use it, so it was driven a total of 737 miles and used 65 gallons of fuel." I was ordered to make books balance by showing the Jeep not used at all while deadlined, as required, and adding entries elsewhere to cover the mileage and fuel consumed. This required rewriting daily entries and changing the monthly and the quarterly figures, all of them having to coincide for a quarter (93 days).

On June 22 it was after 9 p.m. and I was still at the motor pool when I started my letter. I told Joan, "I worked until 10 p.m. last night, and then Charles prevented me from writing you when he began dropping his rockets in our midst. I think he has hit us three out of the last four nights. He

At C Battery's motor pool, Glen displaying a captured enemy machine gun (Ernest Brown).

has been sending in rockets instead of mortars recently and the rockets are much worse." I was also concerned because the rockets were also coming closer too.

The enemy's success in placing rounds depended upon the accuracy of their reconnaissance, which sometimes involved closeup spying. All civilian workers on our firebase went through a search before they were allowed to leave at the end of the day, of course to prevent theft, and more importantly, to prevent would-be saboteurs from gathering intel that could help pinpoint strategic targets. Recently one of the women who worked in our compound had been caught with a sketch of our area, a map which was avowed to have been pretty accurate to scale. Such occurrences were quite sobering.

The good news I had to share came, of course, from other directions that helped me through more stressful concerns. A friend who was a motor pool mechanic, John Baca, found me another tape recorder in Tan An, so I would send my other one to Joan and she could stop borrowing. And I had "hit the jackpot" during mail call: a letter from my Aunt Ruby, one from my parents, one from Joan's parents, and two from Joan. I also got tapes from my folks and from my friend Bush, some Winthrop College newspapers from its editor who was Joan's sister Mary Ann, and some processed slides.

I wrote with excitement June 24 that I had purchased a camera and accessories for it from another GI, a Minolta SLR, lens, case, deluxe tripod, and four rolls of film—all for just $75. I was full of plans. I would use the Minolta equipment until my Nikkormat came in. Then I would keep the tripod, but sell the rest. I would give first offer of purchase to Joan's uncle Rhonda Brown, an accomplished photographer whose favorite camera line was Minolta. It was exactly the camera he wanted. I could send it to him for about $90 (including shipping and insurance). I would essentially recover my investment, have a nice tripod, and give Rhonda the deal of a lifetime. That model Minolta listed for $275 in the States and $126 in the Vietnam PX. He was under no obligation, but I was certain he would seize the opportunity. If he passed, I knew I could sell the camera and probably make some profit.

I worked June 26 until after 9 p.m. A team from battalion maintenance came to help us prepare for the big inspection next month. "They'll be here for 3 or 4 days tearing us apart," I said, "and then rebuilding us so we'll be working late each night they're here. I'll be glad when all this is over." This "tearing us apart" by the battalion team and the urgency of the imminent IG inspection did not stop requirements of Charlie Battery's normal routine, all of these events being very tiring, especially when combined.

On Sunday, June 29, I went to the motor pool to clean my M16 for the next morning's weapons inspection. It was quiet there and I was going to record a tape to Joan, but another guy came in to write a letter so I deferred "talking" and began a letter instead. I relayed news from Brown. Dianne had moved and they had an apartment and were together again. They were both my friends, and I was "glad he didn't have to come over here even if I did."

Mail call, typically "feast or famine," on June 30 was a banquet. I received nine letters, five of them from Joan. The next day I received two more from her. Overall, the mail service did a remarkable job, but there were errors. A letter from my parents had been mis-sent to another battery before it reached me. One of Joan's letters I received July 1 was postmarked March 2. It had been sent "to E-4-1 (AIT), then to the Holding Btry., then to Oakland, and finally to me here." At least it was forwarded. We wondered how many of our letters, tapes, or packages never made it. There were instances when one of us would reference a subject we had previously mentioned, but about which the other had no knowledge, and there were packages of cookies, etc., that folk back home sent but I never received. I commented about the five-month-delayed letter Joan wrote when she did not know my whereabouts: "at least things aren't nearly as uncertain now." There was a juxtaposition of the anxiety of *not knowing* where I was then and of *knowing* where I was now.

My July 3 letter described an event planned for the following day, Independence Day. Our battery was to have a service "dedicating a sign to some Lt. who was a glory hunter and got himself and 3 other men killed. (He and another Lt. had a bet as to which one could get the biggest body count—VC dead—so they both poked around in places they had no business.) Anyway, a colonel and some other brass are supposed to be here and we have to have clean fatigues, spit-shined boots etc. Big deal. Tomorrow night I have guard duty so I won't have any time to write then either." Writing letters home—especially to Joan—was as important to me as receiving them. At times the situation I was in, like now, made writing impossible, and I would become irritated when prevented from the activity which kept me mentally balanced.

15

Independence, Illness, Inspections

"*Wet, muddy, cold, and quite peeved*"

I PERSONALLY "CELEBRATED" JULY 4—INDEPENDENCE DAY—by working all day on the logbooks and then pulling guard duty that night. When I returned to my hooch the next morning, I found yesterday's mail had come in while I was on duty. There was a letter from Joan about a magazine article she had written and photographed for *Sandlapper*. "I am very proud of you," I wrote back, stating I was very pleased "but not a bit surprised" that the popular new independent travel and history publication subtitled *The Magazine of South Carolina* had purchased her work and was interested in more.

There was serious doubt now, I reported, that any of the camera lenses that I had ordered from the PX at Dong Tam would come in. "All the Americans are pulling out of there and it's being turned over to the South Vietnamese army, the ARVNs," I stated. "If my stuff comes in from Saigon, I'll be satisfied." During the rest of my tour, I would experience American facilities closing or being transferred to the South Vietnamese and a consequential shuffling of personnel. Although President Nixon's policy of Vietnamization's initial withdrawal of troops from the 9th Division did not include troops from my brigade, we began feeling its effects.

I vividly remember the situation I described in my July 10 letter. That day I was still running a 100° fever that I had run the day before after having run several days of lower grade temperatures, "but in order to be given bed rest in the Army, one must have 101°. Consequently, I had to work all yesterday and then pull bunker guard last night." Only persons on bed rest did not have to go to work. During guard duty, "It poured rain, the wind howled and we all were wet, muddy, cold, and quite peeved. The only cover on the bunker is an old moldy, holey tarp that we put up and which really doesn't help."

After sleeping most of the next morning and still feeling bad, I went to the Aid Station. My temperature was 102.6° so I was given pills and told to go to bed. Back in my hooch I lay miserably "on a bed that smells of old sweat, in a damp dank building that smells of wet lumber and rats, with no one around to really give a damn," and I could not help but long for fresh linens, hot soup, and kindly treatment at home.

I closed my letter with a lengthy postscript to answer questions Joan had asked:

A mid-afternoon monsoon rain creating the appearance of darkness.

1. *There are two motor pool clerks—a PLL clerk & a TAERS clerk. The Prescribed Load List clerk is a parts clerk & he must requisition all the parts needed for our vehicles. I am the equipment records clerk. I must keep all of the paperwork up to date. I must log out the vehicles each day, make sure the drivers lube and service their vehicles, mark a part off the books when it comes in, make sure when a part is repaired or replaced it goes in the log book, etc., and about a million other things. I am also in charge of writing up and turning in all reports. And, yes, I have an office for my records only.*
2. *I work every day from 8 a.m. until 4:30 p.m. normally but we've worked practically every night for the past 3 wks.*
3. *I haven't been to a church service since I left Dong Tam. I think they had one here once but I couldn't leave my work to go. I do read the Bible and say my prayers each night for us.*
4. *We do have movies sometimes over in the EM Club but I've never gone to one. What little free time I have I like to spend writing you.*
5. *In Tan Tru (our compound, not the nearby village) there is an infantry battalion—5 companies—a 155 mm self-propelled howitzer btry., a mortar btry., our 105 mm btry., headquarters, and a radar section. I don't know how many people that would be.*
6. *When my camera comes in, the PX will drop me a card and I'll have 30 days or so to come and get it.*

15. Independence, Illness, Inspections

Before I sealed the letter, I wrapped around it clippings from a catalog of stereo equipment I wanted to get us.

July 12, a Saturday morning, I returned to the Aid Station on sick call. I was still running a fever and was told to go back to bed. I felt slightly better but had been running a temperature for eight days. I began working off and on when the degree of my temperature allowed it. I described to Joan a crazy incident in the battalion during that time. Sunday afternoon the battalion's maintenance supervisor, a warrant officer, telephoned me that he was flying in from Tan An either that night or Monday morning "to look over our books and help us out."

To my astonishment, about 6 p.m. while I was working alone on my daily reports, the supervisor who had telephoned staggered into my office: "drunk, cursing, and spitting on the floor. His eyes are bloodshot, and he can hardly sit up straight. This infuriates me, but I can't say anything, so I walk out to take my reports to the orderly room."

About 15 minutes later I returned and discovered that the supervisor had informed the motor sergeant, who had just arrived, that we were to have a Command Maintenance Management Inspection (CMMI) the next morning. This was a surprise, and battery reaction was quick. The sergeant informed the BC, who immediately called a formation and addressed all the battery when hastily assembled. I described the scene: "We all stand out in the rain and the mud and listen as he tells us that everyone will stay up and work all night to get ready for the inspection." We were dismissed, and everyone was immediately "running about like crazy," and the whole battery was in turmoil.

After about 30 minutes of bedlam, it was determined that the supervisor was "talking through the bottle and that no CMMI was scheduled for the next day." The battalion assistant commander, a major at headquarters in Tan An, got the supervisor on the phone and relieved him of his duties. Our BC, a captain, gave the supervisor a direct order to go to bed, and the rest of us were told to get in out of the rain. "Can you believe that?" I asked Joan. "I certainly will feel that we both will have given enough and suffered enough for our country when I finish my term!"

I had guard duty July 14 and "for a change I stayed rather dry," but afterward I did not get the customary half-day off, since the following day was the AGI inspection. Furthermore, I said, "We may have another inspection (CMMI) Sunday, but we won't know until the last minute. Shakespeare would have tabbed it 'much ado about nothing.'" Saturday night, July 17, I wrote, "What a horror show!" They told us last night that we would have CMMI today. Consequently, I had to work until 12 p.m. I had to be at work at 7 a.m. today and did not know until almost 10 a.m. that we were "*not* getting the inspection. Grrr!" I added, "Maybe now all this garbage has ended I'll have some time to write." However, it would not be that night. I was scheduled for guard duty.

My July 21 letter exalted, "Summer is half over and that means in ti-ti (opposite of boo-coo) time, school will be starting and the teacher will become a student. Autumn will drift into winter, and I will be *short* (fewer than 100 days left in the Army). Winter will warm into spring, and I'll be home. How sweet it will be!"

The day before we expected the CMMI, I said in my July 21 letter, my friend Dudley had left C Battery. "He really lucked out," I said. "He is now in charge of the photo lab at Tan An. He has no guard duty, no details, no formations to attend, and the photo lab is an air-conditioned trailer. He has to keep it open until 10 p.m., but he doesn't have to open it until about noon and can sleep in the mornings. I'm glad he got it because he was being 'dumped on' here by the BC and 1st SGT. He was one of my best friends here, however, and I hated to see him go."

I turned to the subject of "care packages" from home. I had received one from my mother and father that contained juices, potato sticks, etc., and a can of boiled peanuts. "It was uncanny; I had been craving boiled peanuts. They were not as good as fresh peanuts but they were good." I asked Joan to discourage anyone from sending "candy, cookies, or anything sweet. Things like that usually arrive in damaged condition."

Lee Dudley (left) and Glen in Jeep, taking a break in C Battery (Ernest Brown).

15. Independence, Illness, Inspections

Shifting from the mundane to the spectacular, I remarked at length on a major world event: "Gosh, what about the moon shot! I've been listening to it on the radio today and I just watched some coverage of the lift-off on TV. The moon walk itself is supposed to be shown later tonight. This whole thing awes me. It's really difficult to conceive of men really walking on the moon. It's really wonderful but I still would rather see peace on earth—South America, Israel, Korea, Vietnam—before man gets so enthused over the prospect of inhabiting the moon and Mars. I guess interplanetary war will be a thing of the future. Maybe *Star Trek* isn't so fictitious after all."

News of friends followed. I had received a photo magazine and a letter from my hometown friend Summers Till, who wanted me to get him a telephoto lens for his Ricoh SLR. His big news was that he and wife Rose were expecting again. "Can you believe it?" I asked Joan. "It really doesn't seem that it has been so long since the four of us were double-dating at Winthrop and you, Rose, and I were still in college and Summers had just graduated. Time does fly. I just wish these next 8 months would hurry and fly by and then I could *fly*—back to you."

When I wrote my July 22 letter, I had just spent from 7:30 to 10 p.m. on a new kind of duty for me—starlight guard. "I don't have to pull bunker guard anymore," I said, "but I have to pull starlight guard *every night* for 2½ hours." Rotating shifts ran from dusk to dawn in order to man a recently acquired night-vision "starlight scope," located on top of the hooch in gun section 6. The guard sat behind the scope, which was mounted on a tripod and swiveled to scan a large area. With the appearance of a large, bulky six-pound telescope, the scope was battery-powered to amplify ambient light and allow the viewer to "see in the dark." The image in the viewfinder provided an eerie, greenish view, but with a minimal amount of moonlight or starlight, we could detect enemy movements across the paddies to the tree lines along the river. The guard used a radio telephone to communicate anything out of the ordinary.

One night the starlight guard spotted several VC setting up a mortar tube near some hooches by the river. He called in, and our leadership tried to get clearance to fire on the VC. Since those hooches were inhabited by "friendlies," we were denied permission to fire unless or until we were fired upon. We were allowed to aim a tube at the VC to be prepared, then we had to wait. The VC did fire into our camp with a mortar that caused little damage, but the group had disbanded by the time we fired on them, so I think they got away.

On July 25 I began a letter to Joan at 4 p.m. I had finished work then and it was pouring rain—"boo-coo wet." I had to march with a group over to the 2/60 Infantry Battalion Headquarters "with polished boots, of course" to listen to 9th Division Commander Gen. Harris W. Hollis's farewell speech. I commented that I remembered nothing memorable.

I mentioned plans to go to Dong Tam to division finance to straighten out Joan's allotment, which had not yet increased. My July 28 letter I informed her it was straight. She would receive $130.60 a month and would get all back pay in one lump sum, but it would take about six weeks to get it. I drew a sketch of the starlight scope and mentioned that sometimes I took my recorder and made voice tapes while scanning the horizon. With howitzers on both sides of the hooch where the scope was located, any fire missions proved interruptive.

On July 30 I wrote Joan about an action I had taken since she was still anxiously awaiting word from grad school about the availability of a loan or an assistantship for her in the fall. I wrote to R.L. Osborne, who lived in Orangeburg and was chairman of USC's board of trustees: "I asked him if he might be able to assist you in obtaining a teaching assistantship for the next year. It was the only thing I could think of to do." I otherwise felt helpless being so far away from her problem.

I was again disgusted that the lifer who was supposed to pick up the mail didn't—two days in a row, July 31 and August 1. He went into Tan An as usual for whatever reason he went, and he simply neglected to get the mail. On the other hand, the motor sergeant had been gone for two days, "and it has been great not having him around. He has been in almost 22 years and is only a Staff Sgt. (E-6—just two grades higher than me)." NCOs like him and like the supply sergeant expressed bitterness being "stuck in rank," and we all saw that they would not do anything to help others advance. Because of my job and my constant overtime efforts to straighten out the records, I should have been in line for a promotion to Specialist 5, but the motor sergeant was my immediate supervisor, and I knew he would never recommend me. Once, at a later time, the battery commander mentioned he would approve my being promoted if the motor sergeant recommended it. The sergeant never did.

"This is a big Saturday night, and I went to the movies," I wrote August 2. "Well, anyway I went to the EM Club where they show a movie almost every night." I had not been before but wanted to see the film *Bonnie & Clyde*. I described the event: "The picture is shown on the wall, the films and projector are in bad repair, and something breaks down every five minutes. And, of course, if there's a love scene the guys go wild."

Responding to a letter about Joan's clothing purchases for grad school, I wrote, "I'm glad you bought all those clothes. I know you've deprived yourself of threads because of other expenses. New clothes will undoubtedly cheer you up immensely." I quipped, "Just think of all the money we're saving on clothes for me while I'm in the Army," adding, "I used to like green but when I get out I bet I'll wear the brightest, wildest clothes money can buy." As usual, I expressed yearning to finish my Army stint, observing it will be "the first time since we met that we will have nothing ahead of us but our lives. There will be no school, no military obligation, nothing hanging over our heads. We'll just have hundreds of years of happiness to look forward to."

I launched on a rather Pollyanna financial vision on my return, when we would have acquired several thousand dollars' worth of camera and stereo equipment. "Of course the value I quote is U.S. value," I said, "but we'll be living in the U.S., won't we?" Additionally, "we'll also have about $1,500 in cash that I will have saved." I suggested taking some of it for down payment on a house and buying "some numba-one living room furniture." Then we'd have all our photo equipment (except darkroom equipment), our stereo, a house of our own, nice furniture, and money in the bank. "Not bad, huh?" My logic may have been skewed, but ambitions were clear. Looking back before the Army came into our lives, I reflect that Joan and I had been envisioning a far different plan for ourselves—living abroad in multicultural areas to study, teach, write, and photograph before "settling down" at home and raising a family. Now nowhere seemed more appealing than home.

My letter August 4 reported my working hard that day in a different way: "I mixed cement and poured a walkway down the side of the office. This place is looking more like stateside every day. Almost every hooch has a concrete walk going to it. Of course, the sidewalks lead to the road which is mud and we have formation in the road each morning and police call in the mud etc. so it really doesn't do too much good. However, the way the Army works—an item doesn't have to work; as long as it looks good, it's ok."

Although I did not expound, I must have wondered about the contradiction between the government's Vietnamization policy for withdrawal of troops and construction activities such as I described. Not only were such projects creating unnecessary and expensive work for soldiers, surely it was creating among the Vietnamese a belief that we were going to be there for a long time.

I added to my letter that there had been "a USO show here this afternoon and I went." I took some black and white photos of the show, featuring a former Mouseketeer, Sherry Alberoni. "It wasn't the best show I've ever seen but it wasn't too bad and it did get us away from work for an hour." I also mentioned I had heard on the radio a new hit song that I liked a lot, "Sweet Caroline" by Neil Diamond, and I thought Joan would like it as well.

"I was quite angered when I read your first letter tonight," I began my

August 5 letter. I learned that the USC loan office reported Joan was eligible for a loan, but they were unable to provide one because of "lack of funds." Then upon reading her second letter, I "was much relieved" for her that she might be able to get a loan from the Southern National Bank. This was my bank in Orangeburg from which I had borrowed—and to which I was repaying—money for my own education. I provided names of two people at the bank who had been very helpful to me. To her comment that she could get a part-time job if a loan were not possible, I replied if her need was that serious, I would forego the camera and stereo equipment to allow me to send her additional money monthly. "You know that education means more than those tangible things. I can't be there with you night and day to give you instant help and advice, but I'll do all I can to help you get through grad school," I assured her. It may have been wasted effort, but I was very glad that I had written R.L. Osborne that letter.

Two days later I responded happily to news that Joan had been approved for a loan from the Orangeburg bank. "I knew that they would help you if they had the money. I know practically all of the people who work there and I had an account there when I first went to work in the summer of 1963. Our credit is above reproach in Orangeburg and Camden, too."

Rhonda Brown had written me that he wanted to buy my Minolta whenever I was ready to sell it. I wrote Joan concerning some of the photos I had sent home. I was interested in "capturing the people"—scenes showing them in their environment "doing their thing," and close-ups showing their faces. I mentioned two I especially liked, one of a mama-san sitting in front of the orderly room "biting her fingernail," the other of a baby-san. A baby-san could be anyone from a baby to a young unmarried girl; a boy-san was an adolescent male; a papa-san was a man; and a mama-san was a mature woman. One woman I photographed worked in our camp as a sandbag dollar.

The young girl in another photo worked in our executive post, sweeping, cleaning, etc. I said, "The Vietnamese try to learn your last name because it is sewn on your shirt. She has tried to learn my name but can't say *Inabinet*, so she calls me Buddha because of my short hair and round stomach. She started that and now all of the other Vietnamese call me Buddha or 'same-same Buddha.'" The Vietnamese used the slang *same-same* to indicate *like* or *just like*. I explained the reason I had so many photos of women was because "there are no Vietnamese men here on post. The only ones we see are the ones who come through to collect the garbage." I wanted to get "more close-ups of faces—especially of the children and of the very old—they have the most unique expressions."

There were many scenes I did not photograph. The South Vietnamese

15. Independence, Illness, Inspections

Workers from nearby Tan Tru Village entering the Tan Tru compound.

Sandbag dollars in the back of an M35 truck, awaiting transport back to their village.

Army had a small compound on the road between our position and Tan Tru Village. Recently the ARVN "brought back two dead VC. They carried them tied to poles like one would carry a dead hog. They just put them

Near Tan Tru firebase, the ARVN compound that was later attacked by VC sappers who caused numerous casualties and considerable damage to armaments and buildings.

down on the ground and left them," I think as a warning on the side of the road. In a later incident involving this ARVN unit, one night some of their bunker guards were asleep when nine VC sappers attacked their compound. Some breached the perimeter, killed seven or eight ARVNs, and, with satchel charges, destroyed a couple of howitzers and the Fire Direction Control Center. Four of the VC got away, two were captured, and three were killed. Two were stopped on the wires. Claymore mines blew away their lower bodies, leaving only their torsos hanging there. The next morning some of our guys went there with their cameras and photographed the grisly scene. I did not go. I certainly did not need that kind of photo souvenir to take home.

Friday night, August 8, I had planned to go to bed early but being unable to sleep, I began a letter at 11:30 p.m. I had worked outside all afternoon "moving drums of tar (about 400 lbs. each) from one place to another and then shoveling rock and sand. Then tonight we had to unload 2 generators and six 55 gal. drums of fuel oil off a truck. Oh, well, so much for another day in the Nam."

I wrote Sunday night, "Tomorrow will be the 11th and thus will mark 5 months that I've been in the Nam." I told Joan that living with us in our hooch we now had a dog that one of our guys got from someone from the 1/84 Arty., which had left for Hawaii. "She is brown and her name is Lulu,"

I said. One of the guys took a Polaroid photo of me with Lulu in front of the maintenance office. I told Joan I would send the photo to her, "but don't show Lady," our dog living in a large pen in her parents' backyard. "She might get jealous." Our apartment did not allow pets.

August 12 I had the morning off after pulling bunker guard duty. "We don't have the big starlight scope anymore so I'm back on perimeter guard again," I wrote. Having had only an hour and a half of sleep, "I'll probably crash early tonight." I described an out-of-the-ordinary occurrence: "Yesterday was 'C' day—all MPC was converted to another series of MPC, thus making the 'old' MPC invalid. There was no warning that this would be done and we found out yesterday morning at formation. The KPs and all the other Vietnamese were taken home and no one was allowed in or out of the compound until the conversion had been completed. The Vietnamese were not allowed to convert the MPC they have, so any MPC in their possession is worthless." I continued, "In a way it seems cruel to the Vietnamese, but actually they are not supposed to have MPC and the main purpose of this is to invalidate MPC on their black market. Needless to say there will be boo-coo teed-off native people in Vietnam today—especially the prostitutes who are usually paid in MPC."

I had written a letter of thanks to the Orangeburg bank's vice president, a man long familiar to me, for assisting Joan in getting a student loan approval in case she should not get an assistantship and need a loan. After recent frustrating experiences with USC's administrative office during registration, I recognized her becoming more skeptical of the school as a whole. I reminded her, "There are really some good professors at USC. I hope you are fortunate to get them. The professors are much better than the administrative help." From my time there, I explained that in the fast-growing university, "many of the staff members are women whose husbands are in school there. They may work one semester or one year but seldom longer. Therefore, there is constantly a tremendous turnover of personnel, and a secretary seldom occupies a position long enough to learn her duties, much less to learn what her department is supposed to be doing."

I announced myself "angry" at the beginning of my August 14 letter because "once again the lifers did not get the mail." I elaborated, "This lifer that goes to Dong Tam practically every day is supposed to pick up our mail at Tan An on the way back. However, he has a girl in Dong Tam and he stays down there late and then has to rush back in time to get here before the road closes." Everyone had to be off the road at 6 p.m.

Otherwise, I was upbeat. I had gotten some of my photos back. "All in all they're not too bad," I reflected. Often I had to shoot from a moving truck, having to mitigate shutter speed and depth-of-field realities, especially in low light. Even where we could stop to compose and focus, it was not safe to do so. I was also encouraged that that recent mail had brought me a letter from USC board chairman Osborne, replying that he had asked USC to see if an assistantship might be available for my wife. I enclosed his response, along with my rough draft request, hoping those efforts were not in vain.

My August 16 letter began with sad news from Orangeburg. One of the two sons of my high school band director had committed suicide. The young man, a teacher in another town, I did not know well, but the family lived directly across the street from my parents, who sent his obituary. I remarked to Joan that while I had been in Vietnam, he was the second person I knew from my hometown to have died in that way. The other was a year or so older than me, and we had been in the same Boy Scout troop.

I added current tragic news near me. "Last night the VC mortared some of the hooches down near Tan Tru Village," I said. "Two of the girls who work here were hit. One who worked in the orderly room is not expected to live; she had part of her head blown away. I'm not sure about the other one who is the sister of Bah, the KP who does my laundry." Also, the ARVN husband of another one of the KPs had been shot by the VC the previous night. "All in all, enemy activity has been stepped up recently," I commented. "So far we've only gotten a couple of rockets and/or mortars in but we're being very cautious."

Battalion maintenance had showed up at the motor pool day before yesterday for "an on-the-spot inspection," I wrote on August 21. "My records and most other things were in pretty good order but we got some gigs on the vehicles and consequently have been working again at night. I had bunker guard night before last and then worked last night and tonight" because anything done to the vehicles had to be reflected in my records, which had to stay in balance.

My letter also mentioned receipt of brochures I had requested. One was from a photography school, the other from Pioneer about their stereo components. Writing letters and keeping myself a part of home life, while seeking information on changing technologies of my interests in photography and "good quality sounds," continued to help balance my head amid the humdrum and the terrifying realities of daily life in Charlie Battery.

16

Penta Prime, Photography, Pestering

"I was on a treadmill"

THE FOLLOWING DAY'S MAIL ON AUGUST 22 brought "fabulous news" that USC had offered Joan a teaching assistantship in the English Department. "This is what I hoped for. I wanted this so much for you. I am so very happy," I responded. About the room she took at Mrs. Sloan's home, "It sounds just right for you—air conditioned yet! I certainly won't be worried about you living there. You'll be close to USC and to Jak and Betty. I think you'll find Mrs. Sloan to be an interesting person with whom you can talk and share ideas." The location seemed "a good atmosphere in which to study and write.... No doubt you will meet many interesting and offbeat people."

My postscript mentioned, "Do write Mr. Osborne and tell him what developed and thank him. I'll do likewise." Joan's agreement to teach two freshman English classes each semester would cover her tuition costs and student fees, provide basic texts, and pay a stipend. She would not need to take out a loan, and her military allotment would cover rent for our apartment and her room as well. I agreed with her opinion that teaching students just a year or two older than her recent ones she would enjoy as "challenging" and "interesting."

The night of August 25, I described what had been a difficult day. It began, as did every Monday in Vietnam, with our lining up to take "THE PILL" to prevent malaria. From there it went downhill. "We had to load the penta prime trailer 3 times today," I said. "I picture you frowning and scratching your head, asking ... *a penta prime trailer?*" I described it, pulled behind a deuce-and-a-half truck, an enclosed tank trailer with a gravity-powered spray arm behind it, a trailer which we had to fill with 55-gallon drums of an oily black, very warm tar-like substance called penta prime. "Each drum weighs about 400–450 lbs. and we usually have only 4–6 people to fill the trailer," I said. "It takes about 3 full drums to fill it one time. We must slide each drum up a steel ramp and hold it [above an opening] until its contents drain into the trailer." The truck driver would pull the filled trailer up and down, sprinkling the substance on the road "to (purportedly) keep the surface hard."

I well recall that this practice held down the dust somewhat, but the blazing sun kept the penta prime sticky, and it mixed with the mud beneath it from monsoon rains. We had to walk in the penta prime mixture, stand formation in it, and vehicles had to drive across it. A tremendous amount of backbreaking physical labor was required to create a horrible mess, not to mention an undoubtable environmental problem.

On one occasion, the Beverly-Hillbillies-like truck that the Vietnamese used to collect our garbage slid through the oily mess into a ditch. Some of our guys hooked one end of a heavy chain to a deuce-and-a-half and the other end to the trash truck. As the latter had no bumper, the chain was attached to the axle. The tow vehicle strained and yanked the front axle completely from the chassis. I could not understand what the trash truck's driver was saying, but he was jumping up and down and obviously shouting every obscenity in his vocabulary. I felt truly sorry for him, but it was a scene made for a cartoonist's pen.

My story of the "paving" detail continued, "Imagine filling the penta prime trailer in 120° heat," which was, I said, "'cooler' today than yesterday when it was 125°." I told more about the extreme heat. "Yesterday afternoon about 5 p.m., several of us went down to the river and swam. The water is very deep and very swift, so we would not venture out far. We had to wear our boots because of sharp objects and grossness on the bottom. It was quite refreshing. Except for the one-time swim class in Dong Tam, it was my first swim since last summer before I came in the Army."

My letter did not mention that during the swim we had taken turns standing guard on the riverbank, nor did I relate a unique episode. The pilot of a loach spotted us in the water and dropped down to have a better look. "Apparently we seemed to be having fun, so the copter hovered right above the water's surface and another guy stepped on the skid and jumped into the water with us. When he had cooled off, he climbed back onto the skid, re-entered the cabin, and the hovering loach ascended into the sky." The night of my letter, "Charlie probed our perimeter down by Alpha Co. A lot of automatic weapons fire and tracers were flying everywhere. I hope that was the extent of tonight's activity. Up until tonight, things had continued to be calm here although enemy activity has increased elsewhere."

A brief note to Joan on August 26 remarked on the date, stating, "Just think. Tonight 3 years ago I was in Orangeburg scheming and planning exactly how to go about proposing to you the next night." I wrote that the

16. Penta Prime, Photography, Pestering

love I felt then had not been diminished by the great distance which separated us now. We had for some time accepted the fact that we would be unable to arrange an R&R together in Hawaii. Thinking of when we would be together again, I had a few days earlier reminded Joan to make her grad program timing suit her and her situation, since "neither of us knows what my status will be. I may be a civilian in April or I may have to serve until September next year."

I reported August 30 that uncertainties continued on my pending orders for camera and stereo equipment. I had learned from the PX contractor that the current wait time on most Nikon items was 3–7 months and at least a year on some. Among the uncertain was an 85 mm lens I especially wanted for its f:1.8 aperture. Research convinced me that some of the items I had ordered in Saigon would not come in at all. In Hong Kong, China, however—just one and a half hours away from me by air—there was an enormous Naval PX where I could purchase equipment on the spot. I was investigating how to put myself on that spot.

Meanwhile, I wrote on September 3, two overdue lenses were awaiting my pickup at the Saigon PX. I wanted to wait a while before going there, however, hoping that the long-awaited Nikkormat might also arrive, the use of any lenses requiring, of course, a camera body. The day brought more hard labor. "After supper another guy and I unloaded a 2½ ton truck which was loaded with sand. The sand is being pumped out of the river at Ben Luc and is similar to beach sand," I said. I had no idea what was to be done with the sand. "All of us had to go on police call and trash run, and then we had to unload some furniture off another 2½ ton truck."

The presence of real furniture seemed unreal in our battery, where everything was made from something else. "All of the lifers are getting Hollywood beds, chest-of-drawers etc. from Dong Tam," I said. These were apparently being transferred because that big base was being turned over to the ARVNs under Vietnamization. None of the furniture was given any of the EMs. Instead we anticipated an extra police call the next day because of commotion over a big event. The lifers were frenzied over significant visitors, including the battalion commander, the brigade commander, and especially General Creighton W. Abrams, Jr.—the commander of forces in Vietnam since 1968. (Afterward I wrote nothing about General Abrams's visit.)

September 9 was "another gross day." I was on a detail of about a dozen men tasked with putting a tin roof on a bunker. We worked all day through a driving monsoon rain trying to get the roof on, "only to have our sorry 1st Sgt. decide he didn't like the way it looked, so we have to tear it down in the morning and start over again just to suit him."

We received no mail September 11, I wrote that day, for more serious cause than neglect of pickup. "Last night Chuck blew out one of the bridges on the road between here and Highway 4," I reported. The damage interrupted all commerce along unpaved Thunder Road, which ran between picturesque rice paddies cultivated by peasants and water buffalo, and where usual sites were hooches with chickens, ducks, an occasional pig, and children playing. There were several bridges across the creeks and rivers along the way. Since Thunder Road was the only way in and out of Tan Tru, "there was no traffic at all today. We were brought our daily rations by helicopter and are supposed to have our mail flown in tomorrow."

I had other news too, more important to me personally. It was a long-discussed situation, so I did not need to make much explanation for my announcement. "I 'extended' in order to get out in 19 months," I related. Joan understood that I meant I had officially volunteered to stay an extra 36 days in Vietnam, and I had done so in order to have fewer than six months left on my commitment when I got home. At that point, with an "early out," I would be placed in a military "reserve" category. Therefore, "Instead of coming home March 10, I won't get back to the States now until April 19 or 20. However, when I do come home it will be for good."

What changes a year can make! My letter on September 13 marked exactly one year I had been in the Army. I had been in Vietnam six months. Joan had left her classroom, moved into a rented room in Columbia, entered graduate school, and accepted an assistantship which required her to teach classes of freshman English. Joan's life was moving ahead; I was on a treadmill. One thing that had not changed was my disdain for the institution which controlled my life. After 365 days I didn't like it any more than I did the first day. "Out of 365 days," I pointed out to Joan, "I've been with you about 20. That's *sorry*!"

I continued, "By about noon tomorrow the bridge should have been replaced." The VC's destruction of the bridge across Thunder Road greatly inconvenienced us. "The old one couldn't be repaired so it was removed in four huge sections by a flying crane (helicopter)," I said. "We could watch the crane hover over the old bridge (less than two miles away) and then follow its course as it carried each section to the junkyard right outside our perimeter." Those flying cranes were capable of transporting a tank, so the bridge parts were easy for them. I drew a crude cartoon of the scene, accompanied by another sketch of a scene we recently witnessed of a Chinook under which was suspended "a slick which evidently had been shot down."

My September 16 letter noted something new and something "same-same." I had moved into a new bunker with almost 30 other people, and lifers were to wake us at 6 a.m. tomorrow so we can "have the joint 'clean' by formation." Three days later, I wrote that I was ill again.

The symptoms were "same as the other time—fever, soreness of body, and slight stomach pain." Two days earlier, I had been given three shots—cholera, plague, and typhoid, and I began feeling bad Thursday morning when I awoke, "so this may be an aftereffect," I said. "The medic found I had 103.4 degrees of fever, so he put me on bed rest, and gave me some other medicine. I do feel much better tonight, and I think I'll probably be completely recovered and back to work by morning, so don't worry about me."

The next night, September 20, I revealed, "I had a reaction this morning to the medicine I had been given [Compazine]. I had a convulsion, but the doctor gave me a shot [Atropine] and after about two hours I was ok. He said the shot would cause blurred vision temporarily and it has. I will not try to write anymore." By the time I wrote the following night, I was fully recovered. I had the morning off and due to rain had stayed inside. I made improvements to my area of the hooch, nailing ammo boxes to the wall for cabinets and cleaning out my footlocker. Although I had gotten two lenses and a leather carrying case from the Saigon PX, my camera body had still not come in. I had pre-shopped for Christmas through the PX catalog, and I offered to order from it most of our gifts we planned for family members. I knew Joan was busy with school, and I could get bargain prices. Everything would be shipped directly to her to wrap and distribute. My letter listed items and prices.

I began my September 22 letter "amused but sympathetic" reading of Joan's run-around during USC's registration day, a process I always recalled as "akin to a Chinese fire drill." As darkness fell on my bunker guard post, I ceased writing until the next morning. "What a night!" I remarked without elaboration. "About 1 hour of sleep!" I continued that I was pleased that class sizes Joan would be teaching were limited to 25, and that she herself would be in a poetry class taught by Writer-in-Residence James Dickey.

Writing the next day reflecting on plans for my future return home, I mentioned a recent letter from my father's friend Mr. Caldwell, offering Joan and me a welcome-home vacation in his mountain cabin at Hendersonville, North Carolina, my family's favorite spot for years. Joan and I had been exchanging letters too about a vacation offered us by her uncle and aunt Jak and Betty at their Holden Beach, North Carolina, summer house, her family's favorite spot. Both offers promised happy times to anticipate together. Since Hawaii was not possible for us, I had told Joan that for photographic interests I wanted to apply for R&R closer to me in Hong Kong. Dudley suggested we go together in November. Dud knew the clerk in Tan An who handled R&R allocations and would take care of arrangements. I made a list of required clothing and asked Joan to select from my items at home and to ask brother Byron to package them for mailing.

I wrote September 24 that I was glad that Joan was pleased keeping our Camden apartment and living in Columbia with her teaching, her coursework, her office, and "your pad at the Sloans' house." I joked that I was "a bit envious" but "just as excited and pleased as if it happened to me." I also mentioned feeling self-conscious that she had been showing some of my Vietnam photos to Mrs. Sloan, whose husband had been a noted photographer. Despite issues from shooting in low light from moving vehicles with low ASA film, I was taking shots anyway "because some may be once in a lifetime shots."

My Sunday, September 28, letter complained that mosquitoes had "almost devoured me whole" on Friday night guard duty. I repeated a joke making the rounds: The GI on guard heard two mosquitos buzzing overhead. "Should we eat him now or carry him home for later?" asked one. "Naw," replied the other, "We'd better eat him here. If we take him home for later, the bigger 'uns will take him away from us." I think I had heard that conversation more than a few times.

I wrote that Dudley had come from Tan An on the previous day with assignment to take photos of the battery's return from an air mobile operation. One thing I dreaded about those missions when we helped load and unload the Chinooks was a design feature of the choppers that sent the fiery exhausts of their turbocharged engines surging rearward like a blast furnace. It was grueling to have to cross that scorching exhaust. Dud and I "shot the bull" for a long time, I said. He admired and tested my new lenses on his Nikon. Today he returned to photograph a change-of-command ceremony for a new battery commander. We discussed our Hong Kong plans, and I changed the list of clothing for Joan to send me once I learned that it was rather chilly there the time of year we expected to go.

September 29 my letter-writing, describing favors for fellow camera enthusiasts and requesting information about old friends, was interrupted. "The lifers called four of us out for a detail—unloading a 2½ ton truck which was loaded with gravel," I said. "Of course it was 7 p.m. and already dark. Only convicts and EMs have to do things like shoveling gravel in the dark, and I kind of doubt if convicts do such things."

Another month began, but unlike October at home with crisp cool weather, it was still hot and wet in Vietnam. Only the name on the calendar indicated a change. I had bunker guard duty the first night of the new month and was trying to catch up on sleep the next morning. I mailed the Minolta camera I had been using to Rhonda on October 1 and sent him a letter telling him to expect it in about 10 days. Although my Nikkormat had not yet arrived, Rhonda's paying me back for what I had spent in the Minolta purchase and what it cost me to ship it to him, would help me with new purchases. That was the way I tried to help friends with personal

16. Penta Prime, Photography, Pestering

camera acquisitions—as a middleman looking for good deals they wanted and letting them reimburse the costs without my taking a profit. I thus was part of a network of camera friends looking out for each other, and I benefited by their reciprocal looking out for deals for me, too. Besides, I piled up a lot of photography knowledge and some new friends that way.

Lately I had made another friend with whom I had had some similar background unrelated to photography. John Nesavich, who was in Fire Direction Control, had graduated from college and had also been immediately drafted. He had completed BCT at Fort Leonard Wood and AIT at Fort Sill. Although he had been trained in artillery, he was assigned to infantry OCS at Fort Benning, as I would have been had I not opted out. His cycle had been told they would have desk jobs, but he learned just before the end of OCS that they were to be sent to Vietnam instead as infantry platoon leaders in the field. He and 15 others refused commissions and were sent to Vietnam as enlisted men. He had arrived in Charlie Battery a couple of months earlier.

One of the stories Nesavich told caused me to recall the incident of the civilian worker who had been caught with a handdrawn map of our camp in her possession. He and a buddy finished their shift at 0600 hours and emerged from FDC to go to breakfast. Having forgotten something, Nesavich turned and reentered the bunker. He heard an explosion. His buddy had tripped a booby trap that had

A mama-san with her children near the Vàm Cỏ River in Tan Tru Village.

been set by one of the women who washed laundry for the GIs. Nesavich stated, "The South Vietnamese soldiers came immediately and collected all the clothes washer women. I never saw them again."

On October 5 I wrote I was glad I had taken those impromptu shots in Tan Tru Village back in July because we no longer went to the village. "They meet the Vietnamese at the gate every morning and take them back to the gate every afternoon. So I very well may never go into a small Vietnamese village again," I said. Incidents like the worker with the map and booby trap explosions brought about tighter security measures that affected GIs and Vietnamese workers.

That same day the lifer did not get the mail again. There was rumor of a movement in Charlie Battery to "hang" several lifers, not a joking response to neglecting mail but meaning to expose misdeeds and bring judgment for them. I do not know what charges, if any, were ever brought, prosecuted, or convicted. When I arrived, I began hearing that some lifers there were involved in shady behavior, like sums stolen from the EM Club, sales of SP packs (each worth $100+ on the black market), and parts being stolen and sold from scrapped equipment. The alleged ringleader of nefarious deeds was said to be careful to sell only to Vietnamese who would not testify against him in court.

There were other incidents—tools that showed up in our

In Long An Province, a female gracefully walking in her traditional ao dai with a parasol for protection from the scorching sun.

motor pool stamped with initials that matched no one in our battery, as well as generators, lots of generators. Our battery was allocated an exact number—and power—of generators. Charlie Battery exceeded the number and the size. Some generators were hidden behind sandbag enclosures. One lifer had an air conditioner put in his office/bunker with a generator outside to power it. Like the joke of nuisance mosquitos, a joke had emerged about one sergeant. It went: "Two C Battery GIs were talking about how they looked forward to being out of the Army." One vows that he's going to keep tabs on a certain sarge because when he learns of his death, he intends to go to his grave and piss on it. The other GI replies, "Not me. Once I am out of this Army, I never want to stand in line again."

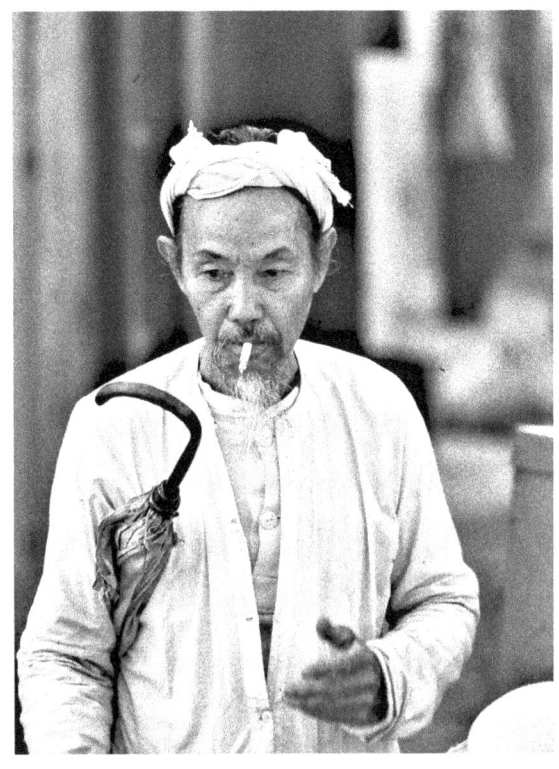

A papa-san wearing long johns beneath his long-sleeved shirt and carrying a parasol in the market of Tan Tru Village.

A "fragging" incident occurred which I distinctly remember but cannot place within a time frame because I did not mention it in letters. It happened before the lifer air-conditioned his hooch because at its back there was a small ventilation window about 20 inches square. One night someone attempted to lob a hand grenade into the window. Apparently, to avoid being spotted, the perpetrator did not get in front of the window and therefore threw the explosive at an angle. His aim was good but because of the thickness of the walls, the grenade hit the side of the window and bounced back outside where it exploded harmlessly on the ground. Our entire battery came to life, thinking Charlie had attacked, and everyone was on alert. The next morning there was a detail assigned to install a grate in the window. There were whispers among us about the culprit's identity, but to my knowledge, no one was ever accused or caught.

I wrote on an unspecified Monday in October that I might have to be a witness in a court-martial. "One night when I was on guard duty, one of the other guys on guard left the bunker and they found him in his hooch asleep. I think they're trying to charge him with being drunk and leaving the guard post. I had to submit a written statement today." I do not know what happened in regard to this, but I never did have to appear in a court-martial.

Knowing I had six more months to be in-country, I did not expect to be anywhere else but in Charlie Battery, although I revealed to Joan the glimmer of a chance for a change. About five days earlier when I was in Tan An, I had dropped by to visit Dudley. He introduced me to the NCO in charge of the Photo Lab, who said, after conversation and discussion, that he wanted me to come to Tan An and work with them. I told Joan, "He said that he would do all he could to get me there, but the decision is really up to my BC. I am going to talk to the BC tomorrow and ask him to let me transfer." I added, "I'm trying not to get my hopes up," although my head was spinning about how much I could learn about developing and printing, and how much I would enjoy the air-conditioned lab with first-class equipment as well as opportunities to take many photos. Plus, I mused, "I would not have to make formations or worry about details."

However, I also knew that "I'm the only person in the battery who knows anything about the logbooks." I cautioned Joan and myself, "If someone were to take over my job, I would have to teach him what to do. I can offer to remain until after the big inspection the end of the month." The next night I wrote, "Just as I had feared, when I talked with the BC that afternoon, he had said he could not let me go because he had no one else who could take over my job." In my letter, I could only comment in the Spanish of my real college major: *"Así es la vida."*

My October 22 letter gave Joan the planned R&R dates to Hong Kong—November 18 to 24. Four days later I wrote divulging two pieces of information unexpected to me. First, USC's football team was 5–1 overall and first in the Atlantic Coast Conference. The second was that I would *not* be going to Hong Kong next month. I said, "Another guy in my section has an R&R about the same time, so we can't both go. Since he has been in-country longer than I have, our section chief told me I'd have to wait." This was just the thing I had feared would happen had I planned to go to Hawaii to meet Joan. The next day I told her that Dudley was disappointed but said that he would try to get some stuff for me in Hong Kong when he went.

In an October 28 letter I responded with interest to news that Joan had gone to a "fire sale" at the Fort Jackson PX and bought a simple movie camera and projector. October 30 I revived an idea we had discussed before service intervened, which was living in Spain for a year. I had learned I could enroll in an MA program in Madrid, Toledo, or Salamanca, since I could use my VA education benefits anywhere as long as the institution was accredited. I suggested that Joan could teach or write, and "we might be able to swing it. I could probably sell some of the pictures that I'll take to make a bit of extra money. What do you think of the idea?" I had mailed her a box of old letters, negatives, slides, color prints and even a pair of chopsticks. While in Tan An, I had visited Dudley at the photo lab, and again I waxed on about camera equipment.

The first day of November I began my letter with a comment that I had watched TV for "about the third time since I've been here." It was an episode of *The High Chaparral* that I had seen a couple of times back in the States. "It brought memories of the many times you and I watched THC." The image of something as mundane as watching TV "with my wife in our home" prompted one and a half pages of sentiment and appreciation for "beautiful memories of the past 5½ years" and our "wonderful life together." I reproached the contemporary trend of people seeking to "'find themselves' or discover life through drugs. All I have to do to find myself or to know what life is all about is to turn to you. Through you I experience everything that is good, true and worthwhile. What better way to discover life than through a warm and beautiful person who appreciates life as you do."

The following day was Sunday and "I slept late—until almost 8 o'clock." A chaplain came and conducted services in the EM Club. "I attended," I wrote. "I had not been to any type of religious services since I was at Dong Tam when I first came in-country. Of course, this was the first time we've had services here since I came out of the field so I really had not had the opportunity to attend before. I think we'll be having worship services every Sunday, or at least more frequently." Despite the dearth of organized religious conventions, I had maintained a close association with God and had felt His presence and His protection.

I could not start my next letter until November 6. I assured Joan I had not forsaken her, explaining I had been "sent off on the spur-of-the-moment" Monday afternoon to Tan An airstrip for a TAERS clerk school at the Go Devil Academy. That was the new name for the Reliable Academy, lately transferred in the Dong Tam withdrawal under Vietnamization. I had not been told how long I would be there and had taken only the clothes I was wearing and my shaving kit, expecting to be there just one night. It turned out to be two days of instruction with "gross" accommodations like those at the Long Binh 90th Replacement Battalion when I first came in-country. I spent "two very miserable nights on a bare mattress, with neither fan nor mosquito net to protect me from wrath of the mosquitoes." Furthermore, as with military schools I had experienced, "I really learned nothing." Getting back yesterday, "Yep, you guessed it—I had guard duty last night."

The following night, November 7, I hurried through an incident that occurred right after I concluded the account of the TAERS school ordeal followed by bunker guard. "One of the lifers had run his truck into the paddy and gotten it stuck. They couldn't just abandon the truck so they picked ten of us to go out there and guard it so the VC wouldn't blow it up," I said. "So we spent the night out on the road staying up most of the night keeping watch. There was a lot of action going on around us but nothing that affected us directly. I guess we were actually safer there because the compound got mortared." That account in the letter I recognize as understated and incomplete, written not to alarm Joan. I recall that incident very clearly, as well as the details that follow.

There was apprehension when we were informed that the distribution run had not come back late in the afternoon with the 6 p.m. curfew looming. No U.S. military personnel were allowed outside the firebase unless part of an authorized night mission. Any Vietnamese nationals moving around outside their villages were considered probable enemy. The U.S. military controlled South Vietnam during the daylight hours, but the VC owned the night.

Most of us EMs had scant affection for the lifer who was out missing on the run as he was constantly involved in schemes that frequently enriched him and his cronies to our detriment. However, driving Sarge that day was a fellow well-liked by us. When we received word that the run had been ambushed by VC and had swerved off the road into a paddy about three or four miles from our firebase, several others and I quickly volunteered to hasten to their rescue. We grabbed weapons and ammo and rushed out onto Thunder Road as daylight faded into dusk. It was thought the ambush had been a typical "hit and run," in which a couple VC fired a few rounds, then quickly disappeared, the attackers intending to await darkness to close in on the vehicle and pilfer its contents.

We had had no idea what to expect when we arrived at the scene, but to our relief the vehicle was not under fire, nor did we encounter any resistance. I do not know what I expected other than to rescue our two comrades and return them to safety. However, upon our arrival, Sarge jumped into our rescue vehicle and ordered the rest of us to stay there with the mud-stuck deuce-and-a-half until we were relieved the next morning.

The Sergeant quickly departed, leaving the rest of us to spend a sleepless night on the paddy, tensing at each night sound as our imaginations loomed nearly as large as our prayers. Our prayers were answered as we met the dawn unscathed and were ourselves rescued. The disabled truck was extracted from its muddy resting place, and all returned to the firebase. We felt a sense of anger and betrayal but were thankful to have survived.

Soon after that event, three of C Battery's guns were sent on an air mobile operation in the Plain of Reeds, and those of us not on guns had to sleep in their three hooches to guard them. I had been assigned to sleep in 3rd section's hooch the night of November 7 and the following night I had guard duty again. Since Sunday night, I had not slept in my own bed when I wrote next that "it looks as if I won't be sleeping there again until Sunday night—if then." I told Joan that I went into Tan An and "just kind of goofed off," something I seldom was able to do. "I took care of your anniversary present today," I said. "You should get it exactly on December 18th so if possible stick around the apartment." I expected that about that time she would be leaving Columbia and returning to Camden for the holidays.

My November 10 letter began like most—sentiments about how much I missed Joan. There had been "too many nights without you, too many nights that I've had to sleep with my rifle in my arms instead of my wife." Things were pretty tense, with increased enemy activity "around this area and all over Vietnam." We had been on special alerts at night due to suspicion that another enemy offensive was in the making. We were expecting "a mortar attack/ground attack/sapper attack tonight and have doubled guards, special guards, etc. I have to guard our hooch from 2–6 a.m." I wrote that it was 11 p.m. and I guessed I should get some sleep, "but I don't really think I can sleep although I am tired." Half of our battery was still in the Plain of Reeds. That meant that the half remaining in the area had to do the same amount of work expected as if all were there.

On November 14, I reported that the VC had blown up another bridge on Thunder Road the day before yesterday, "so once again we're isolated. Supplies must be flown in by chopper. The bridge Charles destroyed this time was longer than the other and will take 10–15 days to replace." The day after the sabotage, Army engineers constructed a temporary pedestrian pontoon bridge for use by the locals and us. We GIs, perhaps half a dozen, would ride in a deuce-and-a-half from our compound to the bridge and meet another truck bringing supplies from Tan An. We would walk across the pontoon bridge, get an armload, and recross the river to load our truck. It was physically demanding—and awkward—work. The pontoon was unsteady, and the swift-moving water made it even more precarious. We did not eagerly anticipate repetitive days of that detail.

While I may have been mistaken thinking the monsoon rains were subsiding, reports that enemy activity was increasing appeared to be accurate. In addition to the bridge demolition, "A Co. 2/60 (the one I had been with as RTO) killed 11 enemy about two miles from here today. This is the largest number of enemy to be killed by any company in this battalion in the last four or five months. Chuck is definitely in the vicinity, and I think he will make his appearance known more frequently."

I wrote a long letter November 15 reacting to news that Joan's brother Rob on the DMZ in Korea might get home for leave in time for Christmas. I sincerely hoped for them, "Maybe this Christmas will be just like Christmas used to be before you met me—with all your family at home."

17

Shorthanded on the Guns

*"Don't know ... if I'm a clerk
or a cannoneer"*

WITH CHRISTMAS A LITTLE MORE THAN A MONTH AWAY, my November 15 letter shifted to more pleasant topics like gift items that Joan told me had begun to arrive at home. I had requested she send nothing to me, but I knew "Lulu would appreciate some doggie chews" and she could send "some flea powder, too," for her and her new puppies, four males and four females. To Joan's suggestion about sending some gifts for the local children, I replied in the negative, adding, "They don't celebrate Christmas as we do and besides, I seldom go to the village or anywhere anymore."

I concluded with a telling remark: "It is after 11 p.m. and although tomorrow is Sunday I think I'll be quite busy. We're so shorthanded on the guns right now that when they have a fire mission everyone has to help out, so I don't know from one moment until the next if I'm a clerk or a cannoneer these days." One thing that was unchanged was the conduct of—and our disdain for—the lifer who, I growled on November 17, "didn't bring the mail again today."

If my recent observation of dust and no rain for several days suggested that the monsoon was ending, that thought was washed away over the next days. "I had guard duty last night and it rained," I wrote on November 19. "Actually, it began raining about 4 p.m. and continued until about 10 p.m. It began raining again this afternoon about 4 and rained until about 8." Dudley had gone to Hong Kong and was to bring me a Nikkormat if he could find one, so I hoped to resume my photo-taking again in a week or so. Without the Minolta I had sold and sent to Rhonda and with no arrival yet of the Nikkormat I had ordered, I had lenses in need of a camera! I was spending spare time reading, and Nesavich was teaching me to play chess. Anytime the first sergeant would see us playing, he would sneer "*college boys*" as he passed by.

I announced good news November 21: "The bridge has been rebuilt

Glen digging to drain monsoon rainwater from under his TAERS office, as barrels of excrement from the latrine at left burn in background (Ernest Brown).

and the road is once again open." Within a week I would try to go to Tan An to see Dudley and find out if he was able to get a camera for me. "If he did, expect the slides to begin pouring in 'cause the kid will be back in business again." I looked forward to using my telephoto lens to capture shots that I had been unable to get when I had just the 58 mm lens on the Minolta I sold Rhonda. Resuming my idea of going to study in Spain, I thought I would seek guidance from a friend and former USC professor from Cadiz, still at USC. Joan had run into him on campus recently. We might want to consider an institution on the Mediterranean coast rather than in Madrid, I suggested. Former interests still came to mind.

The next day, "just a normal day in the Nam," I remarked on the number of people leaving this battery. "We lost three today and about 30 more will go home between now and the end of December. It will be good to get some new guys in. We have one new guy in maintenance who just came in-country—he only has about 350 days to go." Sunday, November 23, was my 26th birthday. After Saturday night guard duty, I observed my birthday sleeping in until nearly 2 p.m. I was cheerful because my alma mater USC defeated archrival Clemson 27–13 to win the ACC football championship with a 6–0 conference mark. Even without being able to hear games themselves, just hearing sports scores, kept minds connected with the world.

I had guard duty the night before Thanksgiving, November 26, and slept the next morning. Despite the fact that Joan and I had to be apart, I said "I'll be most reverent and thankful for the blessings we have been given, for our wonderful past, and for an even happier future." By now, another change was in the air. My November 27 letter stated that I had to wear a field jacket on guard duty, and that a guy who leaves in eight days said this was "the coolest weather he's seen over here." Having become accustomed to 90 to 100+ temperatures, it felt "strange to find myself in 75° weather."

About Dudley and his R&R, I had bad news about his attempts to make photography purchases for me. He had been unable to cash my money orders anywhere, even the First National Bank of Hong Kong. They required identification from both him and me. Furthermore, he had been unable to find exactly what I wanted. I was becoming accustomed to responding "*Así es la vida.*"

Friday, November 28, I went to Tan An. There Dudley and I went to the post office and together cashed the money orders I had given him, so that "at least I have the money now even if I don't have a camera." I was able to see the equipment he purchased in Hong Kong. "It was beautiful," I said, a Nikon Photomic FTN, three lenses, a flash, case, and filters. I had really lost interest in taking an R&R, but now I realized I would have to go myself in order to get the camera gear I wanted. I vacillated between going to Hong Kong or to Tokyo, Japan, since photo equipment was slightly less expensive in the latter, although everything else was more expensive.

On December 2 I began a lengthy letter to Joan: "I was interested in your comments about the observations other people have concerning Vietnam and the situation here." As an instructor of freshman English, Joan had a small office with regular times for student conferences, a process of teaching composition. Students who went there to talk to "Mrs. Inabinet" about their essays would see a small, framed photo of me on her desk. Typically, they assumed I was a professor or a grad student, the usual situation of married female staffers. A student being told that I was serving in Vietnam was typically surprised since campuses were "anti-war" in popular attitude, and might utter something to the effect, "I don't know *anyone* in Vietnam." One varied that response, "I don't know anybody who *knows* anyone in Vietnam." Some of her students were involved in protests on campus, often kids following a crowd without understanding or experience, she said, so signs complaining about dorm rules and cafeteria food popped up amid those of more serious sentiments. The rest of my letter was essentially a treatise about the impact of U.S. public opinion not only upon political and military policy, but also on the policies and behavior of the enemy both at the negotiating table and on the battlefield.

That same day I wrote another letter describing a local mission for which I had volunteered. For this purpose five other guys and I from C Battery went to Tan An and spent the night. At 8 a.m., Sunday, December 30, along with men on four other trucks from the battalion, we picked up 50 children from a Catholic orphanage in Tan An and took them to Saigon on a sightseeing trip and picnic with us. The children wore "Sunday best," and Vietnamese interpreters were our guides.

Glen lifting an orphan into an M35 truck during the battalion-sponsored picnic in Saigon December 30, 1969 (Lee Dudley).

All of us enjoyed the day. We passed slowly by the stately Presidential Palace, which "is really something to see." We stopped by one park where some Vietnamese Boy Scouts were camping, and another park named for John Kennedy, adjacent to an old Catholic church. We visited an ornate Buddhist temple, scented with distinctive incense. We spent the bulk of our time, three hours, at the Saigon Zoo, taking the kids around to see exotic animals. We returned the children to the orphanage at 6 p.m., spent the night in Tan An, and

17. Shorthanded on the Guns

Glen in charge of two orphans at the Saigon Zoo during the December 30 trip (Lee Dudley).

returned to Tan Tru about 11:30 the next morning. I was glad to have had this positive experience.

My letter December 3 was in quite a different tone, reporting "a bit of action here. Three VC sappers were detected trying to enter our compound and were killed trying to crawl through the barbed wire. We were put on 50% alert after that, so I did not get to sleep until after 3:30 this morning." Writing December 7, on Pearl Harbor Day and also the day before Joan's birthday, I explained I had been unable to write much lately, having had guard duty "three nights out of the past six—Monday, Thursday, and again last night." I commented on the article about the Mai Lai Massacre of March 1968 that I had read about in *Time* magazine, which had

Gates of the Presidential Palace in Saigon, by which Glen's truck of zoo-bound orphans passed, and through which NVA tanks crashed April 30, 1975, during the fall of Saigon.

brought forth reports about brutal actions in an enemy village for which now a lieutenant named Calley was facing charges. I had not witnessed any incidents that bad, I said, but I had seen "some sick minds in positions of authority in the military." While acknowledging that the enemy had been guilty of greater atrocities than My Lai, the United States had historically held itself to a higher standard. Revelations such as those at Mai Lai were alarming in perspective.

    My letter the following day wished Joan a happy birthday and told her I had been thinking of her all day "as always." My day had not been special, but rather a normal Monday complete with THE pill although "lifers are going to get us up in the middle of the night to play games." I closed the brief letter to try to get some sleep.

December 10 my letter mentioned Christmas food packages I had received from family and friends, commenting, "I swear I'll be a fat pig when I come home." I had also received a Christmas card from Vernon McGuffy, the supply clerk who had lived in our hooch. Having left Vietnam for California three weeks ago, he wrote that he was doubly happy—out of the Army and married. I had watched part of a movie, *The Heart Is a Lonely Hunter*, enjoyed what I saw, and thinking Joan would like it, suggested we watch it after I came home.

Describing "a new innovation in psychological warfare," I enclosed in my December 12 letter a white stock card, approximately the size of a playing card, with the profile of a red devil's head imprinted with "GO" in black. "Greetings" is printed at the top, and "GO DEVILS" at the bottom. The other side reads, in English first and then in Vietnamese, *"FRIENDS RETURN TO THE GOVERNMENT BEFORE THIS HAPPENS TO YOU."* The 2/60 Infantry here, known as the Go Devils, were using those cards, not a practice I knew of when I was RTO with them. "When they kill an enemy," I said, "they place one of these cards in the victim's mouth and leave the body for the victim's confederates to find."

I alerted Joan in my December 14 letter that she might be mailed a money order from James Palmer, "one of my best friends here." I was sending Joan money, but Jim was going into Tan An and would purchase the order for me, as it could be done only at a post office. I wrote her the following account about Palmer, the stuff of which movies are made: "He was in the army and came to Vietnam a couple of years ago. While here he met a Vietnamese girl, and they fell in love. He left Vietnam with his service over. Shortly afterward he flew to Saigon to try to get married, but there was too much red tape involved, so after several fruitless days in Saigon, he went back to the USA. His only hope was to come back to Vietnam as a GI and try to get all the details worked out, so he reenlisted. He has gone through one ordeal after another, but finally love triumphed, and he and Mai got married. After that, there were many obstacles, but finally she left Vietnam last Sunday for Hawaii, where Palmer's mother had flown to meet her. In two more months, he will go home, and they will be together."

On December 15 I responded to Joan's news that her brother Rob, leaving Korea, had requested duty in Vietnam rather than reassignment in the States, as his family had hoped he would accept. "I'm sorry to hear about Rob," I said, "but I guess he wants to come here so don't worry about it. He would probably have requested Vietnam after he reported to Fort Benning anyway. He has to see it for himself so let it go at that. I think that Rob still thinks that war is exciting and glorious. There's nothing glorious about this place. I think he'll be disappointed at what he finds here unless he happens to get in an exceptionally good unit. Of course, if he is a sergeant, it won't be quite as bad. Anyway, I doubt that he will spend a full year over here if talks of more withdrawal materialize." I concluded, "I know you and your family are disappointed in this change of plans, but it's what he wants, so accept it."

I began my December 16 letter hoping Joan would relax when she got out for school holidays in three days. Then I wrote about camera prices in Japan and in Hong Kong. Later, writing by flashlight, I reported "excitement" here: "One of our generators and all of our supply of diesel fuel and gasoline caught on fire, and the whole motor pool—except for the office where I work—was destroyed."

Two days later on December 18, our wedding anniversary, I wrote Joan an anniversary card and a letter. I proclaimed that the past three years (Army time excluded) had been "the most wonderful of my life … and I am deeply honored to be your husband." The following day's letter reminisced about many of our shared memories. "I'll be thinking about you there in our apartment during Christmas and New Year, and I'll be wishing I were there with you. I can hardly wait for 118 more days to go by." My December 21 letter thanked her for anniversary and Christmas cards she had sent me, and also for "something else which said *do not open until Christmas*, so I shall not—although I must admit I'm curious."

As I wrote my letter December 23, I imagined Joan at her folks' house, warming by the wood-burning fireplace in the room with their Christmas tree. I knew they all were happy that Rob was coming home and inquired about the time of the family Christmas party. The Armed Forces Radio Network was "playing quite a bit of Christmas music and I have the tree and holly that you sent me displayed, but I really can't get in a Christmas mood. The only thing I have to look forward to this year is for Christmas to pass quickly, and for 1970 to get in gear. The sooner April gets here the better I will like it." On December 24 I wrote, "On this Christmas Eve '69, I pledge eternal love and devotion to you. I am yours and forever will be. Know that my thoughts, prayers, and love go with you."

The following day's letter stated, "I think it will make you happy to know that even though we are apart, even though the circumstances are such that they are, I awoke bright and early this morning (4:45 to be exact) and opened my two gifts with the same anticipation that I've always had on Christmas morning." I commented, "I have been cheerful today because of the knowledge that you are home—in our house, in your folks' house, and possibly with my folks—observing Christmas much in the same way we have observed it since our first Christmas as husband and wife in 1966."

The day after Christmas, I mused that when I arrived in Vietnam, I felt there were three large challenges to go through and I dreaded all of them for varied reasons—monsoon season, Christmas, and Tet. Two were

17. Shorthanded on the Guns

past, leaving only one to go—Tet, the Vietnamese New Year observed for five to seven days about the first of February, a period which since 1968 had been synonymous with enhanced offensive action of the enemy.

I had arrived in Vietnam shortly after the 1969 Tet offensive, less deadly than the previous year, but still resulting in 1,140 Americans and 1,500 South Vietnamese killed during three weeks of fighting. I hoped predictions I had heard would be true, that this year's Tet would be mild. However, since the VC had tried to overrun our fire support base here last year, I did not intend to take Tet lightly. I assured Joan, "I will keep my M16 close at hand." December 27 found me hearing rumors about "which and when" divisions were to be withdrawn from Vietnam, and I could not help wondering how various withdrawals would affect my homegoing. Having found that rumors in the Army were as endemic to military life as details and harassment, I also knew rumors were often unfounded. All I could do was wait and see.

My last letter of 1969 responded to Joan's delight with the set of rose-patterned china dinnerware I had sent her to mix and match with the formal china patterns and crystal of our wedding presents. I had ordered it from the military Pacific Exchange's PACEX catalog, and the set had been shipped home, so I had not seen it. On New Year's Eve, Jak and Betty were departing from the USA upon an ambitious, self-directed, 90-day around-the-world trip, sightseeing and taking photographs to be published in *The State* newspaper with Jak's inimical art and storytelling. Joan passed on to him the information from me that, with his passport, he could purchase camera equipment less expensively in Japan than in Hong Kong.

18

Tet 1970, a Two-digit Midget

"We were keeping vigilant"

MY FIRST FEW LETTERS IN 1970 WERE BRIEF IN LENGTH and sparse on details about events in Charlie Battery or in Vietnam in general. I was getting excited about going to Hong Kong and was making arrangements for my R&R. By January 6 I was a "two-digit midget," the term for a short-timer with fewer than 100 days left in-country. The next day I went to Tan An to mail Joan a box of letters for safekeeping and a small pair of stereo speakers I had purchased from a guy in my hooch. In Tan An Dudley "filled me in on where to stay, where to shop, what to look for, and what to look *out* for in Hong Kong."

While speculating about the time frame for processing out and arriving home at the end of my Vietnam service, I had learned an important regulation. "From the day I 'ETS' I have *five* days in which to re-register with my draft board, give them my separation papers, and get reclassified," I told Joan. "If I don't register with the board within five days, I could be fined, imprisoned, and/or recalled to active duty." I ended that with an emphatic "*NO!!*"

My January 11 letter stated that we had "moved our maintenance shop office into another building, for the third time since I've been here." A number of adjustments had been made in the past month since the motor pool had been destroyed by fire. I remember no changes made to my office, which had stayed where it was. I reported, "Today we had a change-of-command ceremony. We have a new battery commander, the fourth one since I've been here." I also stated a fact of greater personal relevance: "Today I begin my 11th month in Vietnam."

The next night, January 12, I had relayed other important news. There was the official announcement that my brigade was *not* scheduled to be withdrawn. Consequently, I would remain in-country through my extended date and indeed I could "ETS." GI slang had converted into a verb the name of the status for which I aimed. There were two acronyms for personnel leaving Vietnam—DEROS and ETS. The former (Date Estimated Return from Overseas) applied to those returning stateside with time remaining in service. The latter (Expiration Term of Service) indicated those, like me, who were going home and getting out.

On the subject of leaving, I was scheduled in one week to leave the battery for R&R. I would fly to Hong Kong, only a one and one-half hour flight from Saigon's Tan Son Nhut Air Base. When I returned from R&R, January would almost be over. Although February would include Tet, I said, "I will be glad to see it come and go (especially *go*). Thank goodness it has only 28 days."

I mentioned having been surprised by a recently arrived gift from stateside buddy Bush Williams. I had received "four sleeves of Kool Aid," popular in various flavors at home and in Nam for making a soft drink out of water. Kool Aid was manufactured by General Foods, the corporation that employed him. I quipped, "I guess he blitzed it for free, and I appreciate it, but gosh—288 packages (each one flavoring two quarts of water). I hope he doesn't expect me to drink it all." I did enjoy handing out the packages to everyone who wanted one.

My January 13 letter was brief for serious reasons. I was extremely tired because "Last night we had to go out on the guns at 11 p.m. and hump ammo. Then again this morning early we had to do it again. All in all, the guns fired almost 1,400 rounds on one fire mission and at one target. They were supposed to be firing at an NVA Regiment headquarters. I hope they're mistaken, because if that's true then that means there is an NVA Regiment (about 1,500 men) within 7 miles of our camp. And with Tet less than a month away, this is not a pleasant thought." I mentioned that I had guard duty the next night also.

The intensive firing apparently stifled retaliation for the time. Brief letters the next few days mentioned regular duties and planning for upcoming R&R, with a sad report made in my January 15 letter on a recent event. "There were three female dogs in the battery, and two of them (not Lulu) were pregnant. The lifers decided we had too many dogs so they took all three females up to Saigon and put them out. We still have Lulu's two pups, both males. They're really cute but they're growing too fast." I followed with a statement of looking forward to being home, away from living under decisions made by the lifers.

Although January 18 was a Sunday, I said, "Had there not been a calendar around I could have sworn that today was a Monday." I had finished several reports in addition to carrying out other work requirements, and that night I packed and was ready to leave for R&R. "I think I'm looking forward to taking a hot bath more than anything else," I wrote. "It has indeed been a long time since I've felt clean." I lamented that I had not received mail the past two days and I would have none until after I returned—some 10 days away. However, I was really looking forward to the trip ahead.

My travel orders directed me to report on Monday, January 19, to Go Devil Academy in Tan An, and from there on January 20 to transient Camp Alpha at Saigon's Tan Son Nhut Air Base. I vividly recall being among several GIs walking into the largest restroom I had seen since Oakland. Like little children, we moved from urinal to urinal, pulling the flush levers and exclaiming, "Wow!"

I likewise remember taking my first hot shower there in more than 10 months. I watched in amazement as soap and hot water sent my wonderful suntan down the drain. About the overnight sleeping quarters and rations at Tan Son Nhut, I remember nothing, but I clearly recall being lined up and thoroughly frisked before being allowed to board the plane to Hong Kong. None of the persons on the plane were people I knew.

On thin stationery imprinted "The Grand Hotel, Carnarvon Road, Kowloon, H.K." and dated by me January 22, I stated: "Here I am in exotic Hong Kong. We left Saigon yesterday at 4:30 and arrived here at 6:30." A GI I met from Minnesota, Mike Smith, and I had walked around the streets and explored last night. I wrote excitedly, "There must be a million camera stores within four blocks of our hotel. (Well, gee, Joan, I didn't count them all. Maybe there are only about 800,000.)" The next morning, instead of writing "FREE" as usual on my letters, on an airmail Grand Hotel envelope, I attached an 18¢ Andrew Jackson stamp and mailed it as I set out on a shopping expedition, beginning with the China Fleet Club.

The next night I reported, "I bought a Nikomat (different spelling from the identical Nikkomat intended for export) and have been taking lots of slides and prints." It was good having a working and familiar camera back in my hands again. Mike and I were going on a tour of H.K. Island tomorrow morning, I said. "We got a package deal of 3 tours for $45 Hong Kong (about U.S. $7.50)." I had found expenses "quite moderate" and most hotels, restaurants, and clubs "very plush, complete with doormen, etc." I was enjoying H.K. but missed Joan immensely. I told her, "This is really the most fantastic place I've ever visited and I'm resigning myself to come back with you someday."

Sunday morning, January 25, I wrote that yesterday's tour was "very interesting but really a bit too long—4½ hours." We still had two tours remaining but might opt for shorter ones (about 2½ hours each). We had eaten a variety of fish, pork, rice, and vegetables last night and I had managed using chopsticks "with some difficulty." I was experiencing difficulty sleeping. I guessed that "the bed is too comfortable or something. I suppose when I come home I'll have to sleep on the floor for a while until I learn to be a human again." I mentioned another problem: "I had a bad nightmare last night. I thought I was still in VN and we were undergoing a bad mortar attack." I hoped I was not having premonitions of Tet next month.

I was disappointed trying to telephone Joan about 10:15 Sunday night, 9:30 Sunday morning at home. She was on semester break and I thought she would likely be at our apartment. When I got no answer, I did not try again, as I had no way of knowing whether she might be at the home of her folks, my folks, the Sloans, or maybe elsewhere. Each separate call required a lengthy hassle. There had been only one other occasion when I was in Vietnam that I had had a possibility of speaking to her. I had gone to Dong Tam and found a Military Auxiliary Radio System (MARS) setup. From the station there, one would speak into a phone, and the call would be relayed by volunteer Ham Radio operators across the globe until the call reached its intended recipient. I got in a line of men waiting to make a call. When there were only two guys ahead of me, I was notified that my ride was ready to leave. I had no choice but to leave the line.

I wrote two postcards Sunday. The one picturing a panorama of Hong Kong I addressed to our apartment and mentioned "outstanding food." The other, portraying junks in the harbor, I addressed to her Columbia pad, describing our misty tour of Victoria. The weather was quite cool, misty, or foggy much of the time I was there. Taking the tram to Victoria Peak, I found the famous breathtaking view obscured by fog.

On January 27 I arrived back at Tan Son Nhut Air Base about 8:30 in the morning. "I had a rather hectic day trying to get a ride," but I eventually reached Charlie Battery at 5 p.m. I wrote the next day, "I found boo-coo mail awaiting me" and spent the bulk of the evening reading, unpacking, and "trying to get squared away." I was excited about getting short, and I told Joan, "After catching a glimpse of the outside world, I don't know if I'll be able to take 77 more days ... '77 and I'll be in heaven.'"

The night of January 29 I wrote a 12-page letter. As promised, I provided details about R&R: It was "really great to get away" from Vietnam, but harsh reality to have to return. Temperatures in H.K. were "in the 50s and 60s, and even with my wool clothing I was cold—particularly on the cruises." We took a sunset cruise which took us by the Aberdeen fishing village, where thousands of people were living on junks. We ate an eight-course meal at one of the world's renowned floating restaurants. My hotel was "plush and the service was extraordinary." I could not believe the number of places to shop. I had purchased the camera and a 200 mm lens, filters, and a strobe, souvenirs for Joan's and my families, and "maybe some little thing for my sweet wife." I did not tell her about the beautiful strand of Mikimoto pearls that I bought at Lane Crawford and planned to give her when I returned home. I did tell her I had purchased "a 150-watt stereo receiver which is now on the way to #6 Park Ct. Apts.," a crate which I requested her not to open until I returned.

Part of my long letter reported that on my return from R&R, I found waiting a postcard from Rob giving me his APO address in Vietnam. He was in Phu Bai. My friend Palmer told me that when he was in Nam the first time, his unit had spent some time in Phu Bai, which was just south of Hue. When I wrote Joan, I said that "Rob's impressions of Nam will be quite different from mine; there is a world of difference between where he is and the Delta—not just the terrain, but the people and the war."

Palmer would be leaving Vietnam for home in 15 days. His orders were for Fort Benning, but he was going to try to get reassigned in the area of Washington, D.C., mainly because of the large number of Vietnamese living there. He thought it would be better for his wife, who was already in the States with his mother. I told Joan, "I'll really miss him.... He and I have been quite good friends ever since I came out of the field."

When I wrote Joan on February 4, I had been in Vietnam 331 days and had 70 days—quiet ones, I hoped—to go. "The last big obstacle begins tomorrow—Tet. And wouldn't you know, I have guard duty tomorrow night.... Once I get through Tet *maybe* all will be downhill."

I reported the next morning, "Tet has begun! Everything was quiet last night and I hope it will continue that way." Palmer and I had watched Tennessee Williams's *The Glass Menagerie*, one of Joan's favorite dramas. I planned to box my civvies and some other things to send home so I would have less to carry through "all the out-processing procedures" coming home. Another practical matter was stirring in my head. "Joan, I have to get a job when I get home but I really don't know what," I wrote. "There will be no more money coming in so I will have to find employment almost immediately so we will be able to pay the rent and eat." We needed to decide whether Joan would attend summer classes, or work on her M.A. thesis, and whether I should seek employment in Camden or Columbia while she was finishing her degree. I am sure many more practical concerns were also in my mind after months of dreaming of possibilities when I was "free."

On February 10 I sent Joan a "short timer's calendar" to help her count down the days until I came home. I had one that I marked faithfully. I had gone to Tan An yesterday and mailed at the airstrip post office my civvies and the lenses I bought for Rhonda and for Summers' father. I also saw Dudley. When I was on R&R, he had taken a 7-day leave to Tokyo where he bought "a beautiful 500 mm Nikkor mirror reflex lens ($180) that

18. Tet 1970, a Two-digit Midget

I would love to have." Joan had sent me Valentine cookies, "quite good." I had been unable to find a "store-bought" card so I had to be resourceful and fabricate one.

Two days later I again addressed my future plans: "I really don't know what I want to do when I return and this concerns me greatly. I would like to return to school for some courses, and I would like to study photography, but these things will come later. What I *must* do immediately when I get back is find a job. Once I out-process at Oakland, my income and your allotment will cease." The money I had been saving each month totaled $1,300 and was intended to be used as a down payment on a house or a piece of property. If I left it in the account an additional 90 days after I returned, it would draw interest at the rate of 10 percent compounded quarterly. However, if we needed money for rent and groceries, I would soon need to notify the authorities in writing several weeks before my ETS in order to withdraw the funds immediately, but without interest.

While I was concerned for our future, the battery's brass was concerned about tomorrow. Some colonel was scheduled to come for a 30-minute visit, "and the lifers have gone completely wild. Even I can't believe the extremes to which they are going." My friend Palmer would miss that affair as he was leaving tomorrow, with about 18 months of Army life to put up with when he returned to the States.

On February 15 I reported that I was back on starlight scope duty for 1½ hours every night and would not pull bunker guard anymore. I preferred the latter because it tied up only two nights per week. I announced, "Tomorrow I have eight (yep, count 'em) weeks left in Charlie Battery. Eight weeks from tomorrow I shall leave Tan Tru. Fifty-nine days left in Vietnam. I'm coming home. Wheeee—" here I interrupted my writing for duty.

Returning from starlight scope guard, I resumed my letter. Before the colonel's visit, "the BC and 1st Sgt. had asked me to take pictures of this blessed event. I rapidly assessed the situation and replied, 'OK, if you'll let me take them in to the photo lab (Tan An) to have them developed.' They agreed." My account continued, "So I shot a roll of Tri-X of the lifers and went in that afternoon to Tan An. Dud had gone to Saigon, but one of the other guys showed me how to develop the negatives so I did that. I had to leave about 4 p.m. so that's as far as I got. However, I went back yesterday about 2 p.m. and worked in the darkroom until 8:30 p.m.—printing first a contact sheet and then making 8 × 10 prints (24 of them)."

After a break at the EM Club, I returned to the lab and developed negatives of two more rolls of Tri-X, this time my own, and made contact sheets. I worked until 11 p.m. and spent the night there, returning to C Battery about 11:00 the next morning. I was well pleased with my first efforts in the darkroom and so were the lifers. They wanted more prints made, "so I know I'll be going again soon, and from the way the BC talked I may be doing this again. I really enjoyed the break from my normal routine, and the experience will prove to be invaluable." I intended to have a darkroom in our house when I got home.

I provided Joan an image of the recent event: "You really would have cracked up at the sight of me covering the colonel's visit—my Nikomat complete with strobe in one hand (I took some shots of them inside) and the BC's Asihi Pentax Spotmatic (he wanted me to take some slides for him) hanging around my neck." Had it not been for my uniform, I might have passed for a photographer for the AP or UPI. I had permission to go to the photo lab tomorrow to process and print the lifer film. While there, I planned to do some of my own. Other than taking photos (and my new interest in printing them), I was enjoying reading. I had read James A. Michener's *Sayonara* last weekend. I had seen the movie long ago, but I really enjoyed Michener's writing style.

After spending the entire day Monday in the photo lab, I returned the next day, February 17, "developing some film for the battery and some for myself." The only printing I did was making a contact sheet. Last night I had taken some shots of our battery's Fire Direction Control Center. "Battalion wanted photos of the set up there." I did not know who at the battalion level had requested this. Neither did I care. I was just happy to be able to pursue my interest in photography and, as a bonus, get away from C Battery for a few hours. I was not getting out of all my duties, however. I had starlight watch that night at 11:00.

On February 18 I stated that I had not written anything yet about My Tho "because I didn't want to alarm you." I thought Joan would recognize the name if it appeared in the media, and it might cause her worry. There had been major enemy action at My Tho, near Dong Tam, causing deaths and severe damage. I did not know if the news media in the USA had covered it. Although we were only 10–15 miles from My Tho, I assured her "we've had no trouble here," adding, "the ARVNs are more dangerous than the VC. They (ARVNs) 'erroneously' dropped several 105 mm howitzer rounds on Bien Hoa Air Base which killed two Americans and wounded 13." Although it was relatively quiet in our area, it was still Tet, and we were keeping vigilant. Two guys were leaving tomorrow "so we who remain are pulling 1 hr. 45 min. starlight guard shifts now."

I was keeping busy as "unofficial battery photographer." I took photos February 19 of an ARVN captain who came to our battery with some other ARVNs "to observe some of our techniques." I took more photos in the afternoon, accompanying the BC to the ARVN compound near here. "Our battery is supposed to work with them as part of the Vietnamization program," I explained. I expected that I would go to the photo lab in a few days to process the film. "I'll try to slip in a few personal prints while I'm at it."

I had begun reading another interesting book, Alice Ekert-Rotholz's *The Time of the Dragons*, translated by Richard and Clara Winston. I finished it three days later, at 479 pages "the longest book I have read in quite some time." The battery had quite a library of books sent in care packages from home or from our SP packs.

On February 23 I went to Tan An "and developed the negatives for some more lifer pictures." Dudley was fine, and very happy to be going home in 15 days. He would ETS. "Had I not extended I would be leaving Nam one day before he does or 14 days from now but I wouldn't be ETSing."

I am not sure whether the battery commander or the battalion commander had the initial idea to send me out to photograph in-field action, but both told me afterward they were "very pleased" with the results. On February 25 Charlie Battery embarked "on a 10-day air-mobile operation to a place with the distinctive name of VC Island, located way out in the Plain of Reeds near the Cambodian border. They have the task of slowing the infiltration of men and supplies from North Vietnam and Cambodia via the Ho Chi Minh Trail." This was Operation Chickamauga.

I was sent out Wednesday, the first day, on the first chopper with the advanced party in order to photograph steps of the entire operation. I was to be out two days and then return for what I called "much work and fun" in the photo lab in Tan An.

On this type of maneuver in such a remote area, a perimeter had to be established, with guards and claymores placed. This the advanced party must do before Chinooks would be allowed to bring in the howitzers and ammo. Back at our compound, we had a relatively secure perimeter which had been established over time, as well as the support of the infantry units there. I vividly remember photographing the unloading of Chinooks and the setting up of the guns, with men scurrying all around. Once everything was in place, I photographed the subsequent activity of fire missions. Those processes being familiar to me, I knew the significance of individual steps and where to aim my camera.

When my two days of filming were up, my ride back to the compound was on a LOH. When I was in the field, I had observed this type of light observation helicopter overhead spotting the enemy position in order for us to call in artillery fire or an airstrike. I learned more inside the loach. It could fly 175 mph and was nimble and capable of maneuvers impossible for other aircraft. At other times, the craft would ferry around high-ranking officers. Any observers that day surely imagined that the person sitting in the back seat being flown around was a special dignitary—rather than just me, merely a specialist.

The afternoon that I returned to Charlie Battery, I was detailed to remove the claymores in front of the bunker so that we could burn the grass there. According to intelligence reports, we were supposed to be hit and were on alert since "an NVA officer was captured with papers which stated that Tan Tru was the #1 target

A peace sign being flashed by the pilot as a Chinook readies to head air mobile "Operation Chickamauga" to establish a firebase on VC Island in the Plain of Reeds, its M60 machine gun protruding and a 105 mm howitzer and equipment ready to be attached.

To set up the firebase, a Chinook lowering a firing platform for artillerymen to level.

18. Tet 1970, a Two-digit Midget

The Chinook setting a 105 mm howitzer onto a leveled firing platform.

for an attack." Fortunately, the predicted attack did not materialize. We remained on alert but carried on as usual.

February, the shortest month, had truly dragged but finally had run

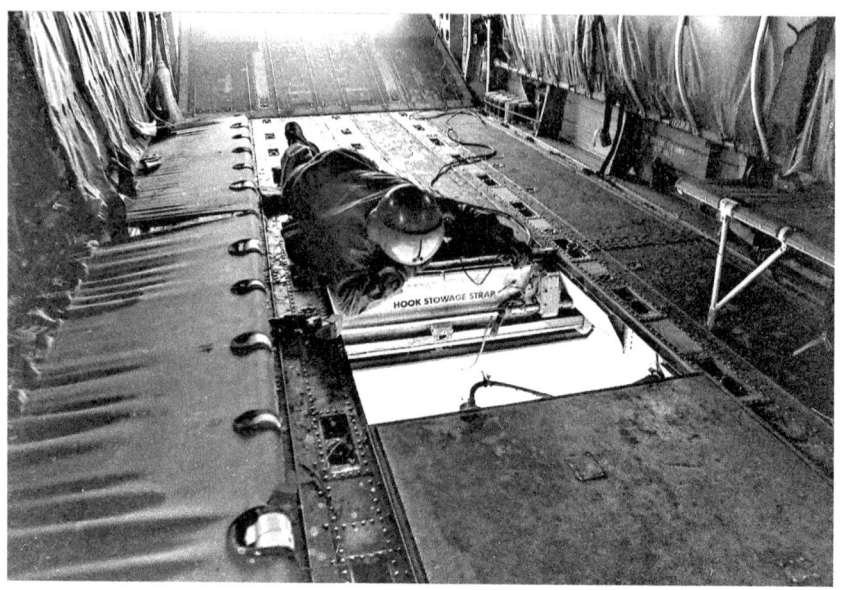

Inside a Chinook, a crewman looking through the open hatch.

With Glen photographing down through the hatch, a view of the load suspended from the Chinook.

18. Tet 1970, a Two-digit Midget

A Chinook lowering bags of ammo to be unhooked by personnel on the ground before the howitzer is set down.

With the area secured, a Chinook landing to enable artillerymen to unload supplies.

Artillerymen dumping contents from boxes to stack ammo ready for use.

its course. Mail call on the 28th included a letter from Jim and Dianne Brown. He was expecting to get a three-month early out to go to grad school in September. If all went well, they hoped to drive to South Carolina

18. Tet 1970, a Two-digit Midget

Artillerymen shoveling mud into empty ammo boxes to construct protection.

to visit us before the start of fall term. In my next letter I inquired if that met with Joan's approval. She responded that she certainly looked forward to meeting the couple who in AIT had befriended me so far from home.

The first of March, I was sent back out to the Plain of Reeds on a resupply helicopter to view and photograph latter phases of the air-mobile operation. "I kinda enjoyed flying over the P of R knowing I wouldn't have to get out and hump," I wrote. I planned to go to

Other artillerymen shoveling mud into sandbags.

Gun section setting up their firing position (note stump on right to orient next photo).

The howitzer in position being readied for firing, with a bunker constructed of filled ammo boxes, sandbags, and metal sections, and with tubes of projectiles stacked nearby (note stump from previous photo in right corner).

18. Tet 1970, a Two-digit Midget

Artillerymen studying map in tent serving as the battery's command center for operation.

With a "water buffalo" (water trailer) visible at left and the command tent at right, a gun section commencing a fire mission in Operation Chickamauga.

Returning to camp at the end of another air mobile operation, a Chinook lowering its ammo bag and howitzer, having been directed in by a yellow smoke grenade detonated by a soldier on the ground waiting to unhook the cargo.

Saigon tomorrow to get the two Nikon lenses I had ordered nearly ten months ago. I had just been notified that at last they were in. "This is going to be a fun trip," I said. "I won't be going on any lifer business." The day's mail also included a letter from Jim Palmer, stationed now at Fort Myer, Virginia, just outside of Washington. He said that it had been worth all the hassle required to marry Mai and get her back to the States. I also had a letter from Patrick McReynolds, who had several more months in Korea and planned to get married in August.

Two surprises awaited me when I made the trip to Saigon. One came when my companions and I went to Tan Son Nhut to eat lunch at the USO, planning to order "cheeseburgers—almost like back in the world." To my great surprise, when we walked in, I saw a female USO civilian employee

18. Tet 1970, a Two-digit Midget

from Columbia, who had been in several of my college English classes. There she had been active in USC's drama presentations, and here she was in Vietnam as the associate director of the Tan Son Nhut USO. Those USC classes had been smaller, upper-level ones, so she remembered me as I did her. To this point, late as it was, she was the first person I had known "back in the world" that I saw later in Vietnam.

My second surprise came when I arrived at the Cholon PX in Saigon to pick up my long-awaited lenses. I discovered that the even longer-awaited Nikkormat camera that had been my first order nearly a year ago in Vietnam had also finally arrived with its ultra-fast f:1.2 lens. Wallet flat, I left with a camera, three lenses, and a dilemma. I had purchased the Nikomat twin in Hong Kong, and Joan had my old camera at home, both of which could share my lenses. I had really busted my budget and had more equipment than I needed. When a fellow GI admired my new purchase, I, with some reluctance but with prudence, exchanged the new camera and its ultra-fast lens for the price I had paid.

I worked in the photo lab all day March 3 and had to spend the night in Tan An because the people who were to take me back to Tan Tru left without me. I imagined I would not see Dudley again as he would be leaving in a few days. The BC was pleased with the photos I had made and assigned me to return to the Plain of Reeds March 7 to take more. I was to return to Tan Tru the next day, I wrote, and "I'll probably have a lot of work to do in the photo lab next week." Since I had unexpectedly stayed in Tan An, I had missed mail call back in the battery.

I wrote happily the next day, "Guess what was waiting for me when I returned from Tan An today? Give up? MY ORDERS TO COME HOME!" Typewritten on the page dated 3 March 1970, in capital letters was SPECIAL ORDERS NUMBER 62, but to me it was "NUMBA 1." On April 15, I was to report to "90th Repl Bn Long Binh RVN." This abbreviated destination, which was indecipherable a year ago, was now crystal clear. And, for the first time, I learned that I would process out at Fort Dix, New Jersey, on the East Coast and closer to home. On the bottom of the copy I sent Joan, I ink-stamped the caricature of a hobo with one hand holding a suitcase and the other grasping a pole with a bag tied to the other end. Stamped over his head was "I SHOULD BE HOME SOON" and beneath his feet "___ DAYS LEFT." I had "42" the day I got the orders, but when I would mail the copy home 12 days later, I would fill in the blank with "30."

On March 6, I thanked Joan for sending me information I had requested about jobs. I planned to follow up promptly. I expected that "lifer harassment is going to be on the upswing around here. We've been getting in boo-coo new guys—some of them lifers and we got a new first sgt. yesterday. I guess I can take anything for 40 more days—only FORTY DAYS. Can you believe it, Joan?" My camera and photo lab work were helping make the slowly passing days more bearable.

19

Extension
"36 days remaining"

THE DATE OF MY LETTER MARCH 10 MARKED ONE YEAR completed in Vietnam. I stated its obvious significance. "Tomorrow I begin my extension and have only 36 days remaining." The week had been miserable so far: I had a stomach virus. I had to rush to the latrine at 3 a.m. Monday. "Since then I've been back at least 30 times (really)." I was writing Tuesday night and "I've only eaten once since Sunday night (dinner today), but my stomach is so bloated I look as though I'm pregnant." I had received news from my folks that my father had retired and his company had presented him with a portable color TV. My parents also had traded their '63 Plymouth for a '67 Fury III with air conditioning.

March 13 found me lamenting the letdown of the recent USC–NC State game, especially after such a great year. I was referring to the ACC championship game, 42–39 in double overtime. The University of South Carolina had begun the 1969–70 season ranked number one by the Associated Press. They had won the regular season conference crown with a 14–0 record, which was extremely impressive, yet meaningless. Only the team that won the conference tournament would advance to the regional playoffs.

I wrote on March 15 that I had gone to Tan An with "practically all my belongings" to get packaged as hold baggage, bulky items shipped free by the military. "You won't believe it when they arrive—4 wooden crated boxes," I said, which should take about 30 days to reach home. I warned Joan to "be prepared!" when she got notice to pick up the shipment. She would need to borrow her father's shop truck "and the services of Podner and Herbert," two of his strong employees who should have no difficulty in moving the heavy boxes. "Put them in the dining room until I get home," I wrote, not wanting them opened until then. I had filled out the forms for our savings to be sent with interest 90 days after my ETS. "So—if we can hold out until then we'll be all right."

On March 18 I said that for the first time in a while, "I worked all day in the motor pool. I've been going to Tan An almost every day. I have many reports due in a few more days, BUT these are the last monthly reports I'll ever do for the Army." I asked about news from Jak and Betty on their world trip and when they were to return home. They had sent me a postcard from Japan. "I hope someday that we can take a trip like that," I said. "I do want you to see this part of the world. I know you would really be intrigued by it." For now I was more interested in *my leaving* that part of the world. I was down to 28 days and "have everything together so well that I think I could pack and be ready to leave in five minutes' notice."

I expected to go to Tan Tru village tomorrow to pick up the barber. Since GIs were no longer allowed to go there, we brought the village barber into our compound for haircuts. I planned to take a camera "and get some shots of the marketplace." I was glad for the opportunity because I had doubted I would get another chance to visit the picturesque place.

Two days later, I advised Joan not to send mail after April 4. "That will allow 10 days for me to receive any mail before I leave," I explained. "Any mail that arrives after I leave, I may never receive." I had gone to the Battalion Aid Station for two shots—my last two. "I shall never get shot in the army again," I quipped. I had also had my teeth checked and was surprised that the dentist found no cavities, only a couple of dark spots that should

At the market in Tan Tru village, locals selling various types of goods.

Near the market in Tan Tru village, a typical street scene with rutted muddy streets lively with children and other civilians.

go away "if I brush my teeth frequently," which in-country I had not been able to do consistently.

I went to Tan An to pick up parts and took some equipment to Ben Luc on March 21. We ate dinner—water buffalo steak—at the Hong Kong Club, a local spot in Ben Luc. I confirmed that I took every opportunity now to run battery errands and to "go on the road" as often as possible to get away. "When I go on the road the day really goes by quickly—and there are no lifers to harass us," I said. "Besides they haven't found any mines on the road lately so it's not too dangerous now." I was now driving a Jeep that was redlined (needing work but safe to drive, unlike a deadlined vehicle), and I frequently picked up the mail. I made certain that nothing would detain me and cause the guys in the battery not to get their mail. By March 22 I had completed all of my monthly reports and was left with just "daily deadline reports, but they are no sweat." I had been "on the road seven of the past eight days." I had never been issued—nor was I ever asked about—a military driver's license.

March 25 marked the first time in a week I did not go on the road, but "just stayed around here and goofed off." I hoped to spend all day tomorrow in the photo lab. I still needed to print photos I took when I went to the Plain of Reeds. I had printed few of my own shots, but I had developed the film and made contact sheets so that I could make prints when Joan and I had our own darkroom at home. Tonight I was going to watch *Gone with the Wind* projected onto a sheet hung on the wall of the EM Club. Nothing like watching a "numba one" movie in a "numba ten" venue.

I went to Tan An and Ben Luc March 27 to pick up tires, tubes, and tools we had turned in for calibration. Joan had written she was busy at home getting the apartment put back in order after the manager had it painted. She had been teaching Joseph Heller's *Catch-22* in her classes and had sent me a copy. I wrote March 29 that I had been reading it and expressed appreciation of "many basic truisms." In other reading, I had enjoyed that Michener "shows the military as it is," although "the only way anyone can *really* know is to serve in it."

I reported March 30 that I had "been bothered for a couple of days by a sore throat." Gargling with salt water and aspirin and using throat discs had not alleviated the problem so I had gone to the Battalion Aid Station. The doctor found pus on my tonsils and gave me penicillin pills. I avowed that should work. I was concerned too about the national mail strike back home. The battery had been getting "very little mail" for the past couple of days and I had not received a letter in three days. "And if the mail situation weren't bad enough," I said, "the air controllers had to go on strike and now some major airports are way behind schedule. They had best be on schedule when I get back. I don't want to have to wait one extra minute to get back to you." I was cheered the next day when the battery got "boo-coo mail," and I had letters from my folks, her folks, and three from her.

"Here it is," my April 1 letter to Joan began, "the month we have been anxiously awaiting. This is OUR month." We had first met in April and were to be reunited in April. Yesterday, I had mailed her the page from my daily calendar with each day of March X-ed out. "Guess what?" I said. "It poured down rain tonight. The monsoon this year will be earlier than that of last year. It may rain several more times before I leave." I thought the monsoon may already have begun "up north" where Rob was.

When I went to Tan An for the mail April 2, I wrote, the road wasn't quite as dusty because of the rain. I related several incidents that had just occurred. "Last night out at Tan An airstrip, where new replacements process into the brigade, one of the replacements at Go Devil Academy was shot between the eyes by a VC sniper as he lit a cigarette," I said. "The guy was pulling bunker guard at the time. He had been in-country only 12 days."

"Also at Tan An last night," I continued, "movement was spotted outside the compound, and when the guards fired, they shot 2 VC. Maybe these two incidents indicate something, maybe not. I should add that I don't pull bunker guard *or* starlight anymore. My nights, for the most part, are spent right here in the bunker."

19. Extension

Because we were shorthanded—especially of experienced personnel—I was now posting the guard each evening. There was even a joke that since we had no sergeant of the guard that I was "specialist of the guard." Another "joke," as I took it, was that the BC would frequently call me in and offer me a promotion to E-5 *if* I would re-enlist. It was all I could do not to laugh in his face and tell him where to put that stripe.

Saturday night, April 4, I addressed two envelopes to #6 Park Court Apartments. One contained a letter which began, "Only one more Saturday night in Charlie Battery ... in Vietnam ... in the Army! Two weeks from tonight—if all works smoothly—we should be together." The other envelope contained a copy of a widely distributed typewritten letter popularly circulated on behalf of every American returning home to send from Vietnam. In part it read:

> Dear Civilians, Friends, Draft dodgers, Etc.,
> In the very near future the undersigned will once again be in your midst, dehydrated and demoralized, to take his place again as a human being with the well-known forms of freedom and justice for all, engage in life, liberty, and the somewhat delayed pursuit of happiness. In making your joyous preparations to welcome him back into organized society, you might take certain steps to make allowances for the crude environment which has been his miserable lot for the past 13 months. In other words, he might be a little Asiatic from Vietnamesitis and Overseasitis and should be handled with care. Do not be alarmed if he is infected with all forms of rare tropical diseases. A little time in the "Land of the Big PX" will cure this malady.
> Therefore, show no alarm if he insists on carrying a weapon to the dinner table, looks around for his steel pot when offered a chair, or wakes you up in the middle of the night for guard duty. Keep cool when he pours gravy on his dessert at dinner or mixes peaches with his Seagrams VO. Pretend not to notice if he eats with his fingers instead of silverware and prefers C-rations to steak. Take it with a smile when he insists on digging up the garden to fill sandbags for the bunker he is building. Be tolerant when he takes his blanket and sheet off the bed and puts them on the floor to sleep on....
> Also if it should start to rain, pay no attention to him if he pulls off his clothes, grabs a bar of soap, and runs outdoors for a shower.... Above all, keep in mind that beneath the tanned and rugged exterior there is a heart of gold (the only thing of value he has left) ... get the civies out of mothballs, fill the car with gas, and get the women and children off the streets—
> BECAUSE THE KID IS COMING HOME!!!!!!!!!!!!!
> [*his signature*] L. Glen Inabinet

On April 5 I said that Joan's several-days-delayed letter seemed "as hysterically happy about my coming home as I am." And I was indeed happy. "Just one more weekend, Joan! Just ten (10; yes, count them—1, 2, 3, 4, 5, 6, 7, 8, 9, 10—10) more days."

I was finally a "single-digit midget." The number written on the hobo stamp became "9." It was April 6. "Seven more days in Charlie Battery, I cannot wait," I said. "Every morning now, all of the dirt and rocks in the battery area have to be raked. The lifers are on this kick about haircuts and shined boots etc. again too. Wednesday we all must paint our footlockers. Like I said only 7 more days in Sorry Btry. and 9 more in Nam. It's been a long time coming."

"When you get this letter I should be in Long Binh out-processing and/or waiting to be bused out to Bien Hoa A.B." began my April 9 letter. "Only 4 more days in Sorry Btry.; only 6 more in Nam." I had taken my camera when I went to the village and got some interesting shots. Afterwards I spent the day in Tan An's photo lab processing film and printing pictures. I thought "maybe these will be my best yet as far as print quality goes. This was really the first time I've had all day just to do my own work."

April 11 I was glad to hear that my hold baggage had arrived at home. "I can just picture you trying to guess what's inside those crates," I teased Joan, "tapping on them and trying to budge them etc. You'll just have to wait—Christmas in April." I turned to serious thoughts. By the time she received this letter, I should be "in Long Binh or Bien Hoa or even over the Pacific. And Joan—*just think*—one week from this moment I should be in your arms once again. I have missed you so very much but soon soon soon it will all be over."

My April 12 letter repeated the steps I would take to get home. I was still unsure whether I would re-enter through Oakland or Fort Dix, but it mattered not. What was clear was that "The END is near at hand." My letter Monday night, April 13, began, "Here it is! This is it! My last night in Sorry Btry. has finally come. Tomorrow I can go down Thunder Road for the last time."

I continued my final Delta discourse:

> This will no doubt be my last letter to you from Vietnam. In slightly over two days I shall be leaving this country. Hopefully in five days I shall be a civilian and will be at home with you where I belong.
>
> This has been a difficult time but it was so much easier for me than it has been for others. We have been lucky in the respect that we have had no crises or extreme difficulties. We have remained close to one another in spite of the enormous distance separating us.
>
> I consider myself so very lucky to have you for my wife. Your letters have kept me happy and in good spirits no matter what the conditions were here.
>
> It feels good to know I'm coming home but it really feels wonderful to know I have you to come home to.
>
> I love you with all my heart.
> Sweetheart. I'm coming
> HOME!

20

Coming Home

"Stopped... That was not going to happen to me"

For days I had been bidding farewell to Nesavich and others with whom I had been friends for many months. For weeks I had watched closely as others departed the battery to return home. Some of the guys wanted to grow their hair out in order to look more like civilians when they arrived home. Recently, our 1st Sgt. actually stopped one guy from getting on the truck taking him to Tan An to begin processing out. The poor fellow had to get a haircut that Top approved before he was allowed to leave the battery. That was not going to happen to me. I had gotten the barber to give me a BCT-style haircut.

There had been a popular daily serial on Armed Forces Radio, "The Adventures of Chicken Man," which began with the hero's call that sounded like a chicken with superpowers. Every time Chicken Man came to the rescue or did anything significant, he loudly let out that call. I had learned to mimic that sound around the battery and had gained the nickname "Chicken Man" to add to "Rabbit," as I was still familiarly called. On my last day, April 14, I threw in my gear and climbed into the back of an open bed ¾ ton truck. As it pulled away from Charlie Battery, I heard someone in the area yell something that over the sound of the vehicle revving up sounded like, "Good luck back in the world, Chicken Man." I stood up and let out the loudest Chicken Man call ever heard in Vietnam. People on details around the guns and in other areas of the battery turned and applauded and shouted as I continued my triumphant call until we cleared the main gate. Then I sat down with a raspy throat but with the biggest smile I had had in well over a year.

I have no recollections of processing out at the battalion level in Tan An nor of the travel to Long Binh. The facilities at the 90th Replacement Battalion had been upgraded, and I learned there was a swimming pool. I bought swim trunks at the PX in order to make use of it. I saw a guy from

BCT. We recognized one another and chatted about going home. A very pale-skinned fellow near us was enjoying himself as much or more than we were. He had just arrived in Vietnam and was awaiting his orders. As he splashed around in the pool, we overheard him say, "I think I'm gonna like duty in Vietnam." My old comrade and I just looked at one another and shrugged.

I completed processing out, got my final orders which confirmed I would ETS at Fort Dix. I was transported to Bien Hoa, reversing the route taken in March of 1969, which this time during daylight was much less foreboding. If I had thought the 90th Replacement Battalion had been upgraded, Bien Hoa's facility could have passed for a stateside metropolitan air terminal.

After a wait (perhaps not very long, but at this point any delay was too long), those of us manifested for this flight made our way toward our "Freedom Bird." The last photo I took in Vietnam was of that beautiful plane. We had an uneventful takeoff and began our ascent. The pilot announced on the intercom that we were approaching the coast. I had a window seat, and I aimed my camera to capture the last frame I would take until I was home—the coastline and beaches—and then settled in my seat for an epic flight.

I remember nothing about the flight home. I likely slept with exhaustion through most of it. Reminiscent of my entry in Vietnam, we landed near midnight at an Air Force base (this time McGuire AFB) and were bused to an Army compound (this time Fort Dix). Unlike my arrival in Vietnam, there was no armed escort leading us through heavily guarded checkpoints nor anxiety that enemy saboteurs might attack us. We arrived at Dix and immediately began processing out of the Army. We were led in line from station to station, each of us in turn answering questions and signing forms in triplicate. During this tedious processing, we passed a group of draftees beginning the transition from civilian life to military regimentation. We glanced at long hairstyles, bearded faces, and rumpled clothing, knowing what lay ahead for them. We knew they did not know.

Somewhere around 3 a.m., we were given the number of a nearby building and told to get some sleep. We went to the location, a room with many mattresses without linens. I may have dozed off, but very soon we were aroused to resume ETSing. We went through a dental and medical check. A dentist told me I had a cracked tooth that I could take care of through the VA. A doctor inquired if I had any claims. It was common knowledge an affirmative answer meant the soldier would be detained for further examination and paperwork. I was unaware of any major problems and had no desire to prolong my Army "career," so I answered negative. One of our last steps was a station where personnel used information from

20. Coming Home

Glen's Freedom Bird waiting on the tarmac at Bien Hoa Air Base to take him "back to the world."

our DD-214 separation papers to select insignia, citations, and medals to go on the coats of the winter uniforms we were being issued, all the clothing we had to wear now. The Army wanted us to go home looking "right."

I was informed there were three airports in the vicinity, but Philadelphia was recommended as my best choice. Three other guys, who also were headed south, and I shared a taxi to the Philly airport. I purchased a ticket to Columbia via Atlanta and called Joan with the flight information. I told her to meet me at the baggage claim area, and then waited patiently to travel the last legs of my journey.

I arrived in Columbia about 10 p.m. on April 8 for a long-awaited reunion with my precious wife, which occurred as if a brief dream. I do not recall the routine details of deplaning and entering the terminal. I stepped onto the escalator, hastening my way by taking steps as it moved. I could see Joan below, wearing a miniskirt, her now-long brown hair held in place with a headband matching her skirt. After a hearty embrace, I grabbed my suitcase and said, "Let's get out of here." I was totally oblivious to the presence of anyone else in the terminal except the two of us. I placed money into a pay phone and made a call to my parents to let them know I had arrived, and that we were detouring on the way home for a brief visit to them. After hugs and kisses at my folks' house in Orangeburg, we headed north on U.S. 601 for Camden and home.

Afterword
"Young men taken way too soon"

OUR APARTMENT IN CAMDEN WAS A WELCOME SIGHT. However, I was unable to relax. The lack of sleep on the long flight to New Jersey and during the rapid processing out at Fort Dix, followed by the flight to South Carolina and the excitement of reuniting with Joan and the rest of my family—all had made me a bundle of energy. If I sat for a few moments, I would jump up to explore something in the apartment or to show something to Joan. There the five wooden crates with stereo components and other items which I had written about over many months were waiting for me to show her. I tried unsuccessfully to sleep.

After a few days of unsettled energy, we were able to get away to Holden Beach. Jak and Betty had given us their oceanfront cottage for a few days. Adrenaline and anxiety were swept away by the rhythmic cadence of the waves and breezes. When I finally slept, it was deep and extended. Joan awoke after a night's rest, but I slept on. She kept coming back to the bedroom to check that I was breathing. Finally, after about fifteen hours of uninterrupted sleep, I awakened peacefully, and the world appeared to be correctly spinning on its axis once again.

Before we had left for the beach at the end of that second week of April 1970, I had promptly, as required, reported my present military status (standby-reserve for three years) to my draft board, which had never gotten to draft me and could not draft me now. (The reserves did not call me either.) Returning from the beach, I tended to other necessary matters: business at our bank, filing a copy of my DD-214 separation paper at the county courthouse, and looking for a job by interviewing my last civilian employer, the county school district. Word on teaching vacancies would not be available until the semester ended in some six weeks, but I was hired right away to begin substitute teaching at Camden High School, where Joan was under contract to resume teaching in the fall while completing her thesis, her last degree requirement. My substituting also extended to Camden Junior High School, across the street from CHS. Subbing was not lucrative, but it was employment, and both campuses were a short walk a block from our apartment.

Meanwhile I visited the State Department of Education in Columbia to clarify requirements for fulltime teaching employment. I would need to take and pass the National Teachers Exam. The fact that I had never taken education courses would not matter for a time if my NTE score was adequate. I also met with the Veterans Administration to establish my GI Bill eligibility to pay for the courses I would eventually require. I wanted to earn an employment-related master's degree. The University of South Carolina graduate school said I must take the Graduate Record Exam and choose a specific program of study. Our income needs and goals prevented full-time attendance to study without earning, since Joan and I both wanted to move toward purchasing a house and starting a family. After our time apart, why postpone what now seemed most important to us?

The feasibility of furthering my undergraduate major in Spanish proved slim, its being a discipline much smaller than other liberal arts departments with fewer graduate classes and those being less convenient to schedule. Furthermore, having had little opportunity to practice Spanish in the military, my hard-earned language skills were very rusty. (An amusing fact is that, about a year after my return from Vietnam, the Army eventually recognized my Spanish degree. A postcard from military records announced a change in my Military Occupational Specialty to 13A1L, the "L" suffix designating me a "Language Specialist." My newfound identity would provide a chuckle but no job prospects.)

I had been home from Vietnam only a little more than two months when upsetting news awakened Joan's parents early on a Sunday morning. Rob had been wounded in action in Cambodia along with others of his unit about June 20. Medevacked to a hospital in Japan for surgery and rehabilitation, he had requested that notification to his parents be postponed until he could call them himself from the hospital with reassuring news that his recovery was underway. He said too he would be requesting after recovery to return to Vietnam to finish his tour. The incursion of U.S. military into Cambodia stepped up attempts to counter the flow of communist supplies into Vietnam as more U.S. troops were being withdrawn. Joan and I joined her family to sit together in church the morning of Rob's call as we prayed for his recovery and return. Our prayers for him and others in the ongoing war would be continuing.

Disturbing news of a different type came to our friend and former apartment neighbor Bill Norris at the same time that I was trying to settle my employment. While I was in Vietnam, Bill, a chemist, had changed jobs. His new Camden employer, DuPont's May Plant, had offered a higher wage and a much shorter commute than his previous employer in Bethune. He and Andrea, a Camden High history teacher, had welcomed their first baby to their new home in a Camden suburb. As they were just settling, fluctuations in the fiber industry brought reductions-in-force at DuPont. As one of May Plant's newest hires, Bill got a pink slip and could find no comparable local employment. On offer of a job with a pharmaceutical company near their eastern North Carolina hometown, our friends reluctantly put their house on the market, bade farewell, and moved. Andrea's position in the Camden High Social Studies Department would be vacated in the fall.

Meanwhile, when my satisfactory NTE scores arrived, the S.C. Department of Education, examined my college transcript and sent me certification to teach in two secondary subject areas—Spanish *and Social Studies.* I had no idea I was qualified for the second area any more than I had been to be an RTO or to be a TAERS clerk in Vietnam. However, I promptly accepted the offer of a full-time position at Camden High teaching three classes of United States History and two classes of World History, the assignments that Andrea was vacating. We were sad to see our friends leave Camden, but I was relieved to have a job and, as well, a subject appealing to me for graduate study. In Vietnam I had found that I was quite interested in history, people, places, and current events.

What emerged as my best employment and education plan would be to teach fulltime and to study part-time to earn a Master of Arts in Teaching Social Studies, for which the salary advancement was the same as for an MA or MS degree and required no time-consuming thesis. I would be able to meet required courses in education at an advanced level and enjoy subject area classes of interest to me. The plan had many moving parts, and I was anxious to map out our future efficiently.

During the summer of 1970 as they had promised, my friends since BCT, Jim and Dianne Brown, did visit Joan and me at our home in Camden. We toured them through our community and other parts of the Carolinas. We drove down to sites in Charleston, featuring the opening of South Carolina's Tricentennial exhibits at Charles Towne Landing. We took the coastal route up to Myrtle Beach, where they stood with their feet in the surf, totally awestruck at experiencing the ocean for the first time. Their exuberance I would recall in later years when we were with children or grandchildren first seeing the ocean. In Calabash, North Carolina, Jim enjoyed "the best seafood ever." On our last evening in Camden, we reviewed our adventures and made plans for future reunions. The Browns left the next morning, headed to Florida and across the Gulf Coast to New Orleans, sending us postcards along the route.

Afterword

In the fall I began fulltime teaching and parttime graduate courses. The school year of 1970–1971 was a challenging one throughout South Carolina, the first year of total racial desegregation as federal court–ordered in its public schools. In the previous few years in Kershaw County, a "voluntary desegregation" plan of historic black and historic white public schools had been in effect. Camden High School, which had been a "predominately white" and modest-sized school of perhaps 1200, became a campus of 2200. It became one of the largest single-unit secondary schools in the state.

Meeting the challenges of that change and undergoing pressures of a first-year teacher were difficult, but I found myself coping successfully. Much work, combined with Joan's support, guided me through the year. After all, this was not the first time I had been given a job for which I was untrained. The work I was enjoying, helping support positive growth among the youth of a changing country I had been serving in the military.

Later in the fall Joan and I had very special news which we saved to share face to face with Rob when he came home at the end of his Vietnam duty. Glad to be back, he was joyful to hear that Joan and I were expecting our first baby in the year ahead and to reflect that both of us returned GIs would be enjoying this Christmas together again with family. In February when Joan began maternity leave, her sister Mary Ann, having graduated from Winthrop in December, was happily employed in her place teaching English and serving as editorial advisor of the student newspaper for which I was business advisor.

Last summer when our friends Jim and Dianne Brown left our apartment after their visit to us, our contacts thereafter gave no inkling of what would happen on February 5, 1971. The Browns were driving through the Southwest, visiting law schools for Jim's potential enrollment, when my generous-hearted friend stopped their vehicle to assist a man standing beside an apparently disabled automobile. The car was stolen, and the man was an escaped felon who rewarded Jim's friendly gesture by shooting them both. He took their car, leaving Jim dead and Dianne wounded and widowed.

When his family informed me of Jim's shocking death and requested my service as a pallbearer at his funeral in the hills of Missouri, I immediately agreed. I arranged a substitute teacher and booked a flight to St. Louis. In a way, I reflected on the trip, I had come full circle. Not long after the funeral of my classmate Dickie Kapp who had died in Vietnam, I had taken my first trip to Missouri for Basic Combat Training nearly two and a half years earlier, filled with anxiety over the uncertainty of what lay ahead in military service. My apprehension had been lightened by the friendship offered by fellow trainee Jim Brown. My second trip to Missouri was filled with great sadness for his loss. Although not a combat-related death, his was the result of a senseless criminal act. Both were cases of decent young men taken way too soon.

Life after my homecoming from Vietnam was filled with many heart-felt experiences in that first year of my teaching while beginning new studies. Joan and I felt deeply blessed on July 1, when our first child, Julie, was born. That year was also the beginning of over 30 more years that Joan and I taught together in Camden High School classrooms, sometimes working collaboratively on cross-discipline projects and co-sponsoring student publications. We have been especially proud of our work together in oral history projects, and we still enjoy teaching in an adult Sunday School class. Our spiritual beliefs have continued to maintain us throughout the years, and we deeply appreciate our relationships with our children and grandchildren.

Joan and I enjoy involvement in community groups, especially the Kershaw County Historical Society. Researching, writing, and publishing the stories of our area's long history brings us pleasure and pride in helping to keep alive meaningful human experiences, messages of errors and accomplishments, of losses and gains, of sorrows and hopes. We have been committed to our belief that truth and understanding of both weaknesses and strengths of our past are foundations for sound guidance for the future.

Over the years we have traveled, though not internationally, through various parts of our country with our children and sometimes our students. At times I have also taught Spanish, and cameras have stayed in use by my side always. Joan and I have participated in various educational and historical organizations from local to state to national interests.

Each time I have had the opportunity to view the Vietnam Memorial in Washington, D.C., or the traveling version of it, The Wall That Heals, I locate the names of my friends engraved on it, from Richard W. Kapp to many others whom I was glad to have known. Jim Brown's name does not appear on the wall; yet as I think of the faces represented by each engraved name, I cannot help but picture his smiling face as well. All of them represent a tremendous loss.

Over 58,000 men and eight women, all of the latter nurses, lost their lives as a result of the war in Vietnam. I hope my memoir awakens collective memory of those who were lost, and also respects the contributions of the 2,640,000 Americans who, like me, served in Vietnam and came home.

Bibliography

Chafe, William H. *The Unfinished Journey: America Since World War II*. New York: Oxford University Press, 1986.

Cohen, Steven, ed. *Vietnam: Anthology and Guide to a Television History*. New York: Alfred A. Knopf, 1983.

Collection of 1968–1970 correspondence, photography, and some voice recordings of Louie Glen Inabinet and Joan Anderson Inabinet, family, friends, and others; time-related military paperwork and miscellaneous memorabilia, including news clippings, souvenirs, and other items; later related miscellany. In private possession of the Inabinets.

Herring, George C. *America's Longest War: The United States and Vietnam, 1950–1975*. New York: Random House, 1986.

Karnow, Stanley. *Vietnam: A History*. New York: Penguin, 1984.

MacPherson, Myra. *Long Time Passing: Vietnam and the Haunted Generation*. New York: Doubleday, 1993.

Race, Jeffrey. *War Comes to Long An: Revolutionary Conflict in a Vietnamese Province*. Berkeley: University of California Press, 1972.

U.S. Army, Office of Chief of Information. *9th Infantry Division: 1918–1968*. [Brochure, 1969]

U.S. Army Training Center: Fort Leonard Wood, Missouri. [Cycle book, 15 Nov. 1968]

Index

Abrams, Gen. Creighton W., Jr. 165
Absent Without Leave (AWOL), desertion 61, 63, 78
Adden, Luther 121
Advanced Individual Training (AIT) 10, 12, 15, 18, 34, 39, 42, 43, 44, 45, 48, 49, 50, 58, 60, 62, 63, 68, 75, 118, 134, 135, 145, 149, 169, 199
air mobile operation 146–147, 168, 175, 193–202; *see also* Operation Chickamauga
Alberoni, Sherry 157
Alderson, Jimmy 75
Allman, Margaret 19
Allman, Neil 18, 19, 20, 25, 29, 30, 31, 38, 41
allotment 18, 24, 30, 31
Alpha (A Co.) Company 96, 98, 99, 102, 106, 138, 152, 164, 176; in 2nd Battalion 60th Infantry Regiment (2/60) 96, 155, 176
American public opinion 7, 180
ammunition (ammo): bunker 85, 110; dump 110, 130–131, 135, 141–142; howitzer 59, 60, 92, 93, 107, 108, 113, 129, 130, 133, 142, 146–147, 187, 192, 193, 197, 198; rifle, machine gun 25, 31–32, 36, 38, 52, 90, 92, 104, 109, 113, 120, 138, 174; section 110
Anchorage, Alaska 78–79
Anders, Vincent 58
Anderson, Lewis F. 66, 109, 144, 149, 161, 205, 215; *see also* Inabinet, Joan Anderson
Anderson, Lottie Smyrl 49, 66, 75, 142, 144, 149, 161, 215; *see also* Inabinet, Joan Anderson
Anderson, Mary Ann (later Blaskowitz) 51, 149, 217
Anderson, Robert (Robbie, Rob) 11, 15, 16, 20, 25, 29, 31, 32–33, 34, 40, 49, 51, 63–64, 176, 183–184, 190, 208, 215, 217

antipersonnel "beehive" round 92
anti-war protest 7, 10, 179–180
Armed Forces Radio 132, 155, 157, 184, 211
Army Reserve 18, 25, 166, 214
artillery 10, 42, 44, 50, 51, 59, 61, 75, 83, 89, 96–97, 98, 99, 100, 102, 107, 110, 113, 115, 118, 122, 134, 169, 193, 194, 198, 199, 201; gun crew (section) 51, 53, 60, 93, 107, 108, 110, 129, 146, 155, 200, 201
ARVN (Army of the Republic of Vietnam) *see* South Vietnamese Army
Atlanta, Georgia 12, 19, 54, 56, 66, 71, 213
Atlantic Coast Conference (ACC) 179, 205
azimuth 29; *see also* howitzer

Baca, John 148
barbed wire 36–37, 38, 87, 111, 181; concertina 87, 111, 130
barber 17, 48, 62, 85, 206, 211
barracks 13, 14, 15, 16, 18, 19, 20, 21, 22, 24, 25, 32, 35, 38, 39, 42, 45, 46, 47, 49, 50, 51, 52, 54, 56, 57, 58, 60, 63, 66–69, 71, 74, 77, 81, 83, 85; *see also* hooch
Basic Combat Training (basic, basic training, BCT) 10, 11, 12, 13, 14, 15, 17, 18, 19, 21, 25, 30, 33, 39–40, 42, 43, 44, 45, 47, 48, 49, 54, 61, 66, 70, 71, 144, 145, 169, 211, 212, 216, 217; RVN (Republic of Vietnam) training 73–74
Basic Combat Training Cycle Book 22, 23, 26, 27, 41, 42
battalion 14, 22, 25, 44, 48, 53, 66, 67, 81, 86, 87, 89, 90, 96, 107, 109, 128, 139, 149, 152, 153, 155, 162, 165, 173, 176, 180, 192, 193, 206, 208, 211, 212; commander 193
battalion aid station 110, 152, 153, 205, 208; *see also* health
battalion training aids detail 66, 67, 69, 70
battery (Fort Sill): Echo Battery 44, 47, 48, 59, 60, 61, 62, 63, 136; holding battery 65, 67, 74–75

221

battery (Vietnam): battery commander (BC) 93, 96, 128, 153, 156, 168, 186, 191–192, 193, 203, 209; Charlie Battery 89, 90, 91, 93, 95, 96, 99, 107, 108, 110, 112, 115, 118, 122, 128–129, 133, 134, 138–139, 142, 147, 148, 150, 153, 154, 162, 165, 169, 170–172, 175, 178, 179, 180, 187, 192–193, 194, 207, 209–210, 211
Baum, Joel 58
bayonet 28–29, 30, 40, 52
Ben Luc 88, 90, 117, 118, 126, 165, 207, 208
berm (perimeter) 37, 83, 85, 89, 93, 95, 111, 116, 117, 130, 131, 160, 161, 164, 166, 193
Bien Hoa Air Base, Vietnam 79, 80, 81, 83
bivouac 29, 31, 33, 34, 35, 36, 37, 38, 39, 49, 53
bivouac training: close combat 38; foxhole digging 35; gas warfare 38; individual tactical (ITT) 37, 38; infiltration 36; search-and-destroy 37
blister 31, 32, 33
boat mission 101–102, 117
body count 93, 150
booby trap 73, 101, 103, 104, 105, 108, 113, 169–170
boondocks (boonies) 15, 29, 85, 93, 101
boots: combat 16, 17, 37, 45, 47, 65, 74, 75, 85, 136; jungle 76, 77, 81, 85, 164; polished (spit-shined) 17, 19, 20, 21, 30, 48, 49, 58, 65, 81, 144, 150, 155, 210; rubber (overboots) 30, 45, 46, 53
bridge 103, 125, 166, 175–176, 177–178
brigade 13, 14, 22, 25, 44, 59, 151, 186, 208; brigade commander 165
Brown, Dianne 68, 70, 71, 74, 142, 149, 198, 199, 216, 217
Brown, Jim 46, 49, 57, 60, 62, 66, 67, 68, 69, 70, 71, 74, 76, 134, 142, 198, 199, 216, 217–218
Brown, Lucy (Smyrl) 116
Brown, Rhonda 149, 158, 168, 177, 178, 190
Buddhism 7, 180
bugle 15
bunk (bed, cot) 13, 21, 24, 34, 45, 90, 165, 175, 189, 209
bunker 37, 81, 85, 89, 91–92, 93, 95, 111, 112, 113, 123, 129, 130–131, 147, 165, 166, 169, 170, 172, 200; VC 100
bunker guard 128, 129, 130–131, 151, 155, 160, 161, 162, 168, 172, 174, 191, 194, 208–209
bus transportation 28, 49, 67, 81, 83, 118

C4 explosive 84
C-rations (Cs) 35, 85, 105, 106, 209
cadre 13, 14, 16, 17, 21, 26, 31, 32, 35, 36, 38, 41, 42–43
Caldwell, S.W. 127, 167
Cambodia 5, 6, 113, 133, 193, 215
Camden, South Carolina 1, 9, 10–11, 55, 66, 71, 140, 158, 168, 175, 190, 213, 214, 216
Camden High School, South Carolina 11, 145, 214, 215, 216, 217, 218
camera: Kodak Instamatic 56, 70, 102; Minolta 149, 158, 168, 177, 179; Nikon, Nikkormat (Nikomat) 56, 121, 139, 149, 165, 168, 177, 188, 192, 203
canal 85, 86, 87, 104, 114, 115
cannon 50, 90; see also howitzer
Caribou (de Havilland C-7A) 83
Carver, Maurice 67
Catholicism 7, 180
charge of quarters (CQ) 24, 30, 32, 42
Charleston, South Carolina 40, 216
Charlie 73, 78, 83, 85, 86, 94, 96, 100, 104, 107, 108, 113, 117, 133, 137, 164, 171; see also Chuck; VC; Victor Charlie; Viet Cong
Charlie Battery (C Battery 2/4) 89, 90, 93, 96, 99, 107, 108, 110, 115, 118, 128, 129, 147, 149, 162, 169–171, 172, 186, 189, 191, 193, 194, 209, 211; Service Battery 129–130
Chickasha, Oklahoma 74
Chicken Man 211
Chiêu Hồi program 109
China 6; see also Hong Kong
chow 25, 29, 39, 48, 62, 65, 69, 75, 139
Christmas 34, 47, 49, 55, 56, 61, 66, 70, 167, 176, 177, 183, 184, 210, 217
Chuck 73, 93, 121, 137, 166, 176; see also Charlie; VC; Victor Charlie; Viet Cong
church service 15, 30, 42, 121, 152, 173, 215–216
cigarette 11, 21, 106, 109, 139, 208
citizenship, heritage, service 3, 14, 30, 144
civilian clothes (civvies) 15, 17, 19, 21, 47, 63, 74, 190
cold weather 16, 25, 30, 33, 34, 35, 36, 39, 46, 48, 51, 53, 56, 61, 65, 73, 75, 79, 151, 189
Cole, David 67
Columbia, South Carolina 9, 11–12, 48–49, 54, 66, 71, 72, 141, 166, 168, 175, 189, 190, 203, 213, 215
combat pay 132
command element (flag) 101, 106–107, 118
communism 5–8, 133, 215; Communist Party of Vietnam 8; see also Democratic Republic of Vietnam; North Vietnam; Viet Cong

Index

company 13, 14, 16, 18, 19, 20, 21, 22, 23, 24, 25, 28, 29, 30, 31, 35, 36, 44, 78, 81, 96, 98, 99, 102, 106, 107, 116, 138, 176; commander 27, 31, 41
compass 29, 35, 51
containment policy 5, 6

Da Nang 7, 79
Dallas, Texas 48–49, 71
DD-214 213, 214
Demilitarized Zone (DMZ) 3, 133; *see also* Seventeenth (17th) Parallel
Democratic Republic of Vietnam 5, 6; *see also* communism; North Vietnam
desegregation 11, 217
detail 17, 18, 23, 31, 42, 48, 53, 69, 70, 71, 74, 75, 77, 81, 83, 92, 93–94, 102, 135, 141–142, 154, 164, 165, 168, 171–172, 175, 185, 211
Dickey, James 167
Diem, Ngo Dinh 6–7
Dien Bien Phu 6
Dismounted Drill (DD) 25, 30, 37, 40
distribution run 90, 174
dog 160–161, 177, 187
dog tags 19–20
domino theory 6
Dong Tam ("Dog Town") 83, 84, 85, 94, 95, 102, 109, 118, 131, 132, 134, 135, 151, 152, 156, 161, 164, 165, 173, 189, 192
draft board 9–10, 186, 214; draft (conscription) 9, 10, 23; draftee (conscript) 17–18, 23, 34, 212
dress uniform (dress greens) 21, 23, 30, 58, 62, 74; winter uniform 213
drill 24, 25, 37, 40, 50, 51; instructor (DI, drill sergeant) 25, 28, 29, 33, 36, 37, 41, 46, 60
Dudley, Lee 142, 144, 154, 167, 168, 172, 173, 177, 178, 179, 180, 181, 186, 190, 193, 203
duffle bag 16, 43

Eagle Flight 97–98, 99, 122–123
early out (early discharge) 59, 166, 198
end of service: DEROS (Date Estimated Return from Overseas) 187; ETS (Expiration Term of Service) 186–187, 191, 193, 205, 212; *see also* short-timer
enemy attack *see* ground attack; mortar attack; rocket attack
enlisted man (EM) 62, 90, 144, 165, 168, 169, 174; EM Club 62, 63, 65, 66, 74, 110, 111, 152, 156, 170, 173, 191, 208
enlistment options: college opt 10, 40, 67; deferment 10; delay 10

Evans, Sgt. Robert 99, 101, 104, 106, 114, 118, 138
extension of service 59, 166, 186–187, 193, 205

fan 134, 138, 174
fatigues 16, 21, 23, 30, 38, 49, 67, 74; jungle fatigues 76, 77, 79, 85, 135, 144, 150
Field Artillery Direction and Control (FADAC) computer 107
field fire range 33
field gear 24, 38, 49, 61, 69
field jacket 16, 17, 23, 29, 33, 45, 51, 60, 61, 179
fieldpiece 51, 93; *see also* howitzer
fighter bomber F-105 Thunderchief 95, 115–116
Fire Direction Center (FDC) 107, 160, 169, 192
fire guard 15–16, 21, 30, 41, 49, 69
fire mission 59, 60, 80, 90, 92, 93, 107, 129, 142, 156, 177, 189, 193, 201
firebase 89, 90, 105, 116, 148, 174, 175
firing range (howitzer) 52, 53–54
firing range (rifle) 25. 30, 31–32, 37, 38, 39, 41; record range 33
first aid training 28, 30, 48
first sergeant (1st Sgt., Top) 118, 120, 154, 165, 177, 191, 211
flak vest 93
footlocker 16–17, 21. 24, 27, 30, 52, 53, 58, 60, 61, 67, 118, 142, 167, 210
formation 13, 14, 16, 17, 28, 31, 45, 51, 62, 69, 77, 78, 81, 83, 93, 128, 131, 133, 139, 153, 154, 157, 161, 164, 172
Fort Benning, Georgia 70, 169, 183, 190
Fort Dix, New Jersey 203, 210, 212, 214
Fort Gordon, Georgia 15
Fort Jackson, South Carolina 11, 13, 16, 21, 48 58, 173
Fort Leavenworth, Kansas 76
Fort Leonard Wood, Missouri 12, 13–15, 18, 21, 30, 34, 42, 45, 48, 51, 66, 169; nicknames 15, 30
Fort Myer, Virginia 202
Fort Sill, Oklahoma 12, 42, 44, 45–47, 49, 53–54, 56–57, 64, 67, 74, 77, 90, 107, 135, 136, 138, 169; Centennial 56–57
forward observer (FO) 51, 96–97, 106, 128, 138
fragging 171
France 5, 6
Freedom Bird 212, 213
French Indochina 5
friendly fire 114, 133, 192
Funderburk, Ann 66

Index

Gant, Lt. Robert 99, 138
generator 134, 160, 171, 184
Geneva Accords 6
Geronimo 53
GI Bill 131, 215; *see also* Veterans Administration
Go Devil Academy *see* Reliable Academy
graduate school 95, 121, 140, 145, 166, 215, 216, 217
graduation 9, 10, 40, 42, 60, 61, 62, 85
grenade: hand 36, 37, 38, 81, 84, 97, 171; smoke 116, 202
ground attack 84, 92, 93, 95, 130, 133, 139, 147, 175; *see* enemy attack
grunts (infantry) 102, 128, 147; *see also* infantry
guard duty 25, 30, 36, 51, 52, 59, 67, 77, 117, 129–130, 131, 134, 139, 146, 147, 150, 151, 153, 154, 161, 168, 172, 174, 175, 177, 179, 181, 187, 190, 209; fire guard 15–16, 21, 30, 41, 49, 69, 75; security guard 49–50, 54, 60, 61, 64, 66, 69, 71, 75
Gulf of Tonkin 7
gun 51, 60, 61, 93, 110, 130, 147, 175, 177, 187, 193, 201, 211; *see also* howitzer

hand-to-hand combat 29, 41, 42
Hanoi 5
harassment 28, 29, 41, 42–43, 61, 63, 65, 129, 142, 143–144, 147, 185, 203
Hawaii 141, 165, 167, 172, 181
health: illness (bed rest) 33, 42, 151–152, 153, 166–167, 208; pills (malaria, sodium chloride, water purification) 25, 95, 135, 163; shots (inoculations) 18, 19, 29, 74, 167, 206; sick call 33, 42, 153; *see also* battalion aid station
helicopter (chopper, copter, slick) 73, 83, 84, 94, 97, 98, 99, 100, 101, 102, 104–105, 106, 107, 108, 109, 110, 114–115, 116, 128, 138, 141, 146, 166, 168, 175, 193–194, 199; Chinook (Boeing CH-47) 116, 146, 166, 194–198, 202; Cobra (Bell AH-1G) 114–115; flying crane (Sikorsky H-54 Tarhe) 166; Huey (Bell UH-1 Iroquois) 97, 116; Huey gunship 94, 100, 104–105; LOH "loach" (Hughes OH-6 Cayuse light observation helicopter) 100, 164, 193; medevac 108, 138, 215
helmet (steel pot) 36, 38, 85, 93, 209; liner 21, 24
Helms, Andy 70–71
high explosive (HE) round 107
Highway 4 86, 87, 88, 89, 90, 166
Ho Chi Minh 5, 6, 7, 137, 139; Ho Chi Minh Trail 193

Ho Chi Minh City 8; *see also* Saigon
hobo stamp 203, 209
hold baggage 205, 210
Holden Beach, North Carolina 167, 214
holdovers 65, 68, 69, 71, 75, 76
Holley, Paul 25, 26, 35, 36
Hollis, Gen. Harris W. 156
home on leave 54–55, 71–72
Hong Kong 165, 167, 168, 172, 177, 179, 184, 185, 186, 187, 188–189, 203; *see also* China
hooch 85, 86, 90–92, 94, 101, 110, 111–112, 117, 121–122, 123, 124, 133, 134, 138–139, 142, 144, 145, 146, 152, 155–156, 157, 160, 162, 166, 167, 171, 175; *see also* barracks
hot weather 13, 23, 85, 92, 105, 112, 118, 121, 131, 137, 138, 143, 168
howitzer: 8-inch howitzer 118; 105 mm howitzer 48, 49, 50, 51, 52, 53, 68, 90, 108, 130, 133, 146, 152, 192, 194–195, 197, 200, 201, 202; 155 mm howitzer 53, 110, 152; self-propelled howitzer 63, 110, 118, 152; *see also* cannon; fieldpiece; gun; tube
howitzer park 51, 53, 54, 57, 58, 61, 67

in-country 7–8, 80, 84, 85, 96, 112, 121, 137, 172, 173, 174, 179, 186, 207, 208
Inabinet, Byron, Jr. 49, 55, 75, 121, 134, 167
Inabinet, Byron, Sr. 24, 40, 49, 55, 56, 66, 127, 143, 144, 149, 154, 162, 167, 205, 213
Inabinet, Gertie Metts 24, 40, 49, 55, 56, 66, 143, 144, 149, 154, 162, 205, 213
Inabinet, Joan Anderson viii, 1, 3, 9, 11, 17–19, 24, 95, 96, 109, 123, 131, 140–141, 145–146, 149–150, 152, 156, 158, 161, 163, 164, 165, 166, 167, 168, 173, 178, 179–180, 190–191, 208, 214–218
Inabinet, Julie 218
Inabinet, Ruby 149
Inabinet pronunciation 49
Indochina War (first) 5, 6, 7
infantry 10, 42, 44, 59, 70, 74, 83, 96–99, 106, 110, 114–115, 118, 129, 138, 147, 155, 169, 183, 193; *see also* grunts
insertion 100–101, 103, 107, 116, 122, 124, 127
inspection 17, 24, 25, 27–28, 30, 34, 38, 39, 42–43, 48, 52, 53, 54, 58, 60, 62, 87–89, 118, 134, 139, 142, 144, 147, 149, 153, 162, 172

Japan 5, 79, 80, 138, 179, 184, 185, 186, 206, 215
Jeep (M38, M151) 13, 80, 81, 84, 86, 90, 118, 120, 147, 154, 207
Johnson, Pres. Lyndon 7

Index

jungle school 84, 86; *see also* Reliable Academy

Kapp, Richard (Dickie) 11, 217, 218
Kelso, Barry 61, 62, 63, 67–69, 70, 145
Kennedy, Pres. John 180
Kershaw County, South Carolina 30; *A History of Kershaw County* 1; *Kershaw County Legacy* and *Legacy II* 1
Kershaw County School District, South Carolina 11, 217
kitchen police (KP) 19, 31, 40, 42, 48, 51, 53, 59, 61, 63, 67, 69, 70, 71, 75, 77, 81, 162
Kool-Aid 133, 187
Korea 34, 51, 63, 76, 134, 155, 176, 183, 202

Lambert Field, Missouri 12
landing zone (LZ) 97–98, 99, 116
Laos 5, 6, 133
latrine 35, 40, 46, 47, 48, 53, 62, 69, 78, 80, 81, 178, 205
Lawton, Oklahoma 54, 58, 66, 67, 68, 71, 73, 74, 75, 76
letter writing importance 3, 139–140, 150, 162, 186
lights out 14, 15, 40, 48, 63, 74, 75
Long An Province 86, 89, 103, 123, 124, 126, 127, 143, 170
Long Binh 81, 83, 95, 173, 210, 211; Long Binh Jail (LBJ) 138; *see also* Ninetieth (90th) Replacement Battalion
long johns 34, 45, 51, 75, 171
Love Field, Texas 54, 56, 71

M2 .50 cal. machine gun (Browning) 53, 80
M14 rifle 24–25, 33, 39, 42–43, 49, 52
M16 rifle 30, 39, 40, 43, 84, 102, 111, 120, 133, 135, 149
M60 machine gun 53, 84, 111, 194
M72 rocket launcher (LAW) 53
M79 grenade launcher 53, 84, 97–98, 100, 114–115
Mai Lai Massacre 181–182
mail 15, 17, 19, 24, 40, 48, 66, 74, 76, 79, 85, 90, 96, 112, 118, 121, 134, 149, 156, 161, 165–166, 170, 177, 188, 189, 206, 207, 208
mail package 17, 19, 49, 70, 116, 118, 133, 135, 136, 149–150, 154, 167, 183, 193, 205
Manual of Arms 24
march 14, 16, 17, 21, 22, 24, 28, 29, 31, 32, 33, 34, 35, 37, 38, 42, 48, 49, 53, 61, 78, 155; road march (howitzer) 138, 142
marijuana 139
Marion, Francis (Swamp Fox) 104
Martin, Paul 33, 63, 65, 118

McGuffy, Vernon 183
McGuire Air Force Base, New Jersey 212
McReynolds, Patrick (Pat) 45, 46, 47, 50, 63, 67, 70–71, 74, 75, 76, 134, 202
medical evacuation, medevac "dustoff" 108, 138, 215
Mekong Delta, Vietnam 3, 79, 83, 86, 88, 89, 90, 98, 107, 113, 123, 190; Mekong River 84, 85, 123
mess 11, 15, 31, 48; mess hall 14, 16, 17, 18, 22, 23, 24, 29, 31, 32, 48, 59, 65, 66, 69, 75, 78, 110, 111, 133, 137
Military Auxiliary Radio System (MARS) 189
Military Occupational Specialty (MOS) 42, 215
military payment certificate (MPC, scrip) 84, 116, 161
military/standard time 11, 12, 15, 77
military standby 47, 71–72
Milner, Garret 29
mine: Claymore 87–89, 111, 160, 193, 194; land 48, 90, 101, 108, 207
Mississippi River 12, 56
monsoon 29, 89–91, 103, 112, 129, 132, 133, 137, 140, 144, 146, 152, 164, 165, 177, 178, 184, 208; *see also* rain
moon shot 155
mortar attack 83, 84–85, 86, 92, 93, 94, 95, 100, 104, 107, 118, 130, 131, 133, 137, 139, 147, 148, 155, 162, 174, 175, 189; mortar unit 110, 152; *see also* enemy attack
mosquito 107, 121, 137, 139, 143, 167, 171, 174; netting 138, 174
motor pool 63, 81, 110, 128, 129, 145, 146, 147, 148, 149, 152, 162, 171, 184, 186, 206
movie 28, 31, 39, 42, 62, 67, 74, 90, 152, 156, 183, 192, 208
My Tho 192
Myrtle Beach, South Carolina 41, 216

nametag 17, 49, 158
National Guard 10, 23, 40
National Liberation Front (NLF) 7; *see also* communism; Viet Cong
Nesavich, John 169–170, 177, 211
night vision 33
Ninetieth (90th) Replacement Battalion, Long Binh 81, 173–174, 211–212; *see also* Long Binh
Ninth (9th) Infantry Division ("Old Reliables") 83–84, 88, 109–110, 131, 132, 151, 156, 219; division commander 156
Nixon, Pres. Richard 7, 41, 145
non-commissioned officer (NCO) 14, 65, 93, 156, 172; NCO Club 110, 111

Index

Norris, Andrea 9, 216
Norris, Bill (Billy T.) 9, 66, 215–216
North Vietnam 6–8, 193; *see also* communism; Democratic Republic of Vietnam; Vietnam
North Vietnamese Army (NVA) regulars 92, 107, 139, 182, 187, 194

Oakland, California 65, 76–78, 136, 149, 188, 191, 210; Oakland Army Depot "Building 790" 78
Officer Candidate School (OCS) 10, 30, 39, 40, 58, 59, 63, 67, 70, 75, 145, 169
Oklahoma Turnpike 44
olive drab (OD) 16, 17, 23, 45
Operation Chickamauga 193–201; *see also* air mobile operation
Orangeburg, South Carolina 9, 10, 11, 40, 55, 156, 158, 161, 162, 164, 213
Osborne, R.L. 156, 158, 162, 163
over-garments (OGs) 45, 51, 53
overnight mission 117–118, 121, 122, 124
Ozark Mountains 34, 35

P-38 (opener) 35–36
Palmer, James (Jim) 183, 190, 191, 202
Palmer, Mai 183, 202
Paris Peace Talks 133
Parson, Stanley 129
peace sign 10, 194
penta prime 163–164
People's Republic of China 6
perimeter *see* berm
Philadelphia, Pennsylvania 213
photo lab 154, 172, 173, 191–192, 193, 203, 204, 207, 210; darkroom 139, 157, 191, 192, 208
photography interest 1, 56, 70, 102, 117, 158, 159–160, 162, 163, 169, 179, 191, 192
physical training (PT) 23, 25, 27, 30, 37, 39, 40–41; horizontal bars 26; low crawl 26, 36–37, 39; man-carry 26; one-mile run 24, 26; rifle PT 39; run-dodge-and-jump 26
Plain of Reeds, Mekong Delta 82, 88, 113, 114, 115, 122–123, 146–147, 175, 193–201, 207
platoon 25, 28, 31, 33, 37, 44, 48, 58, 61, 63, 69, 101, 108, 112; sergeant 31
police call 11, 14, 16, 17, 48, 81, 93, 139, 157, 165
poncho 24, 29, 51, 141
Post Exchange (PX) 15, 18, 19, 20, 21, 31, 42, 48, 49, 66, 67, 69, 109, 113–114, 118, 120, 121, 135, 149, 151, 152, 165, 167, 173, 203, 211

post privileges 31, 32, 33, 39, 62, 63
powder-burning 59–60
Prescribed Load List (PLL) clerk 152
processing 11, 13–14, 15, 41, 60, 65, 71, 76–77, 81, 89, 186, 190, 210, 211, 212, 214
proficiency test: AIT 52, 53, 58; G3 40; PTPT 25, 26, 27, 40, 41, 42
PSP (perforated steel planking) 111
psychological warfare 183
pugil stick 28
punji stick 103, 108
pushups 21, 24, 25, 41

R & R (Rest & Recuperation) 141, 167, 172, 179, 186, 187
Rabbit (nickname) 49, 211
Rabon, Bill 145
radio telephone operator (RTO) 93, 96–97, 98, 99, 100, 104, 105, 107, 114, 116, 118, 128, 131, 138, 144, 176, 183, 216
rain 25, 26, 29, 30, 31, 36, 38, 39, 42, 51, 70, 92, 111, 112, 129, 137, 138, 142, 143, 144, 151, 153, 155, 165, 177, 208, 209; *see also* monsoon
rat 122, 125–126, 144, 152
Reception Station/Center 13, 14, 18, 21, 25, 66
reconnaissance (recon) 37, 93, 148; sergeant 93, 96, 97, 99, 106, 118, 138
recruit 11, 12, 13, 14, 15, 16, 17, 18, 24, 28, 41, 74
Reliable Academy 84, 86, 173; renamed Go Devil Academy 173, 188, 208; *see also* jungle school
Republic of Vietnam 6, 9, 73, 76; *see also* South Vietnam
Reserve Officer Training Corps (ROTC) 9, 24
reveille 15, 36; dike
rice paddy 84, 86, 87, 89–90, 98, 100, 101, 102, 103, 104, 107, 109, 110, 112–113, 116, 117, 126–127, 135, 144, 166, 174–175; dike 100, 101, 103, 104, 111, 117, 125, 127
rocket attack 84, 92, 93, 130, 133, 137, 147–148, 162, 192; *see also* enemy attack
rumor, suspicion 34, 137, 170–172, 185

sabotage 89, 148, 166, 169–170, 175, 212
Saigon 6, 8 113, 117, 118–121, 124, 127, 128, 138, 151, 165, 167, 180–181, 182–183, 187, 188, 191, 202–203; Cholon PX 118, 121, 203; Presidential Palace 182; Saigon Zoo 180, 181, 182; *see also* Ho Chi Minh City
St. Louis, Missouri 12, 13, 19
sandbag 81, 83, 90–91, 92, 94, 111, 129, 130, 144, 199–200, 209

Index

sandbag dollar 94, 158, 159
sapper 93, 160, 175, 181
Selective Service *see* draft board
self-immolation 7
service club 15, 19, 74; *see also* United Service Organizations (USO)
Seventeenth (17th) Parallel 6; *see also* Demilitarized Zone (DMZ)
shave 15, 16, 19, 24, 28, 36, 62, 77, 85, 132
shelter half 34, 36
short-timer 154, 190; single-digit midget 209; two-digit midget 186; *see also* end of service
shower 15, 19, 24, 37, 38, 77, 78, 83, 131–132, 141, 142, 164, 188
sleeping bag 34, 36
Sloan, Gene 141, 168
Sloan, Kathleen (Kitty) 148, 163, 168, 189
Smith, Mike 188
Smyrl, Betty 66, 141, 163, 167, 185, 206, 214
Smyrl, Jak (Oscar J. Smyrl, Jr.) 66, 141, 163, 167, 185, 206, 214; *The World of Jak Smyrl* 1
Smyrl, Oscar J., Sr. 51
sneeze sheet 24
sniper 100, 138, 208
snow 39, 42, 44, 45, 47, 50, 70, 71, 72, 74, 75, 78, 79
South Vietnam 6–8, 86–87, 113, 135, 137, 143, 145, 160, 174, 178, 187, 190, 193, 210; *see also* Republic of Vietnam; Vietnam
South Vietnamese Army (ARVN, Army of the Republic of Vietnam) 114, 133, 151, 159–160, 162, 165, 192; ARVN gunboat 114–115
Southeast Asia 5, 6
souvenir 141
Soviet assault rifle AK 47 107
Soviet Union 5, 6
Spanish study 9, 172, 179, 215, 216, 218
Special Orders: "Number 62" 203; "Number 181" 11–12
specialist 132, 156, 194, 209, 215
spider hole 108, 113
spying 148
squad 25, 34, 37
standdown 99, 101, 102, 113, 117, 118, 121, 122, 124, 127, 129
starlight scope, guard 155, 156, 161, 191, 192, 208
Steffens, Bill 63
stereo 131, 134, 153, 157, 158, 162, 165, 186, 190, 214
sundry package (SP) 105–106, 135, 170, 193

TAERS (The Army Equipment Records System) clerk 128–129, 131, 152, 173–174, 177, 178, 216
Tan An 66, 67–68, 70, 102, 107, 112, 118, 142, 148, 153, 154, 156, 161, 167, 168, 172, 173, 175, 178, 179, 180, 183, 186, 188, 190, 191, 193, 203, 205, 206, 207, 208, 211
Tan Son Nhut Air Base 187, 188, 189, 202–203
Tan Tru firebase 88, 89, 90, 94, 95, 97, 109, 110, 112, 117, 118, 123, 126, 152, 159, 160, 166, 181, 191, 194, 203
Tan Tru village 88, 110, 116, 125, 126, 141, 152, 159, 162, 164, 171, 206, 207
tango boat 117
tape, tape recorder 132, 133, 134, 135, 139, 142, 144, 148–149, 156
Taps 14, 15
telephone 2, 3, 12, 18, 19, 20, 34, 38, 40, 72, 73, 75, 76, 77, 189, 213, 215
television (TV) 29, 58, 155, 173, 205; TV war 95
tent 24, 34, 35, 49, 102, 201
Tet 3, 184–185, 186, 187, 189, 190, 192
Thanksgiving 51, 179
Thunder Road 89–90, 166, 174, 175, 210
tide, tidewater 87, 113
Till, Rose 155
Till, Summers 116, 118, 155, 190
trainee 13–14, 21, 22, 26, 27, 28, 29, 30, 31, 33, 34, 35, 36, 37, 38, 41, 42, 45, 48, 54, 59, 61, 67, 69, 74, 75, 217
trainfire 30
troop withdrawal 145, 151, 157, 173, 184, 185; *see also* Vietnamization
truck: deuce and a half (M35) 51, 52, 54, 84, 90, 118, 159, 163, 164, 174, 175, 180; three-quarter ton (M37) 90, 211
Truman, Pres. Harry 5, 6
Truman Doctrine 5
tube 51, 155; *see also* howitzer

United Kingdom 6
United Service Organizations (USO) 75, 120–121, 157, 202–203; *see also* service club
United States (U.S., USA) 2, 5–6, 9, 23, 109, 182, 183, 185, 192, 216, 219; 1968 presidential election 7, 41
University of South Carolina (USC), Columbia 9, 10, 15, 19, 25, 75, 95, 118, 140, 156, 158, 161, 162, 163, 167, 172, 178, 179, 203, 205, 213

Vàm Cỏ River 125, 169
VC Island, Plain of Reeds 193, 194

Veterans Administration (VA) benefits 173, 212, 215; *see also* GI Bill
Veterans Day 40, 42
Victor Charlie 73; *see also* Charlie; Chuck; VC; Viet Cong
Viet Cong (VC) 7, 73, 81, 83, 85, 90, 92, 93, 94, 100, 102, 105, 106, 107, 109, 111, 113, 114, 116, 117, 118, 122, 128, 130, 131, 150, 155, 159–160, 162, 166, 174, 175, 181, 185, 192, 193, 194, 208; *see also* Charlie; Chuck; communism; National Liberation Front (NLF); Victor Charlie
Viet Minh 5, 6
Vietnam 2, 3, 6, 8, 9, 11, 18, 25, 29, 30, 34, 39, 40, 51, 64, 66, 71, 73, 76, 77, 78, 79, 80, 83, 85, 93, 95, 96, 107, 113, 117, 118, 134, 137, 142–143, 144, 145, 161, 163, 165, 166, 168, 169, 174, 175, 179–180, 183, 184–185, 186–187, 189, 190, 191, 203, 205, 209, 211, 212, 215–216, 217, 218; *see also* North Vietnam; South Vietnam
Vietnam Memorial, Washington, D.C. 218
Vietnamese adversaries of the United States *see* North Vietnamese Army (NVA) regulars; Viet Cong (VC)
Vietnamese allies of the United States *see* South Vietnamese Army (ARVN)

Vietnamese currency: dong 84; piasters 84, 116
Vietnamization 3, 7–8, 145, 151, 157, 165, 173, 192–193; *see also* troop withdrawal
Vik, Don 15, 25, 42, 63, 75

wakeup 15, 16, 24, 46, 60, 75, 105, 166, 209
wall locker 21, 24, 27, 52, 118
Wall That Heals 218
WD-40 25
weapon 6, 24–25, 28, 30, 32, 35, 36–37, 39–40, 42–43, 48, 49, 50, 51–52, 53, 83, 90, 93, 102, 106, 107, 120, 149, 164, 174
weapons qualification 32, 33, 39
Westmoreland, Gen. William 30, 34
white phosphorous: illumination 59; marking 107
Wichita Falls, Texas 67–68, 70–71, 74
Williams, Bob (Bush) 40, 117, 149, 187
Williams, Libby 40
Winthrop College 19, 72, 149, 155, 217
World War I 37, 51
World War II 5, 21, 35, 45, 48, 109, 117

Yokota Air Base, Japan 79

zero in 32, 39, 84, 131
zero week 17

www.ingramcontent.com/pod-product-compliance
Ingram Content Group UK Ltd.
Pitfield, Milton Keynes, MK11 3LW, UK
UKHW041946140426
5217IPUK00014B/682